24 DOCTRINES OF THE BIBLE

By Ken Wooldridge

Copyright © 2013

by Ken Wooldridge

All rights reserved.

This book may not be reproduced in any form without the written permission of the author and publisher Ken Wooldridge.

All Scripture quotations are from the original King James version of the Bible.

First printing, 2006

Revised edition, 2013

ISBN: 0979022053

ISBN 13: 978-0-9790220-5-0

Library of Congress Control Number – 2012903746

Ken Wooldridge Ministries

P.O. Box 7312,

Knoxville, TN 37921, USA

www.kenwooldridge.org

Printed by Create Space in the USA

Cover design – Michael Dutton

The Purpose of This Book

The purpose of this book is to make these important

24 Doctrines of the Bible available and understandable.

People need to know the truth about what the Bible teaches.

It helps us to experience, enjoy and proclaim Bible truth.

2 Timothy 3:16

"All scripture is given by inspiration of God, and is profitable for doctrine,

for reproof, for correction, for instruction in righteousness."

Acts 2:42

"And they continued steadfastly in the apostles' doctrine."

1 Timothy 1:3

"I besought thee ... that thou mightest charge some that they teach no other doctrine."

24 Doctrines of the Bible

I trust that you will find this book a convenient and easy source of locating Bible Doctrines.

The Life And Ministry of Ken Wooldridge

Ken Wooldridge was born in Francistown, Botswana of Southern Africa.

He is the son of Fred and Gwen Wooldridge.

His mother received Jesus Christ as her Savior in the aftermath of the revival of John G Lake in South Africa.

She attended the first Apostolic Faith Mission Bible College in South Africa.

Ken's father Fred was saved several years later and became a great man of prayer.

Fred was active in a miraculous new opening of the Gospel in Botswana.

This was more than 100 years after David Livingstone had ministered there.

At an early age this impacted Ken's life.

After experiencing salvation, Ken felt the call of God to the Ministry and became involved in Mission work.

He continued in this work with his dad and then enrolled in Bible College.

He graduated from Berea Theological College and was ordained to the ministry.

He married Marie the daughter of Izak and Annetjie Cronje.

The Lord blessed Ken and Marie with two children, Charlene and Mark.

Charlene was blessed with three children, Dale, Isaac and Eden.

Ken and Marie have pastored several churches and have preached and taught in many countries around the world.

They have one supreme desire and that is to win lost Souls to Jesus Christ, edifying and touching the lives of people.

24 DOCTRINES OF THE BIBLE

Contents

1. The Godhead 1
2. God the Father 23
3. Jesus Christ 37
4. The Holy Spirit 63
5. The Word Of God. 85
6. Man and Sin 101
7. A Great Salvation 121
8. Water Baptism and the Lords Supper 157
9. The Gift of the Holy Spirit. 183
10. The Church of Jesus Christ 201
11. The Nine Gifts of the Holy Spirit 217
12. The Nine Fruits of the Holy Spirit. 243

13.	The Nine Ministries of the Holy Spirit	279
14.	Prayer and Fasting	307
15.	Stewardship	341
16.	Walking by Faith	389
17.	Spiritual Warfare	409
18.	Thanksgiving, Praise and Worship	445
19.	The Purposes of God	475
20.	Heaven and Hell	509
21.	False Doctrines, Prophets and Lying Wonders	529
22.	Gods Restoration Program	553
23.	The Three Dimensions of Man	575
24.	Last Things	601

CHAPTER 1

The Godhead

What a joy it is for me to share the twenty-four Doctrines of the Bible with you.

They will have a profound, far-reaching effect on your life.

They have been passed down to us by the early Apostles.

Acts 2:41-42

"They gladly received his word … and continued stedfastly in the apostles' doctrine."

The teaching of the Godhead is of great importance.

Most people believe in the existence of God.

Those who don't are known as atheists.

However, very few atheists remain atheistic on their deathbed.

The Bible does not try to prove the existence of God.

It simply declares it.

GENESIS 1:1

"In the beginning God..."

The Bible presents God's existence as a fact.

The first thing that we do when studying about the Godhead is to look at several proofs of the existence of God.

Firstly we deal with the proof of CAUSE

Someone created the Universe and caused its existence.

Who else could it be but God and it is His amazing masterpiece.

The earth weighs about **6.6 sextillion tons.** (6,600,000,000,000,000,000,000)

It travels at the speed of 67,000 miles per hour, on a course of 584 million miles around the Sun.

The earth when compared in size within its solar system is smaller than a grain of sand on the seashore. The sun is 1.3 million times bigger than the earth and the smallest of stars is about one million, million times larger than the earth.

The Alpha Centauri is the nearest star to the earth at a distant **4.2 light years away**. A light year is the distance light travels at 186,000 miles per second in one year.

That distance therefore is **5869874304000 miles**.

The equation - (186,000 x 60 x 60 x 24 x 365.26 = 5869874304000 miles)

The Pistol Star is one of the largest stars in the Universe and its radius is about 100 million miles.

Astronomers estimate that there are at least 70 sextillion stars in the Universe. (70,000,000,000,000,000,000,000)

The Earth is therefore a minuscule part of an immense Solar System.

Our Solar System has over a 100,000 million Stars. Its diameter is 7500 million miles. Outside of our solar system there are millions of other solar systems and together they form the Milky Way.

Our Milky Way is about 703,883,520,000,000,000 miles wide and has over one hundred thousand, million stars. Together with countless other milky way's they form the galaxy we belong to.

Our Galaxy is a part of over one hundred billion other galaxies in the Universe.

It is obvious that the vastness of the Universe and the creative ability of God are beyond imagination.

Yet there are people that reason that the Universe came about by chance or some other way. Some even believe that it was the created by Aliens.

I challenge you to intelligently and honestly examine the truth for your own benefit.

Psalm 14:1

"The fool hath said in his heart, there is no God."

This vast, genial Universe becomes even more marvelous and fascinating, when examining what it is made of.

One grain of sand the size of a pinhead, when examined microscopically, proves to be a miniature universe, consisting of millions of atoms.

Each of these atoms is made up of tiny particles that spin around a nucleus.

All material of everything that exists is made up of these atoms.

These atoms are miniature universes in and around us, invisible to the naked eye.

It is evident that Creation is difficult to measure, however large or small!

Second we deal with the proof of DESIGN

Everything is designed and therefore has a designer.

- A dress suit is designed and made by a tailor.

The Godhead

- A watch or clock by a watchmaker.
- A home or building by an architect.

It would be ludicrous and ridiculous to think that all these beautiful things we enjoy everyday come about by mere chance.

The immeasurable Universe has moving planets, stars and galaxies that function with complex mathematical precision.

Its intricate design makes a manufactured watch, vehicle, supersonic jet, rocket, space shuttle and space station look like child's play.

There are many amazing variations in nature that cannot be by chance such as:

- Seasons and climates that continue if perfect continuous sequence
- Earth's temperature sustaining life, due to its exact distance from the sun
- The rotation of the earth, creating days for activity and nights for rest
- The beautiful rainbow colors of blue, red, yellow, orange, emerald and gold
- The wonderful tastes and flavors of fruits, vegetables, berries and wild plants
- The delectable variations of meats and sea foods
- The thirst quenching satisfaction of crystal clear water

- The perfumes of blossoming flowers
- The refreshing smell of early mornings and the approaching rain
- The delicate feel of the softness of wool and the smooth touch of silk
- The clear sounds of the wild and echoing forests

Can anyone doubt *that it is God who planned everything -*

He artistically created a blue sky, white clouds and golden sunsets

He landscaped and adorned the majestic mountains and deep valleys

He blanketed them with green forests and meandering gushing streams

He beautified them with carpets of flowers everywhere

He filled them with colorful butterflies, chirping birds and different kinds of animals

There is no doubt that behind all of this magnificent creation there must be

A Master Designer - GOD

Third we deal with the proof of INTUITION

All humans all over the world have one natural intuition and desire within them –

The Godhead

It is to worship a God and Supreme Being.

We see this in mans behavior in all forms of religion.

They worship the sun, the moon, idols, objects and creatures.

Why?

There seems to be a driving force within man to worship a higher being.

This is also evident in areas where civilization has had no influence.

Where does this intuition come from?

It has been implanted by God who desires to be worshiped by man!

Fourth we deal with the proof of PURPOSE

Everything exists for a purpose.

The sun gives us light and warmth. The clouds give us rain.

The purpose of the creation of human life is defined in mans final destination.

People have been given this choice to make.

An Eternity, with or without God

Eternity is much longer and more important than 70 or 80 years of earthly life.

Grey hairs, decaying teeth, facial wrinkles all indicate a life that is fast approaching its end. Time passes so quickly.

At death each person faces eternity and a real God who has reached out to them with love and friendship. His loving gesture is to be accepted or rejected.

This is the ultimate purpose of life.

What a tragedy that man so often brushes aside God's loving gestures in ignorance.

God expects us to ascribe greatness to Him who created such a marvelous Universe.

Most people are realistic and honest about the aspects of life.

I challenge you to be realistic and honest with yourself about the existence and creative genius of God!

It seems difficult to think that such a great God, can somehow stoop down to the level of man to communicate with him.

It would be like a giant trying to communicate with an ant.

It seems an almost impossible task for God to say to man -

"This is who I am and let us have fellowship."

God therefore had to systematically introduce and reveal the Godhead to man.

He would reveal the three persons of the Godhead

- God the Father
- God the Son and
- God the Holy Spirit

He did this over a period of time.

He revealed more and more about Himself, so that man could slowly receive and understand this revelation.

God pulled back the curtain and man saw more and more of God, as time passed.

Now let us look at this systematic revelation of the Godhead.

A Systematic Revelation of the Godhead

The Godhead is referred to in -

Romans 1:20

"For the invisible things of him from the creation of the world are clearly seen, being understood by the things that are made, even his eternal power and Godhead;"

Over the last six thousand years, God has revealed the Godhead to mankind.

He has revealed God the Father, Jesus Christ the Son and the Holy Spirit, little by little, from time to time.

In this way He has revealed to us who He is, His characteristics and Divine nature.

However in eternity we will see God, face to face as He is and we will find out more about Him.

Because of this revelation we now know about His love, holiness, righteousness, goodness, kindness, mercy, grace, forgiveness, peace, joy, power, truth, justice, omnipotence, omniscience and omnipresence.

Six thousand years ago God first revealed Himself to man as "Elohim"

Genesis 1:1

"In the beginning God (Elohim) created the heaven and the earth."

The word "God" rendered here in the Hebrew text is "Elohim" made up of two parts

- El
- Ohim

El - means **God**

Ohim -is plural for **three persons**

Therefore the first revelation that God gave Adam and Eve about Himself was -

The Godhead

He is a God of three persons.

If God is only one person, the word in this Hebrew text would have been **El-oah**.

Adam knew that he was dealing with Elohim, a God of three persons.

That is why the Godhead is also referred to by man as the Tri-une God or Trinity.

This revelation of the Godhead -

Throughout the Old Testament times, God the Father is revealed.

In the prophecies and Gospels Jesus Christ is revealed.

In the New Testament the Holy Spirit is revealed.

The other different names of God reveal more about His character and nature.

PSALM 9:10

"And they that know thy name will put their trust in thee."

God revealed His names so that mankind could know and trust Him.

From time to time, God revealed additional names to complete this revelation.

Now let us look at this continued revelation of the Godhead.

When Abraham was ninety-nine years old God revealed His second name to the world and it is " **EL-SHADDAI"**

This took place about 1898 B.C.

GENESIS 17:1

"And when Abram was ninety years old and nine, the LORD appeared to Abram, and said unto him, I am Elshaddai."

Understanding His name "El-shaddai"

El - means **God.**

Shaddai - means **almighty.**

Here God reveals that He is God Almighty.

Then God revealed Himself to Moses as "Yahweh". *(Jehovah)*

This took place about 1491 B.C.

EXODUS 6:2-3

"And God spake unto Moses, and said unto him, I am the LORD: And I appeared unto Abraham, unto Isaac, and unto Jacob, by the name of God Almighty, but by my name **(Yahweh)** JEHOVAH was I not known to them."

Then Moses asked God about His name and God answered -

Exodus 3:13

"And Moses said unto God, Behold, when I come unto the children of Israel, and shall say unto them, The God of your fathers hath sent me unto you; and they shall say to me: What is his name? What shall I say unto them?

God answered and said - "I am".

Exodus 3:14

"And God said unto Moses, I AM THAT I AM: and he said,

Thus shalt thou say unto the children of Israel, I AM hath sent me unto you."

He was not referred to as "I was" or "I will be" but rather **"I am"**

This means that God is always in the **NOW**.

God told Moses that Abraham knew Him as El-shaddai.

Now God was revealing Himself as **Yahweh.**

Moses and Israel were receiving a new revelation.

The revelation of Yahweh then continued thereafter with more information.

Nine aspects of Yahweh were given to reveal more of His nature and character:

1. He is Jehovah-Jireh.

GENESIS 22:14
"And Abraham called the name of that place Jehovahjireh:

His Name is Jehovah- Jireh which means **the Lord our Provider.**

2. He is Jehovah-tshuwah.

PSALM 38:22
"Make haste to help me, Jehovah-tshuwah."

The name Jehovah-tshuwah means **the Lord our salvation.**

3. He is Jehovah-qadash.

EXODUS 31:13
"That ye may know that I am Jehovah-qadash that doth sanctify you."

The name Jehovah-qadash means **the Lord our sanctifier.**

4. He is Jehovah-stidkenu.

JEREMIAH 23:6
"And this is his name whereby he shall be called Jehovah-stidkenu.

The name Jehovah-stidkenu means **the Lord our righteousness.**

The Godhead

5. He is Jehovah-raah.

Psalm 23:1
"Jehovah-raah is my shepherd."

The name Jehovah-raah means **the Lord our shepherd.**

6. He is Jehovah-nissi.

Exodus 17:15
"And Moses built an altar, and called the name of it Jehovahnissi."

The name Jehovah-nissi means **the Lord our Banner** who leads us in battle.

7. He is Jehovah-shalom.

Judges 6:24
Then Gideon built an altar there unto the LORD, and called it Jehovahshalom:

The name Jehovah-shalom means **the Lord our Peace.**

8. He is Jehovah shammah.

Ezekiel 48:35
And the name of the city from that day shall be, Jehovah shammah.

The name Jehovah shammah means **the Lord is always with us**.

9. He is Jehovah-rapha.

EXODUS 15:26
"For I am Jehovah-rapha that healeth thee."

The name Jehovah Rapha means **the Lord our Healer**.

By revealing His names to mankind, God was actually revealing that He is:

Our savior, sanctifier, righteousness, shepherd, provider, banner, peace, healer and that He is always with us.

That is why Jesus told us to always regard God's name as SACRED.

MATTHEW 6:9

"Our Father which art in heaven, Hallowed be thy name."

The Israelites regarded Jehovah's name to be so **sacred** that they never spoke His name aloud.

Every time Scribes wrote the name of Jehovah in texts, they would use a new pen.

God commanded the Israelites to have high regard for His name.

EXODUS 20:7

"Thou shalt not take the name of the LORD thy God in vain; for the LORD will not hold him guiltless that taketh his name in vain."

Throughout the generations of the Old Testament the revelation of the Godhead was becoming more complete.

People were seeing a clearer picture of God and understanding more about Him.

During the rest of the period of the Old Testament no other name revelations were given.

God then revealed the second person of the Godhead namely Jesus Christ His Son.

The revelation of Jesus Christ the Son of God

Jesus was with God at the beginning of time.

John 1:1, 14

"In the beginning was the Word, and the Word was with God, and the Word was God. And the Word was made flesh, and dwelt among us."

God prepared Israel for the coming of His son Jesus to the earth.

He gave many Old Testament Prophets, prophecies concerning Jesus the Messiah.

The Messiah's coming was predicted.

Daniel 9:25

"Know therefore and understand, that from the going forth of the commandment to restore and to build Jerusalem unto the Messiah the Prince shall be seven weeks."

Other predictions were made:

He would be born of a virgin.

ISAIAH 7:14

"Therefore the Lord himself shall give you a sign; Behold, a virgin shall conceive, and bear a son, and shall call his name Immanuel."

He would be born in Bethlehem.

MICAH 5:2

"But thou, Bethlehem ... out of thee shall he come forth unto me that is to be ruler in Israel; whose goings forth have been from of old, from everlasting."

He would be rejected of men.

ISAIAH 53:3

"He is despised and rejected of men; a man of sorrows, and acquainted with grief: and we hid as it were our faces from him; he was despised, and we esteemed him not."

He would be sold for thirty pieces of silver.

ZECHARIAH 11:12

"And I said unto them, if ye think good, give me my price; and if not, forbear.

So they weighed for my price thirty pieces of silver."

His hands and feet would be pierced.

Psalm 22:16

"For dogs have compassed me: they pierced my hands and my feet."

He would be given vinegar to drink.

Psalm 69:21

"They gave me also gall for my meat; and in my thirst they gave me vinegar to drink."

Many Israelites wanted to find out more about the Messiah.

These prophetic directives would help them find God's Son.

Then, at God's appointed time, Jesus Christ was born in Bethlehem.

Matthew 1:23

"Behold, a virgin shall be with child, and shall bring forth a son, and they shall call his name Emmanuel, which being interpreted is, God with us."

24 Doctrines of the Bible

Then God sent John the Baptist to prepare the way of Jesus.

MATTHEW 3:3

"The voice of one crying in the wilderness, Prepare ye the way of the Lord, make his paths straight."

Before Jesus arrived on the scene, John told the children of Israel to look out for His appearance.

When Jesus was baptized in the Jordan River all three persons of the Godhead were manifested.

Jesus stood in the Jordan River.

God the Father spoke from Heaven.

The Holy Spirit descended on Jesus in the form of a dove.

MATTHEW 3:16-17

"And Jesus, when he was baptized, went up straightway out of the water: and, lo, the heavens were opened unto him, and he saw the Spirit of God descending like a dove, and lighting upon him: And lo a voice from heaven, saying, This is my beloved Son, in whom I am well pleased."

Jesus was just like His Father.

He had his Fathers nature and characteristics.

He said -

John 14:9

"He that hath seen me hath seen the Father;"

The four Gospels, Matthew, Mark, Luke and John describe the life, work, message, ministry, power and ultimate sacrifice of Jesus.

In his life work -

- Jesus revealed the truth about God,
- did miracles,
- healed the sick,
- cast out devils,
- did many good works and
- manifested the true nature of the Godhead.

When Jesus was about to leave this world, He promised that he would ask the Father to send another **Comforter, the Holy Spirit.**

John 14:16-17

"And I will pray the Father, and he shall give you another Comforter, that he may abide with you forever; Even the Spirit of truth;"

And so Jesus prepared the world for the revelation and coming of the third person of the Godhead, namely the Holy Spirit.

The revelation of the Holy Spirit

On the day of Pentecost, fifty days after the resurrection of Christ, the Holy Spirit was revealed in a new way, introducing a new dispensation.

Acts 2:1-4

"And when the day of Pentecost was fully come, they were all with one accord in one place. Suddenly there came a sound from heaven as of a rushing mighty wind, and it filled all the house where they were sitting. And there appeared unto them cloven tongues like as of fire, and it sat upon each of them.

And they were all filled with the Holy Ghost."

The New Testament describes the following of the Holy Spirit:

- His nature, character and power
- His message, activities and purposes
- His Fruits, Gifts and Ministries

For almost two thousand years, the Holy Spirit has blessed the world.

We continue to enjoy and appreciate His presence and manifestations in our lives and other Christians.

We will forever experience and enjoy the revelation of the Godhead!

CHAPTER 2

God the Father

The Old Testament specifically reveals God the Father.

Since the beginning of time people have wanted to know more about God and His appearance.

Isaiah the Prophet had a vision of God the Father upon His throne.

Isaiah 6:1

"In the year that king Uzziah died I saw also the LORD sitting upon a throne, high and lifted up, and his train filled the temple."

Other scriptures also describe God upon His Throne.

Revelation 4, Ezekiel 1:5-21 and Ezekiel 10:1.

Above God's throne is an emerald colored rainbow.

In front of His throne are the seven Lamps of fire which are the seven Spirits of God and a crystal sea which is like glass.

Around His throne are Seraphim and Cherubim that worship Him night and day.

The following verses of the Bible reveal His greatness and magnificence:

Deuteronomy 33:26

"There is none like unto the God of Jeshurun, who rideth upon the heaven ...in his excellence on the sky."

Deuteronomy 3:24

"O Lord GOD, thou hast begun to shew thy servant thy greatness, and thy mighty hand: for what God is there in heaven or in earth that can do according to thy works, and according to thy might?"

Psalm 104:1-2

"O LORD my God, thou art very great; thou art clothed with honour and majesty.

Who coverest thyself with light as with a garment: who stretchest out the heavens like a curtain:

God the Father

Psalm 145:3

"Great is the LORD … and his greatness is unsearchable."

Psalm 115:3

"But our God is in the heavens: he hath done whatsoever he hath pleased."

Luke 1:37

"For with God nothing shall be impossible."

Genesis 18:14

"Is anything too hard for the LORD?"

Isaiah 40:12-22

"Who hath measured the waters in the hollow of his hand, and meted out heaven with the span, and comprehended the dust of the earth in a measure, and weighed the mountains in scales, and the hills in a balance?

Behold, the nations are as a drop of a bucket, and are counted as the small dust of the balance:

All nations before him are as nothing; and they are counted to him less than nothing, and vanity.

To whom then will ye liken God? or what likeness will ye compare unto him.

It is he that sitteth upon the circle of the earth, and the inhabitants thereof are as grasshoppers; that stretcheth out the heavens as a curtain, and spreadeth them out as a tent to dwell in:"

There are twelve aspects of God the Father that we should know:

1. He is the **Most High God** - El-eliyon

2 SAMUEL 22:14
"The LORD thundered from heaven, and the most High uttered his voice."

2. He is God Almighty - El-shaddai

GENESIS 17:1
"The LORD appeared to Abram, and said unto him, I am El-shaddai."

3. He is a **God of majesty**

1 CHRONICLES 29:11
"Thine, O LORD is the greatness and the majesty:"

JOB 37:22
"With God is terrible majesty."

PSALM 29:4
"The voice of the LORD is powerful; the voice of the LORD is full of majesty."

God the Father

Psalm 93:1
"The LORD reigneth, he is clothed with majesty."

4. He is **immeasurable**

Isaiah 66:1
"The Heaven is His throne, the earth is His footstool and He measures the universe with the span of His hand."

5. He is **eternal** (outside of time)

Psalm 90:2
"Even from everlasting to everlasting, thou art God."

6. He is **immutable** (He never changes)

Malachi 3:6
"For I am the LORD, I change not."

7. He is **indestructible**

Acts 5:39
"Ye cannot overthrow it; lest haply ye be found even to fight against God."

8. He is omniscient (knows all things)

Job 34:21
"For his eyes are upon the ways of man, and he seeth all his goings."

9. He is **omnipresent** (He is everywhere)

PSALM 139:8
"If I ascend up into heaven, thou art there: if I make my bed in hell, behold, thou art there."

10. He is **omnipotent** (He can do anything)

LUKE 1:37
"For with God nothing shall be impossible."

11. He is **self sufficient,**

PSALM 50:12
"If I were hungry, I would not tell thee: for the world is mine"

12. He is **all wise**

ROMANS 11:33
"O the depth of the riches both of the wisdom and knowledge of God!

How unsearchable are his His judgments, and his ways past finding out!"

God the Father has a wonderful Divine Nature.

His Divine nature is:

Holy -

Exodus 15:11

"Who is like unto thee, O LORD, among the gods? …glorious in holiness?"

Glorious -

Exodus 24:17

"And the sight of the glory of the LORD was like devouring fire."

Excellent -

Isaiah 28:29

"LORD of hosts excellent in working."

Righteous -

Psalm 145:17

"The LORD is righteous in all his ways."

Loving -

1 John 4:8

"For God is love."

Kind -

PSALM **117:2**

"For his merciful kindness is great toward us."

Good -

PSALM **25:8**

"Good and upright is the LORD."

Merciful -

PSALM **103:17**

"But the mercy of the LORD is from everlasting to everlasting upon them that fear him."

Gracious -

EPHESIANS **2:7**

"That in the ages to come he might shew the exceeding riches of his grace."

Forgiving -

PSALM **86:5**

"For thou, Lord, art good, and ready to forgive."

Wise -

Romans 16:27

"To God only wise, be glory through Jesus Christ forever."

All knowing -

1 John 3:20

"God is greater than our heart, and knoweth all things."

Just -

John 5:30

"I judge: and my judgment is just."

Truth - He is truth and all truth transcends from Him.

Deuteronomy 32:4

"A God of truth and without iniquity, just and right is he."

Faithful - He will never disappoint or fail us.

Deuteronomy 7:9

"Know therefore that the LORD thy God, he is God, the faithful God."

Impartial -

Job 34:19

"Him that accepteth not the persons of princes, nor regardeth the rich more than the poor."

Joyful -

Matthew 25:21

"Enter thou into the joy of thy lord."

Peace -

Ephesians 2:14

"He is our peace."

Longsuffering -

2 Peter 3:9

"The Lord is not slack concerning his promise, but is longsuffering to us-ward."

Gentle -

James 3:17

"But the wisdom that is from above is gentle."

Caring -

1 Peter 5:7

"Casting all your care upon him; for he careth for you."

The Name "God the Father" is very special.

It reveals the very essence of His relationship with us, namely His Fatherhood.

This Fatherly relationship impacts our life in three ways:

1. God has received us as children so that He can be our Heavenly Father.

John 1:12

"But as many as received him, to them gave He the power to become the **sons of God.**"

2 Corinthians 6:18

"And will be a **Father unto you,** and ye shall be my **sons and daughters**, saith the Lord Almighty."

2. Jesus said that we may pray to God our Father -

Matthew 6:9

"After this manner therefore pray ye: Our Father which art in heaven, Hallowed be thy name."

3. God loves us and cares for all our needs.

MATTHEW 7:11, 6:26
"How much more shall **your Father** which is in heaven give good things to them that ask him?

Behold the fowls of the air: for they sow not, neither do they reap, nor gather into barns; yet your heavenly Father feedeth them. Are ye not much better than they?"

God the Father knows us intimately and thinks about us.

PSALM 139:1-16

"O Lord, You have looked through me and have known me. You know when I sit down and when I get up. You understand my thoughts from far away. You look over my path and my lying down. You know all my ways very well. Even before I speak a word, O Lord, You know it all.

For You made the parts inside me. You put me together inside my mother. Your eyes saw me before I was put together. And all the days of my life were written in Your book before any of them came to be.

His thoughts about us are countless.

PSALM 139:17-18

"How precious also are thy thoughts unto me, O God! how great is the sum of them!

If I could number them, there would be more than the sand."

God always takes very special care of us.

He is concerned with our well being and we are valuable to Him.

Matthew 6:30-32

"Wherefore, if God so clothe the grass of the field, which today is, and tomorrow is cast into the oven, shall he not much more clothe you, O ye of little faith?

Therefore take no thought, saying, what shall we eat? Or, what shall we drink? Or, Wherewithal shall we be clothed?

For your heavenly Father knoweth that ye have need of all these things."

Those who are born again of the Holy Spirit of God, are privileged to be a part of God's family.

Become a Child of God and honor Him as your Heavenly Father!

CHAPTER 3

Jesus Christ

Jesus Christ the Son of God was and forever will be subject to the authority of God the Father.

1 Corinthians 11:3

"But I would have you know ... the head of Christ is God."

Jesus the Son of God existed before His physical birth in Bethlehem.

The Bible refers to this pre-existence and clearly states that He existed before the creation of the world.

JOHN 1:18

"The only begotten Son, which is in the bosom of the Father."

JOHN 16:28

"I came forth from the Father, and am come into the world."

JOHN 17:5

"And now, O Father, glorify thou me with Thine own self with the glory which I had with thee before the world was."

JOHN 8:58

"Jesus said unto them, Verily, verily, I say unto you, Before Abraham was, I am."

When Jesus had accomplished His pre-existent role, four things happened before He came into this world:

1. Many *Prophets* announced that he would come as Christ the Messiah.

2. *Wise Men* from the east looked for and saw the sign of His coming in the sky.

Jesus Christ

MATTHEW 2:1-2

"Now when Jesus was born in Bethlehem of Judaea behold, there came wise men from the east to Jerusalem,

Saying, Where is he that is born King of the Jews? for we have seen his star in the east, and are come to worship him."

3. The *Saints of God in Jerusalem* were waiting for His coming with fasting, praying night and day.

LUKE 2:25

"And, behold, there was a man in Jerusalem, whose name was Simeon; and the same man was just and devout, waiting for the consolation of Israel."

LUKE 2:36

"And there was one Anna, a prophetess. Which departed not from the temple, but served God with fastings and prayers night and day and spake of him to all them that looked for redemption in Jerusalem."

4. *Jesus prepared Himself* for His earthly mission.

From His pre-existent position in Heaven Jesus saw a suffering human race.

He saw the sin, affliction, bondage, pain misery and poverty that satan had inflicted upon mankind and willingly came to rescue humanity.

HEBREWS 2:14-17

"That through death he might destroy him that had the power of death, that is, the devil; And **deliver them** who were all their lifetime subject to bondage.

He took on him the seed of Abraham.

Wherefore in all things **it pleased him to be made like man.**"

This so beautifully describes the feelings of Jesus before He came to this world.

He had feelings of love and a desire to help a dying humanity.

In order to do this He accepted living in a human body.

Before He came, He spoke to His Father about His earthly mission.

These words reflect this -

HEBREWS 10:5-7

"Wherefore when he cometh into the world, he saith ... a body hast thou prepared me:

Lo, I come (in the volume of the book it is written of me) to do thy will, O God."

This is such an incredible statement of Jesus.

He refers to the plan of God for His life that is written in a volume of one of God's books in Heaven.

Jesus yields Himself to the Will of God

The Life of Jesus

The Bible tells of the wonderful birth of our Lord Jesus Christ in Bethlehem.

Luke 2:7

"And she brought forth her firstborn son, and wrapped him in swaddling clothes, and laid him in a manger; because there was no room for them in the inn."

Luke 2:11

"For unto you is born this day in the city of David a Saviour, which is Christ the Lord."

And so we have the miraculous virgin birth of Jesus.

The Holy Spirit came over the womb of Mary and the human body of Jesus was conceived within her. Jesus had no earthly father.

From that moment, Jesus had only one purpose in His life and that was to do His Father's will.

This He revealed to His parents when He was twelve years old.

LUKE 2:49

"Wist ye not that I must be about my Father's business?"

Those words were a summary of His life's work.

His anointed ministry purpose was to do good on earth.

ACTS 10:38

"How God anointed Jesus of Nazareth with the Holy Ghost and with power: who went about **doing good**, and healing all that were oppressed of the devil; for God was with him."

This actually describes what His three years of earthly ministry was all about.

He had a well-planned and organized program.

Each year started and ended at Capernaum.

His twelve disciples and seventy witnesses went ahead of Him to the cities to prepare the people for His coming, saying the Kingdom of Heaven is at hand.

When Jesus arrived, He healed the sick, cast out devils and set the captives free. He raised the dead and ministered to the poor.

His preaching and teaching was phenomenal and there are about fifty discourses in the Gospels that contain a wide range of themes.

He also reveals the mysteries of the Kingdom of God through His parables.

His life on earth was a perfect sinless life and set an example of Christian living to all men.

1 Peter 2:21-22

"Christ also suffered for us, leaving us an example, that ye should follow his steps:

Who did no sin, neither was guile found in his mouth:"

All nine Fruits of the Holy Spirit were demonstrated in His life:

1. Love -

Jesus manifested love in His dealings with men.

When He was told that Lazarus was dead, He wept and the people said that it was because Jesus loved him so much.

John 11:36
"Then said the Jews, Behold how he loved him!"

2. Joy -

Luke 10:21
"In that hour Jesus **rejoiced** in spirit, and said, I thank thee, O Father, Lord of heaven and earth."

3. Peace -

While the Disciples were terrified in the midst of a storm on the Sea of Galilee, Jesus said - "Peace be still."

MARK 4:39
"And he arose, and rebuked the wind, and said unto the sea, Peace, be still. And the wind ceased, and there was a great calm."

4. Longsuffering -

Jesus continued to teach men and patiently endured their unbelief with much longsuffering.

MATTHEW 17:17
"Then Jesus answered and said, O faithless and perverse generation, how long shall I be with you? How long shall I suffer you?"

5. Gentleness -

Jesus revealed His gentleness in His dealings with children.

MARK 10:16
"And he took them up in his arms, put his hands upon them, and blessed them."

6. Goodness -

ACTS 10:38
"Jesus of Nazareth ... who went about doing good."

7. Faithfulness -

After Simon Peter denied the Lord at the death of Jesus, he decided to go back to fishing again, but Jesus faithfully went looking for him, found him and restored him.

John 21:3-4
"Simon Peter saith unto them, I go a fishing and that night they caught nothing.

But when the morning was now come, Jesus stood on the shore:"

8. Humility -

Jesus showed humility by being willing to take on a human body.

Philippians 2:8
"And being found in fashion as a man, he humbled himself."

9. Temperance -

Jesus exhibited temperance and self-control by fasting in the wilderness for forty days and nights.

Matthew 4:2
And when he had fasted forty days and forty nights, he was afterward an hungred."

All nine gifts of the Holy Spirit were manifested through Him:

1. Healing -

MATTHEW 4:23
"And Jesus went about all Galilee, healing all manner of sickness and all manner of disease among the people."

2. Working of miracles -

JOHN 2:11
"This beginning of miracles did Jesus in Cana of Galilee, and manifested forth his glory;"

3. Faith -

Jesus exercised His faith and then explained how it worked.

MARK 11:21-22
"And Peter calling to remembrance saith unto him, Master, behold, the fig tree which thou cursed is. And Jesus answering saith unto them, **have faith** in God."

4. A Word of wisdom -

The very best learned men and lawyers tried to outwit and catch Jesus with difficult questions but failed hopelessly because of His wisdom.

MARK 12:13-34

"And they send unto him certain of the Pharisees and of the Herodians, to catch him in his words.

And Jesus answering said unto them; Render to Caesar the things that are Caesar's, and to God the things that are God's. And they marveled at him.

And no man after that durst ask him any question."

5. A Word of Knowledge -

Jesus demonstrated a word of Knowledge when He saw Nathanael.

JOHN 1:48
"Nathanael saith unto him, whence knowest thou me? Jesus answered and said unto him, before that Philip called thee, when thou wast under the fig tree, I saw thee."

6. Discerning of spirits -

Jesus discerned that a woman's infirmity was satanic bondage.

LUKE 13:16
"And ought not this woman, being a daughter of Abraham, whom Satan hath bound, lo, these eighteen years, be loosed from this bond on the Sabbath day?"

7. Divers kinds of Tongues -

When Jesus raised up Jairus' daughter from the dead, He prayed and spoke in another language.

MARK 5:41-42
"And he took the damsel by the hand, and said unto her, **Talitha cumi;**"

8. Interpretation of Tongues -

MARK 5:41-42
"And he said unto her, **Talitha cumi;** which is, **being interpreted**, Damsel; I say unto thee, arise."

9. Prophecy -

Jesus prophesied of future events.

MATTHEW 24:33-34
"So likewise ye, when ye shall see all these things, know that it is near, even at the doors. Verily I say unto you, this generation shall not pass, till all these things are fulfilled."

The five main Ministries of the Holy Spirit manifested through Jesus:

1. Apostle -

Hebrews 3:1
"Wherefore, holy brethren, consider the Apostle and High Priest of our profession, Christ Jesus."

2. Prophet -

Jesus said that He was a Prophet without honor in His own country.

Matthew 13:57
"But Jesus said unto them, A prophet is not without honour, save in his own country, and in his own house."

3. Evangelist -

Jesus preached the Gospel. (Evangelio) It is the same word that is used for Evangelist.

Mark 1:14
"Jesus came into Galilee, preaching the Gospel of the Kingdom of God."

4. Pastor -

The word Pastor means Shepherd and Jesus is our Good Shepherd.

JOHN 10:11
"I am the good shepherd:"

5. Teacher -

While Jesus ministered on earth, men recognized that He was a Teacher.

JOHN 3:2
"The same came to Jesus by night, and said unto him, Rabbi, we know that thou art a teacher come from God."

Jesus ultimate purpose was to die and destroy the devil and sin.

HEBREWS 2:14

"That through **death** he might destroy him that had the power of death, that is, the devil."

John the Baptist revealed that Jesus would accomplish this as **the Lamb of God**.

JOHN 1:29

"Behold the Lamb of God, which taketh away the sin of the world."

He came as God's sacrificial lamb to die for the sins of all mankind.

He did this in order to save us from satan, hell, sin, sickness, death and poverty.

Isaiah 53: 5-7

"But he was wounded for our transgressions, he was bruised for our iniquities: the chastisement of our peace was upon him; and with his stripes we are healed.

All we like sheep have gone astray; we have turned everyone to his own way; and the LORD hath laid on him the iniquity of us all.

He was oppressed, and he was afflicted, yet he opened not his mouth: he is brought as a lamb to the slaughter, and as a sheep before her shearers is dumb, so he openeth not his mouth."

The fulfillment of this event is recorded in:

Matthew 27:33-38

"And when they were come unto a place called Golgotha, that is to say, a place of a skull, they gave him vinegar to drink mingled with gall: and when he had tasted thereof, he would not drink.

And they crucified him, and parted his garments, casting lots: that it might be fulfilled which was spoken by the prophet, they parted my garments among them, and upon my vesture did they cast lots.

And sitting down they watched him there;

And set up over his head his accusation written, THIS IS JESUS THE KING OF THE JEWS.

Then were there two thieves crucified with him, one on the right hand, and another on the left."

Jesus died so that He could redeem us with His blood.

Revelation 5:9

"Thou hast redeemed us to God by thy blood out of every kindred, and tongue, and people, and nation."

This is what happened when Jesus was physically put to death:

His body was cruelly mutilated.

His back was whipped apart by a flagellum, a roman whip made of nine leather thongs and metal pieces at the end of each thong.

A platted crown of three inch long thorns was forced into His head.

Upon His shoulders a heavy one hundred and ten pound patabellum was tied.

Jesus Christ

(It was the crossbar of the cross)

Our Savior was battered, dehydrated and exhausted.

He was led out of the Fortress of Antonio onto the Via-Delarosa, to stumble His way to Calvary. The centurion Longinus led the procession of sixty soldiers to take Jesus to Golgotha.

They nailed His hands and feet with six inch iron nails onto the cross, piercing His skin, muscles, tendons and arteries.

This experience of His crucifixion took Jesus past natural death to the ultimate price described as the second death.

There is no telling how traumatic this suffering must have been.

We know that His sweat turned to blood and He cried out to God the Father, to let the cup pass from Him.

The blood capillaries under His skin were bursting under the strain and suffering He was experiencing. This medical condition is known today as Hematidrosis.

No human has ever suffered so much.

When Jesus completed His sacrifice on the cross, He spoke these words -

John 19:30

"It is finished."

The sacrifice was made, the price was paid and the work was done.

On the third day after the crucifixion, Jesus arose from the dead

John 20:6-9

"Then cometh Simon Peter following him, and went into the sepulchre, and seeth the linen clothes lie,

And the napkin, that was about his head, not lying with the linen clothes, but wrapped together in a place by itself.

Then went in also that other disciple, which came first to the sepulchre, and he saw, and believed. For as yet they knew not the scripture, that he must rise again from the dead."

On several occasions after His resurrection, Jesus appeared to many people.

Acts 10:40-41

"Him God raised up the third day, and shewed him openly ... to us, who did eat and drink with him after he rose from the dead."

Jesus Christ

1 Corinthians 15:3-4

"How that Christ died for our sins according to the scriptures;

And that he was buried, and that he rose again the third day according to the scriptures:

And that he was **seen of Cephas,** then of **the twelve:**

After that, he was **seen of above five hundred brethren at once**; of whom the greater part remain unto this present, but some are fallen asleep.

After that, he was **seen of James;** then of **all the apostles.**

And last of all he was **seen of me** also."

Forty days after His resurrection Jesus ascended into Heaven.

Acts 1: 9

"And when he had spoken these things, while they beheld, he was taken up; and a cloud received him out of their sight."

Jesus Christ the Son of God was exalted by God the Father.

HEBREWS 1:3-13

"Who being the brightness of his glory, and the express image of his person, and upholding all things by the word of his power, when he had by himself purged our sins, sat down on the right hand of the Majesty on high: Being made so much better than the angels, obtained a more excellent name than they. But unto the Son he saith, Thy throne, O God, is forever and ever: a scepter of righteousness is the scepter of thy kingdom. God, even thy God, hath anointed thee with the oil of gladness above thy fellows But to which of the angels said he at any time, Sit on my right hand."

PHILIPPIANS 2:9-11

"Wherefore God also hath highly exalted him, and given him a name which is above every name: That at the name of Jesus every knee should bow, of things in heaven, and things in earth, and things under the earth; And that every tongue should confess that Jesus Christ is Lord, to the glory of God the Father.

Jesus is now at the right hand of God the Father doing His present day ministry on our behalf.

This ministry includes the following;

- He is our **Savior.**
- He is our **Good Shepherd.**
- He is our **High Priest.**
- He is our **Righteous Advocate.**
- He is our **Intercessor.**
- He is our **Lord.**
- He is our **King.**

Jesus is our Savior.

He continues to save people from eternal damnation.

1 Timothy 1:15

"Christ Jesus came into the world to save sinners."

Hebrews 7:25

"Wherefore he is able also to save them to the uttermost that come unto God by him."

He continues to help and save us every day we need Him.

Jesus is our Good Shepherd.

JOHN 10:11

"I am the good shepherd: the good shepherd giveth his life for the sheep."

Jesus shepherds and takes care of God's children.

He is our High Priest.

HEBREWS 7:17

"For he testifieth, Thou art a priest for ever after the order of Melchisedec."

His High Priestly sprinkling of His blood in Gods Temple in Heaven took care of all sins past, present and future.

HEBREWS 9:12

"But by his own blood he entered in once into the holy place, having obtained eternal redemption for us."

1 PETER 2:9

"But ye are a royal priesthood"

We are priests of God, and Jesus is the High Priest of our priestly activities.

He is our Righteous Advocate.

1 John 2:1

"We have an advocate with the Father, Jesus Christ the righteous."

When satan comes before God in the Courts of Heaven to accuse us, Jesus our Advocate rises up in our defense.

He knows and understands the Laws of God.

He also knows our thoughts, behavior and temptations.

On earth He was tempted and tried in all things just like us and He can help us.

He is our Intercessor.

Hebrews 7:25

"Wherefore he is able also to save them to the uttermost that come unto God by him, seeing he ever liveth to make intercession for them."

Jesus continually sees our needs and prays for us.

He is our Lord.

PHILIPPIANS 2:11

"And that every tongue should confess that Jesus Christ is Lord, to the glory of God the Father."

Jesus is our Lord and Master. We are His servants and we obey his commands.

He is our King.

REVELATION 19:16

"And he hath on his vesture and on his thigh a name written, KING OF KINGS, AND LORD OF LORDS."

As children of God we are subjects and citizens of the Kingdom of God, and Jesus is our King. We owe and pledge our allegiance to Him and are in subjection to Him. Before He returns to this earth to set up His Millennial Kingdom, He will be crowned as King of all Kings.

The glorious promise of His return to earth

We have this glorious promise that Jesus will soon return.

Jesus Christ

Luke 21:28

"And when these things begin to come to pass, then look up, and lift up your heads; for your redemption draweth nigh."

1 Thessalonians 4:16-17

"For the Lord Himself shall descend from heaven with a shout, with the voice of the archangel, and with the trump of God: and the dead in Christ shall rise first:

Then we which are alive and remain shall be caught up together with them in the clouds, to meet the Lord in the air: and so shall we ever be with the Lord."

Revelation 19:11-16

"And I saw heaven opened, and behold a white horse; and he that sat upon him was called Faithful and True, and in righteousness he doth judge and make war.

His eyes were as a flame of fire, and on his head were many crowns; and he had a name written, that no man knew, but he himself.

And he was clothed with vesture dipped in blood: and his name is called The Word of God.

And the armies which were in heaven followed him upon white horses, clothed in fine linen, white and clean.

And out of his mouth goeth a sharp sword, that with it he should smite the nations: and he shall rule them with a rod of iron: and he treadeth the winepress of the fierceness and wrath of Almighty God.

And he hath on his vesture and on his thigh a name written, KING OF KINGS, AND LORD OF LORDS."

There has never been and will never be any person like JESUS CHRIST!

CHAPTER 4

The Holy Spirit

The Holy Spirit is the third person of the Godhead.

1 John 5:7

"For there are three that bear record in heaven, the Father, the Word, and the Holy Ghost: and these three are one."

The Holy Spirit is mentioned together with God the Father and Jesus Christ in scripture.

(Matthew 3:16-17, 2 Corinthians 13:14)

He is part of the **Godhead** mentioned in **Acts 17:29**

The Holy Spirit has several characteristics:

He is Holy.

One hundred times He is referred to as the Holy Spirit.

There must be a reason why this adjective "Holy" is used to describe Him.

It is because He is a Holy Being.

He is called the Spirit of Holiness which is the very essence of His being.

ROMANS 1:4

"And declared to be the Son of God with power, according to the spirit of holiness..."

He is Spirit.

He is a Spirit and does not have a fleshly body or fleshly limitations.

He can come and go like wind, and is like water, rain and fire.

He is a Person.

We know that the Holy Spirit is a Person and has all the elements of Personality.

He has distinctive elements such as a mind, emotions and a will.

He sees, hears, feels, speaks and makes decisions.

He has intelligence, knowledge, reason and feelings.

In all His plans and works there is precision and perfection.

The following scriptures clearly reveal His mind, emotions, will and actions.

The Holy Spirit

Romans 8:27

"And he that searcheth the hearts knoweth what is the **mind of the Spirit**."

Romans 15:30

"And for the l**ove** of the Spirit."

Acts 9:31

"And walking in the **comfort** of the Holy Ghost."

Acts 8:29

"Then **the Spirit said** unto Philip, Go near, and join thyself to this chariot."

Acts 10:19-20

"While Peter thought on the vision, **the Spirit said** unto him, behold, three men seek thee."

Acts 16:6-7

"Now when they had gone throughout Phrygia and the region of Galatia, and were **forbidden of the Holy Ghost** to preach the word in Asia,

After they were come to Mysia, they assayed to go into Bithynia: but the **Spirit suffered them not."**

1 Corinthians 2:10

"For the Spirit **searcheth** all things, yea, the deep things of God."

Revelation 2:7

"He that hath an ear, let him hear what the **Spirit saith** unto the churches;"

Romans 8:26

"But the Spirit itself **maketh intercession** for us."

He is active.

Over one hundred and sixty passages in the Bible reveal the activities of the Holy Spirit and here are some of them:

Genesis 1:2

"And the Spirit of God **moved** upon the face of the waters."

Job 26:13

"By his spirit he hath garnished the heavens;"

It is clear in the Bible, that the Holy Spirit had a significant role in the creation of the heavens and the earth. He was the co-creator of the Universe and helped to garnish and beautify it. He had a part in the creation of man.

Psalm 104:30

"Thou sendest forth thy spirit, they are created: and thou renewest the face of the earth."

Job 33:4

"The spirit of God hath made me."

The Holy Spirit works in the lives of men and women.

People receive special enduements, power and creative abilities from Him.

Here is an example:

Exodus 31:1-5

"And the LORD spake unto Moses, saying,

See, I have called by name Bezaleel:

And I have filled him with the Spirit of God, in wisdom, and in understanding, and in knowledge, and in all manner of workmanship."

The Holy Spirit comes upon men.

He literally clothes them with His presence.

Judges 6:34

"But the Spirit of the LORD came upon Gideon."

1 Samuel 16:13

"And the Spirit of the LORD came upon David from that day forward."

The Holy Spirit rests upon men

Numbers 11:25-26

"And the LORD came down in a cloud, and spake unto him, and took of the spirit that was upon him, and gave it unto the seventy elders: and it came to pass, that, when the spirit rested upon them, they prophesied, and did not cease."

The Holy Spirit moves men into action.

Judges 13:25

And the Spirit of the LORD began to move him at times in the camp of Dan.

The Holy Spirit comes into men.

Genesis 41:38

"And Pharaoh said unto his servants, can we find such a one as this is, a man in whom the Spirit of God is?"

NUMBERS 27:18

"Take thee Joshua the son of Nun, a man in whom is the spirit."

DANIEL 4:8

"But at the last Daniel came in before me in whom is the Spirit of the holy gods:"

There are ninety New Testament references to the Holy Spirit.

He is given sixteen titles that are divided into three groups:

Titles that express His relationship to God namely:

    The Spirit of God

    Voice of the Almighty

    Breath of the Almighty

Titles that express His character namely:

    Holy Spirit

    Spirit of Power

    Spirit of Life

    New Spirit

Titles that express His operations in and through men:

    Spirit of wisdom

    Spirit of understanding

Spirit of power

Spirit of might

Spirit of knowledge

Spirit of the fear of the Lord

Spirit of grace

Spirit of supplication

Spirit of burning

There are also nine symbols of the Holy Spirit given in the Bible.

These symbols are:

1. A Dove

MATTHEW 3:16
"And he saw the Spirit of God descending like a dove."

2. Wind

JOHN 3:8
"The wind bloweth where it listeth, and thou hearest the sound thereof, but canst not tell whence it cometh, and whither it goeth: so is every one that is born of the Spirit."

The Holy Spirit

3. Water

John 4:14
"But whosoever drinketh of the **water** that I shall give him shall never thirst;"

(The Holy Spirit)

4. Rivers

John 7:38-39
"He that believeth on me, as the scripture hath said, out of his belly shall flow rivers of living water. But this spake he of the Spirit."

5. Rain and Showers

Psalm 72:6
"He shall come down like rain upon the mown grass: as showers that water the earth."

6. A well of water

John 4:14
"But the water that I shall give him shall be in him a well of water springing up into everlasting life."

7. Tongues of fire

Acts 2:3
"And there appeared unto them cloven tongues like as of fire, and it sat upon each of them."

8. Oil and anointing

MATTHEW 25:4
"But the wise took oil in their vessels with their lamps."

ACTS 10:38
"How God anointed Jesus of Nazareth with the Holy Ghost and with power:"

9. New Wine

LUKE 5:38
"But new wine must be put into new bottles."

EPHESIANS 5:18
"And be not drunk with wine, but be filled with the Spirit;"

The Holy Spirit reveals Himself in the life of Jesus, in seven ways:

1. The Holy Spirit prophesied about Jesus before His birth.

1 PETER 1:11
"The **Spirit** of Christ which was in them did signify, when it **testified beforehand** the sufferings of Christ."

The Holy Spirit

2. Jesus was physically born of the Holy Spirit.

Matthew 1:18
"Now the birth of Jesus Christ was on this wise: she was found with child of the Holy Ghost."

3. Jesus was anointed of the Holy Spirit.

Acts 10:38
"How God anointed Jesus of Nazareth with the Holy Ghost."

4. Jesus rejoiced in the Holy Spirit.

Luke 10:21
"In that hour Jesus rejoiced in spirit."

5. Jesus died by the Holy Spirit.

He 9:14

"Christ, who through the eternal Spirit offered Himself."

6. Jesus was resurrected, by the Holy Spirit.

Romans 8:11
"But if the Spirit of him that raised up Jesus from the dead."

7. Jesus gave commands to his disciples by the Holy Spirit.

Acts 1:2

"Until the day in which he was taken up, after that he through the Holy Ghost had given commandments unto the apostles whom he had chosen:"

The present day Ministry of the Holy Spirit

The Holy Spirit continues to reveal Himself in this New Testament Church dispensation.

It extends for two thousand years from Christ's ascension to His Second Coming.

This period is divided into seven church periods described in Revelation chapters two and three.

Ephesus was symbolical of the first Apostolic Church and Laodicea of the last end time Church.

The Holy Spirit manifests Himself as seven lamps.

Each lamp represents one of the seven churches.

The lamps are symbolical of the outpouring of the Holy Spirit during the church dispensation.

This is the initial prophecy given for the outpouring of the Holy Spirit:

Joel 2:28

"And it shall come to pass afterward, that I will pour out **my spirit** upon all flesh;"

When Peter spoke of their experience of receiving the Holy Spirit on the day of Pentecost, he spoke of them only receiving a portion. He uses the word **"of"**.

Acts 2:18

"And on my servants and on my handmaidens I will pour out in those days of my Spirit;"

They first Church received the first portion. (The former rain)

The last Church will receive the last portion. (The latter rain)

There are **three** different **seven-fold manifestations** of the Holy Spirit to each Church:

As seven lamps

Revelation 4:5

"And there were seven lamps of fire burning before the throne."

This refers to the **perfect light of truth and revelation** that the Holy Spirit brings.

As seven horns

Revelations 5:6

"Having seven horns and seven eyes, which are the seven Spirits of God."

This refers to the **perfect power and authority** the Holy Spirit brings.

As seven eyes

This refers to the perfect **insight, knowledge and discernment** the Holy Spirit brings.

More specifically the Holy Spirit deals with each Christian in seven ways:

1. He reaches out to change sinful people into Christians.

He convicts them of sin and strives to bring them to salvation.

GENESIS 6:3
"And the LORD said, My spirit shall not always strive with man, for that he also is flesh."

JOHN 16:8
"And when he is come, he will reprove the world of sin."

2. The Holy Spirit causes our spiritual birth.

He does this by giving life to the seed of God's Word that is sown into our hearts.

He causes this seed of the Word to come alive in us.

It becomes a spiritual embryo and we are **born again into God's Kingdom.**

JOHN 3:5
"Except a man be born of water and of the Spirit, he cannot enter into the kingdom of God."

The Holy Spirit

I Peter 1:23
"Being born again, not of corruptible seed, but of incorruptible, by the word of God, which liveth and abideth for ever."

2 Corinthians 3:6
"For the letter killeth, but the Spirit giveth life."

3. The Holy Spirit fills us with His presence, empowers us and seals us.

Ephesians 5:18
"Be filled with the Spirit."

Acts 1:8
"But ye shall receive power, after that the Holy Ghost is come upon you:"

Ephesians 1:13
"In whom also after that ye believed, ye were sealed with that Holy Spirit of promise."

4. The Holy Spirit fellowships with us.

2 Corinthians 13:14
"The communion of the Holy Ghost, be with you all."

He walks and talks with us, teaches, helps and comforts us.

5. He imparts the nine Fruits of the Holy Spirit to us.

GALATIANS 5:22-23
"But the fruit of the Spirit is love, joy, peace, longsuffering, gentleness, goodness, faith, Meekness, temperance:"

6. He imparts the nine Gifts of the Holy Spirit to us.

1 CORINTHIANS 12:4-10
"Now there are diversities of gifts, but the same Spirit.

For to one is given by the Spirit the word of wisdom;

to another the word of knowledge by the same Spirit;

to another faith by the same Spirit;

to another the gifts of healing by the same Spirit;

to another the working of miracles;

to another prophecy;

to another discerning of spirits;

to another divers kinds of tongues;

to another the interpretation of tongues:"

7. He imparts any of the nine Ministries of the Holy Spirit to us as He chooses to use us in His Ministry Program.

The Holy Spirit

1 Corinthians 12:13-28
"For by one Spirit are we all baptized into one body...But now hath God set the members every one of them in the body as it hath pleased him... And God hath set some in the church, first apostles, secondarily prophets, thirdly teachers, after that miracles, then gifts of healings, helps, governments, diversities of tongues."

Ephesians 4:11
"And he gave some, apostles; and some, prophets; and some, evangelists; and some, pastors and teachers;"

He places Christians in their right order and position.

An example is given of the Holy Spirit appointing Paul and Barnabas into Apostolic ministry.

Acts 13:2
"The Holy Ghost said, Separate me Barnabas and Saul for the work whereunto I have called them."

We should recognize, appreciate and reverence the Holy Spirit.

There are three things we should never do:

1. We should never sadden or disappoint the Holy Spirit.

EPHESIANS 4:30
"And grieve not the Holy Spirit of God, whereby ye are sealed unto the day of redemption."

2. We should never hold back or resist the work of the Holy Spirit.

1 THESSALONIANS 5:19
"Quench not the Spirit."

3. We should never speak against the work or person of Holy Spirit.

MATTHEW 12:31
"But the blasphemy against the Holy Ghost shall not be forgiven unto men."

Christians should always enjoy a very personal relationship with the Holy Spirit.

Interesting Old Testament typology reveals this -

- Abraham was a type of God the Father.
- Isaac his son was a type of Jesus Christ God's Son.
- Eliezer Abraham's servant was a type of the Holy Spirit.

Eliezer was a servant of Abraham.**(Genesis 24)**

Abraham placed his child Isaac into the hands of Eliezer his servant, for care and tutoring.

This relationship continued until Isaac reached maturity at thirty years of age.

The Holy Spirit is described as our Spirit of adoption:

Romans 8:15

"But ye have received the Spirit of adoption, whereby we cry, Abba, Father."

In Old Testament times, a child was placed under the tutoring and governing of the servant until the child's maturity. This was known as an adoption process and is very similar to the adoption of children today.

Similarly God the Father has given His children into the tender loving care of the Holy Spirit to help them, tutor them and govern their life.

Galatians 4:1-6

"Now I say, That the heir, as long as he is a child, differeth nothing from a servant, though he be lord of all;

But is under tutors and governors until the time appointed of the father.

Even so we, when we were children, were in bondage under the elements of the world:

That we might receive the adoption of sons.

And because ye are sons, God hath sent forth the Spirit of his Son into your hearts, crying, Abba, Father."

In this adoption process the Holy Spirit does five things:

1. He convicts us of Sin, Righteousness and Judgment.

JOHN 16:8
"And when he is come, he will reprove the world of sin, and of righteousness, and of judgment:"

2. He teaches and guides us in all truth.

JOHN 16:13
"Howbeit when he, the Spirit of truth, is come, he will guide you into all truth:"

3. He brings us to full spiritual maturity.

4. He comforts us.

JOHN 14:16
"And I will pray the Father, and he shall give you another Comforter."

5. He guarantees our inheritance.

Ephesians 1: 13
"In whom ye also trusted, ye were sealed with that Holy Spirit of promise… which is the earnest of our inheritance."

Would you like to have a fruitful and successful relationship with the Holy Spirit?

Then yield yourself to His authority and do four things:

1. Listen to what the Holy Spirit says to you.

Revelations 2:7
"He that hath an ear, let him hear what the Spirit saith."

2. Pay attention to and meditate upon the things the Holy Spirit says to you.

Romans 8:5
"For they that are after the flesh do mind the things of the flesh; but they that are after the Spirit the things of the Spirit."

3. Be obedient and do what the Holy Spirit commands.

Romans 8:14
"For as many as are led by the Spirit of God, they are the sons of God."

4. Live and walk in the presence and anointing of the Holy Spirit.

GALATIANS 5:16
"Walk in the Spirit, and ye shall not fulfill the lust of the flesh."

CHAPTER 5

The Word Of God

The Bible is the written form of God's word to us.

It is the key to finding out who God is and what He says.

It is a communication channel from God to man.

God's first communication with man was with Adam and Eve in the Garden of Eden.

God continued to communicate with people from generation to generation.

After that God gave His Word to Israel in written form:

It is called the Pentateuch.

Moses recorded and gave the Israelites the first five books of the Bible -

Genesis, Exodus, Leviticus, Numbers and Deuteronomy

Romans 3:1-2

"What advantage then hath the Jew? Or what profit is there of circumcision?

Much every way: chiefly, because that unto them were committed the oracles of God."

The word "**oracle**" means "Divine Words."

These Divine Words are perfect, sure and wise.

Psalm 19:7

"The law of the LORD is perfect, converting the soul:

the testimony of the LORD is sure, making wise the simple."

The Bible, God's inspired Word gives man understanding:

Job 32:8

"The inspiration of the Almighty giveth them understanding."

It was Holy Men who received and gave the inspired Word from God.

2 Peter 1:21

"But holy men of God spake as they were moved by the Holy Ghost."

God spoke through His anointed Servants.

One by one the thirty-nine books of the Old Testament and the twenty- seven books of the New Testament were written.

Together they total sixty-six books.

This written form of the Bible is known as the Holy Scriptures.

Jesus said that scripture cannot be broken.

John 10:35

"Unto whom the word of God came, and the scripture cannot be broken;"

Every scripture in the Bible is important and cannot be discarded, because all scripture, is given by God.

2 Timothy 3:16

"All scripture is given by inspiration of God."

The original writings of the Bible were written on papyrus or animal skins and do not exist today.

However there are three ancient copies that do exist today.

The three most ancient copies are:

Codex Sinaiticus

Codex Alexandrinus

Codex Vaticanus

The Codex Sinaiticus and Alexandrinus are in the British Museum and the Codex Vaticanus is in the Vatican in Rome.

In many different ways, the authenticity of the Bible has been verified.

Copies of parts of the original manuscripts have been found in different places and they agree perfectly. Their writers had absolutely no contact with each other.

Thousands of writings and personal letters between people have been discovered. They make reference to scriptures and when pieced together, form the whole Bible that is identical to the three Ancient Copies.

The King James Bible

In 1611, King James the First appointed forty-seven scholars to translate the Ancient Copies of the Bible into English. This resulted in the King James Bible version. There are various other modern translations of the Bible today.

The King James Bible stands out as the most accepted true version.

For bible study or doctrines many believe that it is the best version to use other than the original Greek and Hebrew texts.

As you hold a Bible in your hand you hold God's inspired Word.

The Word Of God

It is God speaking to you!

I trust that you appreciate and value this magnificent Book.

I challenge you to read and enjoy the Bible.

If you don't have one, get a copy today.

Treat every page with due respect and reverence.

Never allow it to become a dust collector on a forgotten bookshelf.

There are two aspects of God's Word:

1. The Word of God is **Logos.**

2. The Word of God is **Rhema.**

First - Gods Word is Logos.

JOHN 1:14

"And the Word was made flesh, and dwelt among us."

Here the word **"Word"** is the Greek word **"Logos"** and means the given, written Word of God.

This Word was made flesh in the person of Jesus Christ the Son of God.

He was the very alphabet of the Bible.

24 Doctrines of the Bible

Jesus said this of Himself:

REVELATION 1:11

"I am Alpha and Omega, the first and the last:"

The alpha and omega are the first and last letters of the Greek alphabet.

Jesus is therefore every letter of every word of the Bible and it comes to life in the person of Jesus.

When we read the Bible it becomes an active force within us:

1 THESSALONIANS 3:13

"The word of God, which effectually worketh also in you."

It is the basis of three wonderful blessings:

a. God's Word causes our spiritual birth.

1 PETER 1:23
"Being born again, not of corruptible seed, but of incorruptible, by the Word of God, which liveth and abideth for ever."

b. God's Word brings truth to us.

JOHN 17:17
"Thy word is truth."

c. God's Word is our Light.

Psalm 119:105

"Thy word is a lamp unto my feet, and a light unto my path."

Second - Gods Word is Rhema.

Ephesians 6:17

"And take the sword of the Spirit, which is the word of God:"

The Greek word here for **Word** is **"Rhema"**.

It means "the spoken Word of God."

Revelation 1:16

"And out of his mouth went a sharp two-edged sword:"

The Spoken Word that went out of Jesus mouth was a two-edged sword and was Rhema.

How Logos becomes Rhema.

The Logos within our hearts when spoken out of our mouths becomes Rhema.

Hebrews 4:12

"For the word of God is quick, and powerful, and sharper than any two-edged sword."

This Rhema Word of God:

a. Is a Powerful Force.

Isaiah 55:11
"So shall my word be that goeth forth out of my mouth: it shall accomplish that which I please, and it shall prosper in the thing whereto I sent it."

b. It will never pass away.

Matthew 24:35
"Heaven and earth shall pass away, but my words shall not pass away."

c. It is forever settled in Heaven.

Psalm 119:89
"Forever, O LORD, thy word is settled in heaven."

Gods spoken Word is everlasting and unchangeable.

The powerful Word of God affects us in ten different ways:

1. It is truth to us.

When it reaches our hearts, it dispels all ignorance and confusion.

The Word Of God

PSALM 119:140
"The entrance of thy words giveth light; it giveth understanding unto the simple."

2. It causes us to have faith in God.

ROMANS 10:17
"So then faith cometh by hearing, and hearing by the Word of God."

As we read Gods Word, faith is stimulated within us.

It rises up causing us to trust and depend upon God as our source for everything.

The Logos in us then becomes Rhema and we speak it out in faith saying:

God is my salvation.

God is my healer.

God is my provider.

God is my victory.

3. It causes us to experience life and health.

PROVERBS 4:20-22
"My son, attend to my words; incline thine ear unto my sayings.

For they are life unto those that find them, and health to all their flesh."

PSALMS 107:20
"He sent his word, and healed them."

4. It is spiritual food and nourishment to us.

1 PETER 2:2
"As newborn babes, desire the sincere milk of the word that ye may grow thereby:"

MATTHEW 4:4
"But he answered and said, it is written, Man shall not live by bread alone, but by every word that proceedeth out of the mouth of God."

We are therefore nourished spiritually:

- By the pure milk of the Word.
- By the satisfying bread of the Word.

5. God's Word is hidden in our hearts.

PSALM 119:11
"Thy word have I hid in mine heart, that I might not sin against thee."

We hear or read God's Word and it is processed deep within our Soul and Spirit.

The presence of the Word within us counteracts all sin coming against us.

This Word within us is the Sword of the Spirit that we use in spiritual battle, against the devil and the kingdom of darkness.

The Word Of God

1 John 2:14
"The word of God abideth in you, and ye have overcome the wicked one."

6. God's Word keeps us from the destroyer.

Psalm 17:4
"By the word of thy lips I have kept me from the paths of the destroyer."

7. The Word of God is our mirror.

James 1:23
"For if any be a hearer of the word, and not a doer, he is like unto a man beholding his natural face in a glass:"

As we read the Bible we see ourselves as we are and who God wants us to be.

It is like looking in a mirror. We discover what needs to be changed, we experience that change and continue in that blessing.

8. God's Word cleanses and refreshes us.

Ephesians 5:26
"That he might sanctify and cleanse it with the washing of water by the Word."

John 15:3
"Now ye are clean through the Word which I have spoken unto you."

As we read or hear the scriptures of the Bible, they are assimilated into our mind, and they pass through the chambers of our observation, reason, imagination, memory, emotion, will and spirit. They have a cleansing and refreshing effect upon our entire inner being.

9. The Word contains all of God's promises.

2 Peter 1:4
"Whereby are given unto us exceeding great and precious promises: that by these ye might be partakers of the divine nature."

These are promises of:

Power

Holiness

Righteousness

Health

Blessing

Prosperity

Joy

Peace

happiness

Through God's Word we partake of these promises.

10. God's Word contains all the Doctrines we need.

2 Timothy 3:16
"All scripture is given by inspiration of God, and is profitable for **doctrine.**"

It is through the Bible that we receive instruction in all the teachings of God.

By these teachings we know what God requires us to do.

God tells us what He has done for us and what He will do for us. These teachings cover every aspect of every subject we need to know while we are here on earth.

Nothing may be added to the Word of God.

Revelation 22:18

"For I testify ... If any man shall add unto these things, God shall add unto him the plagues that are written in this book."

The Word of God has special significance for the end-time Martyrs.

They will overcome the dragon and the antichrist by the Word of God.

It is therefore now timely and most important to read and study the Bible.

REVELATION 12:11

"And they overcame him by the blood of the Lamb, and by the word of their testimony; and they loved not their lives unto the death."

Here are four helpful suggestions:

1. Read the Bible.

If you can't read, have someone read it to you, or get the Bible in audio form and listen to it.

Try to enjoy one chapter a day.

Start at the beginning of the New Testament with the book of Matthew.

2. Meditate the scriptures you read.

David loved thinking about God's Word day and night.

PSALM 1:2
"But his delight is in the law of the LORD; and in his law doth he meditate day and night."

To **meditate** means to think about something over and over again.

When you read the Bible early in the morning, you can meditate and think about the scriptures you have read, throughout the day. While you lay on your bed at night you can meditate the Scriptures you have read.

3. Memorize the scriptures.

Psalm 119:11
"Thy word have I hid in mine heart, that I might not sin against thee."

By memorizing the Scriptures of the Bible, we hide them in our heart. At any given moment you will be able recall to memory a scripture and apply it to any situation or need you may find yourself in. Try to memorize all the promises of God.

4. Study the Word of God.

2 Timothy 2:15
"Study to shew thyself approved unto God, a workman that needeth not to be ashamed, rightly dividing the word of truth."

I encourage you to use every possible method or technology to study the Bible and its Doctrines.

Appreciate the fact that the Most High God has communicated with you through His Word, revealing the truth you need to know!

"The Word of God"

3. Memorize the Scriptures!

Psalm 119:11
Thy word have I hid in mine heart, that I might not sin against thee.

By memorizing the Scriptures of God you will store up in your heart God's Word that will be able to... ... ...
... ...
... you also at ... ... of God.

4. Study the Word of God.

2 Timothy 2:15
Study to shew thyself approved unto God, a workman that needeth not to be ashamed, rightly dividing the word of truth.

It is a challenge to you to search the Scriptures for yourself and to rightly divide God's word of truth.

5. Apply what the Bible teaches in your life as a Christian, emulating Christ with your example. Remember, you may be the only ... ... the truth your friends see.

CHAPTER 6

Man and Sin

After God completed the creation of the universe He crowned it with a beautiful masterpiece, namely the creation of man.

Man - Gods masterpiece:

G‍ENESIS **1:27**

"So God created man in his own image ... male and female created he them."

The Hebrew word "create" in this verse is **"Bara"**

It means - **a new creation**

Never before had any other creature been created in God's image or likeness.

Genesis 1:26

"And God said, Let us make man in our image, after our likeness:"

The words image and likeness have two totally different meanings:

The Hebrew word for "image" is "**Demooth**".

It means - **in resemblance of**

Man has the outward appearance of God and has a face, body, hands and feet.

The Hebrew word for "likeness" is "**Charit** ".

Its meaning is similar to an - **architectural plan.**

An architectural plan of a house shows what it consists of.

It could have several rooms, bathrooms, a kitchen and a living room.

The Godhead is One Being, consisting of three Persons namely:

God the Father

Jesus Christ and

The Holy Spirit

We are made in God's architectural image and have three parts:

Body

Soul and

Spirit

Man and Sin

God is Tri-une and we are Tri-partate.

1 Thessalonians 5:23

"And the very God of peace sanctify you wholly; and I pray God your whole **spirit and soul and body** be preserved blameless unto the coming of our Lord Jesus Christ."

God created Adam's body with clay and then blew the breath of life into his nostrils.

The breath became mans spirit. When the clay and the spirit came together, man became a living soul. Man therefore has a Body, Soul and a Spirit.

Genesis 1: 7

"And the LORD God formed man of the dust of the ground, and breathed into his nostrils the breath of life; and man became a living soul."

This enabled man to have three kinds of consciousness:

1. With his Body he had world consciousness to communicate with the world.

2. With his Soul he had *self-consciousness* and could communicate with himself.

3. With his Spirit he had *God consciousness* to communicate with God who is Spirit.

Why was man created and for what purpose?

There are five reasons why God created man:

1. Man was created to have a relationship with God.

God wanted to walk, talk and fellowship with man.

GENESIS 3:8-9
"And they heard the voice of the LORD God walking in the garden in the cool of the day:

And the LORD God called unto Adam, and said unto him, where art thou?"

2. Man was created to replenish the earth.

God wanted man to have children, multiply and fill the earth with people.

God wanted a large family of billions of people to love and care for.

GENESIS 1:28
"And God blessed them, and God said unto them, be fruitful, and multiply, and replenish the earth."

Man and Sin

3. Man was created to subdue the earth.

Genesis 1:28
"And God blessed them, and God said unto them, be fruitful, and multiply, and replenish the earth, and subdue it: and have dominion over the fish of the sea, and over the fowl of the air, and over every living thing that moveth upon the earth."

Man was placed in Authority and Management over all things on the earth.

4. Man was created to enjoy everything on earth that God provided.

God gave man things to enjoy that were pleasant, good and satisfying.

Genesis 2:9
"And out of the ground made the LORD God to grow every tree that is pleasant to the sight, and good for food;"

Genesis 2:10-12
"And a river went out of Eden to water the garden; and from thence it was parted, and became into four heads.

The name of the first is Pison: where there is gold;

5. Man was created to be under Gods authority and discipline.

God wanted man to recognize and respect His authority.

God tested Adam and Eve's submission and obedience to Him.

They were perfect, without sin and God gave them a command.

He expected them to obey it.

When they were disobedient and showed their disrespect for His authority, they were disciplined and punished by Him.

God clearly warned them of the consequences of disobeying Him.

GENESIS 2:17
"But of the tree of the knowledge of good and evil, thou shalt not eat of it: for in the day that thou eatest thereof thou shalt surely die."

The fall of Man

This is described in:

GENESIS 3:1-8

"Now the serpent was more subtle than any beast of the field, which the LORD God had made. And he said unto the woman, Yea, hath God said, ye shall not eat of every tree of the garden?

And the woman said unto the serpent, we may eat of the fruit of the trees of the garden:

Man and Sin

But of the fruit of the tree, which is in the midst of the garden, God hath said, ye shall not eat of it, neither shall ye touch it, lest ye die.

And the serpent said unto the woman, ye shall not surely die:

For God doth know that in the day ye eat thereof, then your eyes shall be opened, and ye shall be as gods, knowing good and evil.

And when the woman saw that the tree was good for food, and that it was pleasant to the eyes, and a tree to be desired to make one wise, she took of the fruit thereof, and did eat, and gave also unto her husband with her; and he did eat.

And the eyes of them both were opened, and they knew that they were naked; and they sewed fig leaves together, and made themselves aprons.

And they heard the voice of the LORD God walking in the garden in the cool of the day: and Adam and his wife hid themselves from the presence of the LORD God amongst the trees of the garden."

Here satan came in the form of a serpent to tempt Adam and Eve.

He caused them to doubt God's word, disobey God and partake of the forbidden fruit.

They experienced the after effects of their sin, feeling naked, defiled and guilty. They fled from God's presence and hid in the garden.

The results of the fall of man into sin

The sin of Adam and Eve brought about five consequences:

1. Adam and Eve's sin came upon all men.

Sin came upon all Adam's descendants and therefore all people born into this world are in sin.

PSALM 51:5
"Behold, I was shapen in iniquity; and in sin did my mother conceive me."

Man's very nature is sinful.

1 JOHN 5:19
"And the whole world lieth in wickedness."

2. Therefore people continue to experience the process of sin:

This process is described in:

JAMES 1:14-15
"But every man is tempted, when he is drawn away of his own lust, and enticed.

Then when lust hath conceived, it bringeth forth sin: and sin, when it is finished, bringeth forth death."

This process involves:

- An own lust that is in every person.
- This lust becoming a target for satan to tempt.

- Falling into temptation.
- Committing sin.
- Experiencing death.

3. Every person has a weakness or own lust to sin.

Lust is a **negative appetite** for something.

Every person has his or her own lust that craves for something that is sinful.

There are many kinds of own lusts.

When this lust is enticed and yields to a temptation, it produces sin and then death.

Here is an example of a lust for money and how the sinful process works:

- A person has a love for money. (Their own lust)
- They see money and are tempted to steal it. (Temptation)
- They decide to steal it. (Sin actually occurs in the mind.)
- They steal the money. (The fruit of the sin is the deed)

Jesus clearly teaches about this process.

MATTHEW 5:28

"But I say unto you, that whosoever looketh on a woman to lust after her hath committed adultery with her already in his heart."

Our own lust lies in three areas:

a. The desires of the **flesh.** (Sexual and food appetites)

b. The desires of the **eyes.** (Attractions and possessions)

c. The **pride** of life. (Desires of exaltation, fame and pride)

I JOHN 2:16
"For all that is in the world, the lust of the flesh, and the lust of the eyes, and the pride of life."

4. The spirit of man is dead.

GENESIS 2:17
"But of the tree of the knowledge of good and evil, thou shalt not eat of it: for in the day that thou eatest thereof thou shalt surely die."

Adam and Eve did not die physically the day they ate of the fruit.

They died spiritually and their spiritual death passed on to all humanity.

Man and Sin

1 Corinthians 15:22
"For as in Adam all die."

Romans 6:23
"For the wages of sin is death;"

5. Because of sin, man is cursed.

Genesis 3:16-19
"Unto the woman he said, I will greatly multiply thy sorrow and thy conception; in sorrow thou shalt bring forth children;

And unto Adam he said; because thou hast hearkened unto the voice of thy wife, and hast eaten of the tree, cursed is the ground for thy sake; in sorrow shalt thou eat of it all the days of thy life;"

This curse was passed on to all men and women in three ways:

1. It was a curse of Toil and Sorrow.

2. It was a curse of Mortality. (Experiencing sickness, frailty and death)

3. It was a curse of Poverty. (Experiencing lack and want)

The Bible reveals three kinds of sins that could be committed by man:

1. Innocent sin

Innocent sin is better described, as a person unwittingly doing that which is wrong in the sight of God.

HEBREWS 12:1
"Let us lay aside every weight, and the sin which doth so easily beset us."

GALATIANS 6:1
"Brethren, if a man be overtaken in a fault."

This sin occurs when a person is suddenly, unexpectedly or unknowingly mislead by satan into sinning.

We are assured that if we sin innocently, Jesus our Advocate will defend our case before God our Father. That he will procure our cleansing and forgiveness.

I JOHN 2:1
"My little children, these things write I unto you, that ye sin not. And if any man sin, we have an advocate with the Father, Jesus Christ the righteous:"

If we confess our sin, God will always forgive and cleanse us.

1 JOHN 1:7-9
"The blood of Jesus Christ his Son cleanseth us from all sin.

If we confess our sins, he is faithful and just to forgive us our sins, and to cleanse us from all unrighteousness."

2. Willful sin.

Hebrews 10:26
"For if we sin willfully after that we have received the knowledge of the truth, there remaineth no more sacrifice for sins."

We sin willfully when we contemplate, plan and commit sin in spite of the conviction of the Holy Spirit not to do it.

David knew this when he prayed this prayer:

Psalms 19:13
"Keep back thy servant also from presumptuous (willful, planned) sins."

Against his better knowledge, David actually committed a willful sin by committing adultery with Bathsheba and then had her husband killed. From that moment, for the rest of his life David was punished for sinning willfully. His child died. His daughter was raped, his son Absalom arose up in rebellion against him and was killed.

We are warned that willful sin is punishable by death.

Numbers 15:30
"But the soul that doeth ought presumptuously (willfully) the same reproacheth the LORD; and that soul shall be cut off from among his people."

Christians should not commit habitual, planned, willful sin.

When we are born again spiritually we are a new creation in Christ.

We are raised to a higher level of living.

This new culture of Gods Kingdom has higher standards and expectations for us.

Planned and willful sinning should not be a part of the overcoming Christian mindset and life.

1 John 3:9
"Whosoever is born of God doth not commit sin; for his seed remaineth in him: and he cannot sin, because he is born of God."

If a child of God commits a presumptuous sin, the sin may be forgiven but it is punishable.

1 John 5:16
"If any man see his brother sin a sin which is not unto death, he shall ask, and he shall give him life for them that sin not unto death. There is a sin unto death: I do not say that he shall pray for it."

Willful sin is actually called a sin unto death.

It is **not** the sin against the Holy Spirit.

An example of this is Ananias and Sapphira:

They committed a willful, planned sin and it resulted in their death.

Man and Sin

ACTS 5:1-10
"But a certain man named Ananias, with Sapphira his wife, sold a possession,

And kept back part of the price, his wife also being privy to it, and brought a certain part, and laid it at the apostles' feet.

But Peter said, Ananias, why hath Satan filled thine heart to lie to the Holy Ghost, and to keep back part of the price of the land?

Thou hast not lied unto men, but unto God.

And Ananias hearing these words fell down, and gave up the ghost:

His wife, not knowing what was done, came in.

And Peter answered unto her, tell me whether ye sold the land for so much? And she said, yea, for so much.

Then she fell down straightway at his feet, and yielded up the ghost:"

If we irresponsibly continue with planned sin in our life, we will reap what we sow.

GALATIANS 6:7
"Be not deceived; God is not mocked: for whatsoever a man soweth, that shall he also reap."

The Lords Supper and sin:

We should partake worthily of the Lords Supper and those who participate with un-confessed sin will be judged.

1 Corinthians 11:27-30

"Wherefore whosoever shall eat this bread, and drink this cup of the Lord, unworthily, shall be guilty of the body and blood of the Lord.

But let a man examine himself, and so let him eat of that bread, and drink of that cup.

For he that eateth and drinketh unworthily, eateth and drinketh damnation to himself, not discerning the Lords Body. For this cause many are weak and sickly among you, and many sleep."

3. The sin against the Holy Spirit.

This is also referred to as the **unpardonable sin**.

Matthew 12:31
"Wherefore I say unto you, all manner of sin and blasphemy shall be forgiven unto men: but the blasphemy against the Holy Ghost shall not be forgiven unto men."

This sin is described as speaking against the Holy Ghost.

Matthew 12:32
"But whosoever speaketh against the Holy Ghost, it shall not be forgiven him."

Here Jesus was speaking to men who were ascribing the mighty powerful works of the Holy Ghost to that of the devil. Jesus said that in doing that they were sinning against the Holy Ghost.

Matthew 12:24
"But when the Pharisees heard it, they said, this fellow doth not cast out devils, but by Beelzebub the prince of the devils."

Sin is transgressing the Law or Commandments of God:

After being born again into Gods family we experience great change.

It is totally contrary to our new Divine Nature as children of God, to want to break Gods Law.

Ephesians 5:3-4

"But fornication, and all uncleanness, or covetousness, let it not be once named among you.

Neither filthiness, nor foolish talking, nor jesting, which are not convenient: but rather giving of thanks."

1 John 5:18

"We know that whosoever is born of God sinneth not; but he that is begotten of God keepeth himself, and that wicked one toucheth him not."

2 Corinthians 6:17-18

"Wherefore come out from among them, and be ye separate, saith the Lord, and touch not the unclean thing; And will be a Father unto you, and ye shall be my sons and daughters, saith the Lord Almighty."

Jesus gives a special promise of reward to those who overcome sin.

Revelation 3:21

"To him that overcometh will I grant to sit with me in my throne, even as I also overcame, and am set down with my Father in his throne."

God cannot be defeated or fail.

God is an Overcomer.

He has ordained all Christians to be like Him.

We who are God's children are born again of God's Seed which is Overcomer Seed.

Therefore by nature we are overcomers and should overcome.

1 John 2:13

"I write unto you, young men, because **ye have overcome** the wicked one.

What an amazing destiny we have!

CHAPTER 7

A Great Salvation

Paul the Apostle describes the importance and value of salvation:

Hebrews 2:3

"How shall we escape, if we neglect so great salvation;"

He understood the benefits of salvation and treasured its value.

He described it in these words.

2 Corinthians 9:15

"Thanks are unto God for his **unspeakable gift.**"

He had great insight into the teachings of the Bible and regarded Salvation as the greatest experience a person could have.

Jesus said;

Luke 10:20

"Notwithstanding in this rejoice not, that the spirits are subject unto you; but rather rejoice, because your names are written in heaven."

Salvation is more important than having power to cast out devils.

Salvation is great because of three things:

1. Its value.

Matthew 16:26
"For what is a man profited, if he shall gain the whole world, and lose his own soul? Or what shall a man give in exchange for his soul?"

Jesus clearly taught that salvation is more valuable, than all the wealth of the world and that there is nothing that a man can give in exchange for his soul.

2. Its power.

Romans 1:16
"For I am not ashamed of the gospel of Christ: for it is the power of God unto salvation to everyone that believeth;"

A Great Salvation

Salvation has a powerful impact on our lives.

It totally changes and transforms a wrecked, damaged and destroyed life.

It brings complete hope, healing, restoration, success and new direction to a lost sinner.

It changes our destination from hell to Heaven.

A defiled, contaminated, filthy sinner becomes a holy, righteous Saint and chosen Servant of the Lord.

Simeon the Priest in Jerusalem waited his entire life to see God's Salvation come in the person of Jesus.

Luke 2:28-30
"Then took Jesus up in his arms, and blessed God, and said,

Lord, now let thy servant depart in peace, according to thy word:

For mine eyes have seen thy salvation."

3. Salvation has fifteen great experiences.

We may experience and enjoy all of them:

1. We experience God's love.

John 3:16
"For God so loved the world that he gave his only begotten Son, that whosoever believeth in him should not perish, but have everlasting life."

ROMANS 5:8
"But God commendeth his love toward us, in that, while we were yet sinners, Christ died for us."

1 JOHN 4:16
"And we have known and believed the love that God hath to us."

While we were sinners, God manifested and proved his love for us, by sending Jesus to die for us on Calvary.

Jesus procured our salvation even though we did not deserve God's gift of love.

When we experience salvation we personally discover and feel God's love.

We are drawn near to God's heart and feel His warm embrace.

His love fills our entire being and there is nothing in the Universe that can separate us from it.

ROMANS 8:38-39
"For I am persuaded, that neither death, nor life, nor angels, nor principalities, nor powers, nor things present, nor things to come,

Nor height, nor depth, nor any other creature, shall be able to separate us from the love of God, which is in Christ Jesus our Lord."

A good definition of God's love is found in -

Romans 2:4
"The riches of his goodness and forbearance and longsuffering; not knowing that the goodness of God leadeth thee to repentance?"

Its ingredients are goodness, forbearance and longsuffering.

Because of Gods goodness He loves undeserving sinners.

God forebears us through the times that we sin, reject and grieve Him.

In longsuffering He patiently waits for us to change our rebellious, hard hearted and sometimes stiffnecked attitude.

Day by day, week by week and sometimes year after year He patiently continues to reach out to us.

2. We experience God's Grace.

Ephesians 2:8-9
"For by **grace** are ye saved through faith; and that not of yourselves: it is the gift of God:

Not of works, lest any man should boast."

God's grace is the basis of all the gifts He gives to us:

His grace is unmerited or undeserving favor.

He saves us, not because we deserve it but because He wants to.

He is like a lifesaver diving into the water to save a drowning victim.

Paul describes our condition.

We are deprived of goodness and our human nature is evil.

EPHESIANS 2:3
"Among whom also we all had our conversation in times past in the lusts of our flesh, fulfilling the desires of the flesh and of the mind; and were by nature the children of wrath."

We are as filthy rags in Gods sight.

ISAIAH 64:6
"But we are all as an unclean thing, and all our righteousnesses are as filthy rags;"

Regardless of how sinful we are, His grace is sufficient for us.

God's grace is much greater than our sin. It outmeasures our sin.

ROMANS 5:20
"But where sin abounded, grace did much more abound:"

3. We experience God's foreknowledge.

1 PETER 1:2
"Elect according to the foreknowledge of God the Father."

Foreknowledge is knowledge of something before it happens.

Only God presently has knowledge of everything that is in the future.

Time consists of things that are past, present and future.

God is not contained in time and is outside of time.

What we see in the past, present or future, God sees taking place at one time, in the now.

God is called "I am" and sees the beginning and the end of time at the same moment. He sees all our life experiences at the same time.

God's foreknowledge of people was before they were ever created.

EPHESIANS 1:4
"According as he hath chosen us in him before the foundation of the world."

We were in God's thoughts and on His mind before we were born.

We were so important to God that He saw us and chose us to be His children before the creation of the earth.

The decision for choosing us was based on His foreknowledge of us.

It pleased Him to see us before we were born, then living our life, accepting Jesus Christ and serving Him.

He said **"I choose you"** and therefore we should appreciate and enjoy this miracle.

If we were on God's mind before time began, then we are still on God's mind, right now.

Psalm 139:17
"How precious also are thy thoughts unto me, O God! How great is the sum of them!"

4. We experience Predestination.

When a King decides and commands something to be done, he decrees it and says

"So let it be written, so let it be done."

His command will stand and be executed.

Who can remove, obliterate or make of none affect, the Decrees of God?

When God foreknew and chose us He gave us a destination.

That destination was given to us before we were born and that is why it is called pre-destination. Our destination included being saved, serving God, working for Him and going to Heaven.

Romans 8:29
"For whom he did foreknow, he also did predestinate to be conformed to the image of his Son."

It is important for us to get to know what God's plan is for our life in order to reach our destination.

5. We experience God's calling.

Stop for a moment and think about the fact, that you have been called, by the Most High God. This calling of God will lead you to His destination for your life.

Romans 8:30
"Moreover whom he did predestinate, them he also called:"

Every Child of God needs to know that they are called and what His purpose is.

Romans 8:28
"To them who are the called according to his purpose."

God has a purpose and a plan for His children.

We have been given a small part in His great universal plan that is called the dispensation of the fullness of times.

Ephesians 1:10
"That in the dispensation of the fullness of times he might gather together in one all things in Christ."

Our part in God's plan begins the first day that we are saved and never ends.

6. We experience Redemption.

Revelation 5:9
"For thou wast slain, and hast redeemed us to God by thy blood."

Jesus Christ died for us on the cross and by His blood we have redemption.

To be redeemed means to be bought.

1 Corinthians 6:20
"For ye are bought with a price:"

The price Jesus paid for us was His blood.

Jesus went to the bargaining table and paid the payment that was necessary to redeem mankind.

He looked at our lives as valuable treasure and gave all he had to buy it.

Matthew 13:45-46
"Again, the kingdom of heaven is like unto a merchant man, seeking goodly pearls:

Who, when he had found one pearl of great price, went and sold all that he had, and bought it."

Jesus bought us out of bondage and slavery to set us free.

We no longer are under satan's bondage but we belong to God.

If you are a child of God, you are paid for. The transaction is done!

7. We experience Substitution.

A substitute is someone who takes another person's place.

As sinners we needed someone to take our place and save us.

A Great Salvation

ROMANS 3:23
"For all have sinned, and come short of the glory of God;"

We are convicted and pronounced "Guilty". We are guilty sinners.

ROMANS 6:23
"For the wages of sin is death."

We are sentenced to death for our sin.

Jesus cries:

NO! I will be their substitute.

I will take their sin on myself and die in their place.

GALATIANS 3:13
"Christ being made a curse for us: for it is written, Cursed is every one that hangeth on a tree."

Jesus became a curse for us. He took our guilt, punishment and God's wrath upon Himself. He became our substitute and was crucified in our place.

GALATIANS 2:20
"I am crucified with Christ:"

Jesus was saying -

"All you have to do is hang symbolically with me on the Cross and I will be your substitute."

As substitute, Jesus became the propitiation for our sin.

1 John 2:2
"And he is the propitiation for our sins: and not for ours only, but also for the sins of the whole world."

The word "propitiation" means **"appeasement"**.

It means to **satisfy or pacify.**

God is holy and abhors sin and because of this, His wrath was revealed against sinful mankind.

As our substitute, Jesus died in our place to take the brunt of God's wrath towards us. He is our propitiation and satisfies the demands of God's wrath against us.

8. We experience Repentance.

Repentance is a change of heart towards sin. It is a feeling of sorrow and contrition for committing sin.

We need to look at our spiritual condition sincerely and honestly.

When we see our filthy and wretched condition as God sees us, we sorrowfully repent.

Isaiah 64:6
"But we are all as an unclean thing, and all our righteousnesses are as filthy rags;"

In repentance we see ourselves as we really are, change our way and walk in a completely different direction that is pleasing to God.

The word **repentance** is the Greek word **"metanoia"** and it means to change and walk in a new direction.

It is a continuous daily experience throughout our Christian life.

1 John 1:8-10
"If we say that we have no sin, we deceive ourselves, and the truth is not in us.

If we confess our sins, he is faithful and just to forgive us our sins, and to cleanse us from all unrighteousness.

If we say that we have not sinned, we make him a liar, and his word is not in us."

It is a change of attitude towards sin in our life.

When we become aware of our sin, we are sorry, honestly admit it, repent and confess it to God.

9. We experience Faith.

Ephesians 2:8
"For by grace are ye saved through faith."

We experience salvation **by believing** that Jesus Christ died to save us and we receive Him into our lives as our Savior.

This is our first experience of faith and we continue to live from faith to faith.

Romans 1:17
"For therein is the righteousness of God revealed from faith to faith: as it is written, the just shall live by faith."

We embark on a new way of living. We totally trust Jesus for everything.

Galatians 2:20
"I am crucified with Christ: and the life which I now live in the flesh I live by the faith of the Son of God."

Before we were saved we lived by sight. Now we live by faith in God.

2 Corinthians 5:7
"For we walk by faith, not by sight:"

By faith we trust God for salvation, restoration, healing, deliverance, protection, provision, blessing and all things.

10. We experience New Birth.

John 3:3
"Jesus answered and said unto him, Verily, verily, I say unto thee, except a man be born again, he cannot see the kingdom of God."

The moment that we receive Jesus into our life as Savior, we are born again.

We are born into God's family and open our eyes in the Kingdom of God.

God the Father receives us as His child and we receive Him as our Heavenly Father.

JOHN 1:12
"But as many as received him, to them gave He power to become the sons of God."

EPHESIANS 2:19
"Now therefore ye are no more strangers and foreigners but of the household of God;"

2 CORINTHIANS 6:18
"And will be a Father unto you, and ye shall be my sons and daughters, saith the Lord Almighty."

Our names are written in God's Book of Life.

This is God's heavenly register of all His children.

REVELATIONS 21:27
"And there shall in no wise enter into it anything that defileth, but they which are written in the Lamb's book of life."

How does this rebirth take place?

Spiritual birth is very similar to natural physical birth.

It takes place in the spiritual dimension.

It cannot be seen with the natural eye.

In physical birth an ovum is fertilized, becomes an embryo in the womb and nine months later a beautiful baby is born.

Similarly when reading or hearing the preaching of the Word of God, it is sown into our hearts as seed.

Luke 8:5, 11
"A sower went out to sow his seed: The seed is the word of God."

James 1:18
"Of his own will begat he us with the word of truth."

1 Peter 1:23
"Being born again, not of corruptible seed, but of incorruptible, by the word of God, which liveth and abideth for ever."

The Holy Spirit quickens the seed of God's Word sown into our lives and makes it come alive in our heart.

2 Corinthians 3:6
"The Spirit giveth life."

This quickened seed becomes a spiritual embryo and then we are born into God's family as a spiritual baby.

1 Peter 2:2
"As newborn babes, desire the sincere milk of the word, that ye may grow thereby."

As spiritual babies we grow, learn to talk, walk, think and behave as Christians, eventually reaching spiritual adulthood.

11. We experience Justification.

As sinners we are all guilty of sin.

To be justified means to be pardoned of all evil deeds and made just as if we have never sinned.

Criminals are pardoned when the King, President or Governor of a State forgives and sets them free.

When we turn to God for forgiveness of sin, He not only forgives us -

He pardons us and lets us go free.

Isaiah 55:7
"Let the wicked forsake his way, and the unrighteous man his thoughts: and let him return unto the LORD, and he will have mercy upon him; and to our God, for he will abundantly pardon."

Being justified, the sin is removed that separates us from God and we have Peace with God.

Romans 5:1
"Therefore being justified by faith, we have peace with God through our Lord Jesus Christ:"

Once a person has been pardoned, they can never be charged for the same crime they have committed and be punished again.

When God saves us, we are justified and enjoy this same privilege.

ROMANS 8:33
"Who shall lay anything to the charge of God's elect? It is God that justifieth."

ROMANS 8:1
"There is therefore now no condemnation to them which are in Christ Jesus."

12. We experience Sanctification.

Sanctification is a cleansing of sin in our lives.

God is called Jehovah Kadesh - "The Lord our Sanctifier."

When we are saved we experience an initial sanctification.

1 THESSALONIANS 5:23
"And the very God of peace sanctify you wholly; and I pray God your whole spirit and soul and body be preserved blameless unto the coming of our Lord Jesus Christ."

Throughout our Christian life we may experience continued sanctification.

When we sin we may ask God to cleanse us and He sanctifies us with the precious Blood of Jesus.

1 JOHN 1:7
"And the blood of Jesus Christ his Son cleanseth us from all sin."

We have confidence to go to God for forgiveness and cleansing anytime.

1 John 2:1
"My little children, these things write I unto you, that ye sin not. And if any man sin, we have an advocate with the Father, Jesus Christ the righteous:"

God knows that we need an **Advocate**, because we have an accuser satan, who continuously brings accusations against us.

God has therefore provided His son Jesus, a righteous advocate to defend us.

When the Holy Spirit convicts us of sin we confess our sins and we are sanctified by God.

1 John 1:9
"If we confess our sins, He is faithful and just to forgive us our sins, and to cleanse us from all unrighteousness."

Reading the Word of God also has a sanctifying effect upon us.

As we read it, the words cleanse and refresh us.

John 17:17
"Sanctify them through thy truth: thy word is truth."

The verb sanctify is related to the word holiness.

When we are sanctified, we are set apart and filled with God's holy presence.

13. We experience Gods Righteousness.

Here is God's definition of righteousness -

1 John 3:7
"He that doeth righteousness is righteous, even as he is righteous."

Therefore Christians need to **do** that which is righteous.

The Bible says that as sinners, our righteousness is as filthy rags in God's sight.

Isaiah 64:6
"We are all as an unclean thing, and all our righteousnesses are as filthy rags;"

God has wonderfully made provision for us.

2 Corinthians 5:21

"For He hath made him to be sin for us, who knew no sin; that we might be made the righteousness of God in him."

When we are saved we awake to righteousness and are constantly aware of it:

1 Corinthians 15:34

"Awake to righteousness, and sin not;"

We follow after righteousness.

1 Timothy 6:11

"But thou, O man of God, flee these things; and follow after righteousness."

Every step of faith we take we experience more righteousness.

Romans 1:17

"For therein is the righteousness of God revealed from faith to faith:"

We are led to walk the paths of Righteousness.

Psalm 61:10

"I will greatly rejoice in the LORD, my soul shall be joyful in my God; he hath covered me with the robe of righteousness, as a bride adorneth herself with her jewels."

Psalm 23:3

"He leadeth me in the paths of righteousness for his name's sake."

A Christian has a natural desire to seek more experiences of righteousness.

Matthew 6:33

"But seek ye first the kingdom of God, and his righteousness;"

We yield ourselves to God as an instrument of righteousness to do righteous deeds.

Romans 6:13-18

"But yield yourselves unto God, and your members as instruments of righteousness unto God."

This covering of righteousness protects us from the enemy and is our breastplate.

Ephesians 6:14

"Stand therefore, having your loins girt about with truth, and having on the breastplate of righteousness;"

14. We experience God's Glory.

When the Israelites came out of Egypt a cloud and pillar of fire went before them.

It was God's manifest Presence and Glory.

The Israelites had God's glory but the Egyptians did not.

We as children of God have something the world and sinners do not have.

We have the Glory of God.

Sinners come short of God's glory.

ROMANS 3:23

"For all have sinned, and come short of the glory of God;"

When we are saved the Presence of God and God's glory comes into us, shines out of us and makes us look different.

As we grow spiritually, the glory of God intensifies in our life.

2 CORINTHIANS 3:18
"But we all are changed into the same image **from glory to glory**, even as by the Spirit of the LORD."

In this scripture the first Greek word **"glory"** is **"doxe".**

It means **the initial** experience of glory.

The second word **"glory"** is **"doxan".**

It means the **highest form** of God's glory.

We are therefore led from the initial experience to the highest form of God's glory.

As we are changed, we receive more and more of God's glory.

This glory can be seen as was the glory of Jesus.

JOHN 1: 14
"And the Word was made flesh, and dwelt among us, and we beheld his glory."

When Moses came down from the mountain after his encounter with God, his face shone with God's glory.

Exodus 34:29

"And it came to pass, when Moses came down from mount Sinai with the two tables of testimony in Moses' hand, when he came down from the mount, that Moses wist not that the skin of his face shone."

While Steven was being tried before the Sanhedrin, the glory of God was manifest upon him.

Acts 6:15

"And all that sat in the council, looking stedfastly on him, saw his face as it had been the face of an angel."

When Solomon dedicated the Temple, the glory of God filled the Temple so greatly that the priests could not stand.

2 Chronicles 5:14

"So that the priests could not stand to minister by reason of the cloud: for the glory of the LORD had filled the house of God."

The glory of God is our supernatural protection.

Isaiah 4:5

"And the LORD will create upon every dwelling place of mount Zion, and upon her assemblies, a cloud and smoke by day, and the shining of a flaming fire by night: for upon all the glory shall be a defense."

God has promised that the end time church will have a greater experience of glory than the first church.

Haggai 2:9

"The glory of this latter house shall be greater than of the former, saith the LORD of hosts."

15. We experience Assurance.

The songwriter wrote a song with these wonderful words:

"Blessed assurance Jesus is mine. Oh what a foretaste of glory divine."

Many people in the world seemingly only seek financial security.

Christians however may enjoy a higher form of security.

They have spiritual security and it embraces everything.

It is a security of total salvation.

2 Peter 1:10
"Wherefore the rather, brethren, give diligence to make your calling and election sure: for if ye do these things, ye shall never fall:"

God wants us to make our calling and election sure.

He wants us to be totally secure in our Christian walk.

God wants us to be His child forever, not just for a week or a year.

God does not want us to have a fluctuating up and down experience of salvation.

God does not expel his children out of His Kingdom every time they sin.

Though we sin he allows us to remain His child and He expects us to deal with the sin. He wants us to live a Godly life. He wants us to walk circumspectly and in excellence.

Enjoy your salvation and trust in Gods ability to keep you from falling and present you faultless in Heaven. If you do your part He will do His part.

Jude 24
"Now unto him that is able to **keep you from falling**, and to present you faultless before the presence of his glory with exceeding joy."

God has given you a Great Salvation.

Visit and drink out of the wells of salvation!!!

Isaiah 12:3

"Therefore with joy shall ye draw water out of the wells of salvation."

We should value these precious things we have received from GOD

Matthew 16:26

"For what is a man profited, if he shall gain the whole world, and lose his own soul? Or what shall a man give in exchange for his soul?"

Hebrews 6:5-6

"Those who were once enlightened, and have tasted of the heavenly gift, and were made partakers of the Holy Ghost; And have tasted the good word of God, and the powers of the world to come,"

We should hold fast that which we have received.

Hebrews 10:23

"Let us hold fast the profession of our faith without wavering;"

2 Corinthians 6:1

"...I beseech you also that ye receive not the grace of God in vain."

The reality of backsliding:

Many Christians experience backsliding and should be made aware of this unfortunate experience.

1 Peter 2:25

"For ye were as sheep going astray; but are now returned unto the Shepherd and Bishop of your souls."

The consequences of the spiritual backsliding of a Christian can be eternal damnation in hell and should be prevented at all costs.

It is a fact that some Christians backslide and return to their old sinful way of living.

Backsliding can best be defined in two ways:

1. A slipping back.

2. A withdrawing from.

Israel was described as a Heifer that was slipping back. Although she was facing the right direction, the muddy dirt she was trampling caused her to slide back.

Hosea 4:16

"For Israel slideth back as a backsliding heifer:"

Paul also speaks of those who withdraw from the Lord.

Hebrews 10:38-39

"But if any **man draw** back, my soul shall have no pleasure in him."

How do Christians draw back or backslide?

They begin backsliding by neglecting their salvation."

Heb 2:3

"How shall we escape, if we neglect so great salvation?"

There are several things that indicate that a person is backsliding:

- Not attending Church regularly.
- Prayerlessness.
- Neglecting to read the Bible regularly.
- Falling back into old sinful habits.
- Finding fault with other Christians and Church Leaders.
- Totally falling away from Christianity.

There are 5 aspects of backsliding, from the least to the most serious:

1. Being overtaken by sin and continuing in it.

GALATIANS 6:1
"Brethren, if a man be overtaken in a fault."

2. Not abiding in Christ.

JOHN 15:6
"If a man abide not in me, he is cast forth as a branch, and is withered;"

COLOSSIANS 1:23
"Moved away from the hope of the gospel, which ye have heard."

3. Being taken captive by satan.

2 TIMOTHY 2:26
"That they may recover themselves out of the snare of the devil, who are taken captive by him at his will."

4. Falling into doctrinal error and instability.

2 PETER 3:16-17
"Beware lest ye also, being led away with the error of the wicked, fall from your own steadfastness."

A Great Salvation

JAMES 5:19-20
"Brethren, if any of you do err from the truth;

5. Total sinful depravity.

2 PETER 2:20 -22
"For if after they have escaped the pollutions of the world and are again entangled therein and overcome, the latter end is worse with them than the beginning.

For it is better for them not to have known the way of righteousness, than after they have known it, to turn from the holy commandment delivered unto them.

But it is happened unto them according to the true proverb, the dog is turned to his own vomit again; and the sow that was washed to her wallowing in the mire."

1 TIMOTHY 5:12-15
"Having damnation, because they have cast off their first faith.

For some are already turned aside after satan."

HEBREWS 10:29
"He who hath trodden underfoot the Son of God, and hath counted the blood of the covenant, wherewith he was sanctified, an unholy thing, and hath done despite unto the Spirit of grace?"

HEBREWS 10:38-39
But if any man draw back, my soul shall have no pleasure in him. But we are not of them

who draw back unto perdition; but of them that believe to the saving of the soul.

Three examples of people backsliding:

1. Esau.

HEBREWS 12:15-17

"Looking diligently lest any man fail of the grace of God; Lest there be any fornicator, or profane person, as Esau, who for one morsel of meat sold his birthright. For ye know how that afterward, when he would have inherited the blessing, he was rejected: for he found no place of repentance, though he sought it carefully with tears."

2. Hymenaeus and Alexander

1 TIMOTHY 1:19-20

"Some having put away concerning faith have made shipwreck: Of whom is Hymenaeus and Alexander;"

3. Demas.

2 TIMOTHY 4:10

"For Demas hath forsaken me, having loved this present world."

There is hope for the backslider!

Those who have backslidden may return to their Savior Jesus Christ.

1 Peter 2:25

"For ye were as sheep gone astray; but are now returned unto the Shepherd and Bishop of your souls."

Paul in Love reaches out to warn Christians against backsliding.

Acts 20:31

"Therefore watch, and remember, that by the space of three years I ceased not to warn every one night and day with tears."

1 Corinthians 9:27

But I keep under my body, and bring it into subjection: lest that by any means, when I have preached to others, I myself should be a castaway.

2 Corinthians 6:1

We then … beseech you also that ye receive not the grace of God in vain.

Jesus Christ the Good Shepherd seeks lost sheep and welcomes them back into His sheepfold.

Luke 15:4-6

"...Doth leave the ninety-nine sheep going after the one that is lost, until he find it. And when He hath found it, He layeth it on his shoulders, rejoicing ... saying:

Rejoice with me, for I have found my sheep, which was lost."

Isaiah 55:7

"Let the wicked forsake his way, and the unrighteous man his thoughts: and let him return unto the LORD, and he will have mercy upon him; and to our God, for he will abundantly pardon."

Many Christians have been wounded by satan in spiritual battle and have backslidden, but there is hope for their return and restoration.

Always remember that every battle scarred Soldier may recover from wounds.

An example is that of Samson who had lost his power.

A Great Salvation

Judges 16:28

"And Samson called unto the LORD, and said, O Lord God, remember me, I pray thee, and strengthen me, I pray thee, only this once, O God."

Joel 2:12-28

"Therefore also now, saith the LORD, turn ye even to me with all your heart: The LORD your God is gracious and merciful, slow to anger, and of great kindness, and repenteth him of the evil.

There is a way back to God!

CHAPTER 8

Water Baptism and the Lords Supper

Both ordinances of Water Baptism and the Lords Supper relate to the death and the resurrection of our Lord Jesus Christ.

In Water Baptism, Christians are **identified** with the Lords death and resurrection.

In the Lords Supper they **remember** and **celebrate** the Lords death and resurrection.

Water Baptism:

Jesus clearly commanded His disciples to be baptized.

Matthew 28:19

"Go ye therefore, and teach all nations, baptizing them in the name of the Father, and of the Son, and of the Holy Ghost:"

He set an example by being baptized Himself.

Matthew 3:13-16

"Then cometh Jesus from Galilee, to the Jordan unto John, to be baptized of him.

But John forbad him, saying, I have need to be baptized of thee, and comest thou to me?

And Jesus answering said unto him, suffer it to be so now: for thus it becometh us to fulfill all righteousness. Then he suffered him.

And Jesus, when he was baptized, went up straightway out of the water:"

Jesus went to the Jordan River to John the Baptist to be baptized of him.

John felt that he was not worthy to baptize Jesus, but Jesus insisted.

Jesus said that by being baptized He was fulfilling all righteousness.

John went ahead and immersed Jesus in the water.

When Jesus came up out of the water the Holy Spirit came upon Him in the form of a dove.

God the Father spoke out heaven saying that He was pleased with His Son Jesus.

Jesus also personally baptized many disciples.

John 4:1

"When therefore the LORD knew how the Pharisees had heard that Jesus made and baptized more disciples than John."

Baptism fulfils righteousness and is a part of the experience of salvation.

Mark 16:16

"He that believeth and is baptized shall be saved; but he that believeth not shall be damned."

Water Baptism relates to four things:

1. It is an outward sign of an inward experience of cleansing.

The baptism of water on the outside symbolizes our cleansing with the Blood of Jesus on the inside.

Acts 22:16
"Arise, and be baptized, and wash away thy sins, calling on the name of the Lord."

2. It is symbolical of the burial of our old sinful life and a resurrected new life in Christ.

When we are saved, we are symbolically placed on the Cross with Jesus, because He died in our place as our substitute.

GALATIANS 2:20
"I am crucified with Christ: nevertheless I live; yet not I, but Christ liveth in me:"

In salvation God sees us crucified with Christ.

In baptism God sees us buried and resurrected spiritually with Christ.

Baptism helps us to establish the exact time of our spiritual burial and resurrection.

After we have been saved we should do two things:

1. Reckon ourselves crucified with Christ and dead to sin.

2. Be baptized to experience burial and resurrection with Christ.

ROMANS 6:11

"Likewise reckon ye also yourselves to be dead indeed unto sin, but alive unto God through Jesus Christ our Lord."

Romans 6:4

"Therefore we are buried with him by baptism into death: that like as Christ was raised up from the dead by the glory of the Father, even so we also should walk in newness of life."

When Jesus died on the cross He was taken off the cross and placed in a tomb.

After the third day He was resurrected and came out of the tomb in a glorified body.

Symbolically we are taken from the cross, buried with Him in a water grave. We rise up out of the water and are resurrected with Him in the Name of the Father, Jesus the Son of God and the Holy Spirit.

The Greek word for baptism is **"Baptiso".**

It means to **immerse or dip into.**

When one is immersed or dipped into water by baptism, it is a form of burial.

3. Baptism is a public confession that we are true followers of Jesus Christ.

In baptism we openly testify to the world that we are disciples of Jesus Christ.

4. Baptism plays an important part in our deliverance.

The children of Israel were in captivity in Egypt and God delivered them from bondage.

The night of their deliverance an amazing thing happened. (Exodus 12)

The blood of the killed Passover Lamb was smeared on the doorposts of the houses of the Israelites to protect them from the destroyer that passed by.

That night they were delivered from Egypt.

Jesus was the Lamb of God who was crucified for us.

By accepting Jesus Christ as our Savior we were also delivered from bondage.

His shed blood was sprinkled on our hearts to save and deliver us.

Then the Israelites had to pass through the Red Sea to be completely delivered from Egypt and Pharaoh.

The Red Sea is a type of our deliverance in baptism from the effects and the bondages of sin.

1 Corinthians 10:1-6

"Moreover, brethren, I would not that ye should be ignorant, how that all our fathers were under the cloud, and all passed through the sea;

And were all baptized unto Moses in the cloud and in the sea;

Now these things were our examples."

Baptism is the part of Salvation that brings us deliverance.

1 Peter 3:20-21

"When once the longsuffering of God waited in the days of Noah ... eight souls were saved by water.

The like figure whereunto even baptism doth also now save us."

In baptism Christians experience deliverance from their old sinful life and bondage.

By faith they experience deliverance from all the old sinful habits and begin to walk in a new life.

Ephesians 4:22-24

"That ye put off concerning the old man, which is corrupt according to the deceitful lusts;

And be renewed in the spirit of your mind;

And that ye put on the new man, which after God is created in righteousness and true holiness."

The Israelites practiced the baptism ceremony in Old Testament times.

When someone who was diseased with leprosy completely recovered, they then had to show themselves to the priest, be baptized and cleansed in water.

When John the Baptist arrived on the scene he preached repentance and baptism.

Because baptism was not strange to the Jews, thousands came to the Jordan River and were baptized.

Baptism was also practiced and preached by New Testament Christians.

ACTS 2:37-41

"Now when they heard this, they were pricked in their heart, and said unto Peter and to the rest of the apostles, Men and brethren, what shall we do?

Then Peter said unto them, Repent, and be baptized every one of you in the name of Jesus Christ for the remission of sins, and ye shall receive the gift of the Holy Ghost.

Then they that gladly received his word were baptized: and the same day there were added unto them about three thousand souls."

Phillip the Evangelist went down to Samaria to preach the Gospel, many men and women were saved and immediately baptized.

ACTS 8:12

"But when they believed Philip preaching the things concerning the kingdom of God, and the name of Jesus Christ, they were baptized, both men and women."

Then Phillip ministered to the Eunuch in the desert; he believed on Jesus and asked Phillip to baptize him. After he was baptized he went on his way rejoicing.

Acts 8:36-39

"And as they went on their way, they came unto a certain water: and the eunuch said, See, here is water; what doth hinder me to be baptized?

And Philip said, If thou believest with all thine heart, thou mayest. And he answered and said, I believe that Jesus Christ is the Son of God.

And he commanded the chariot to stand still: and they went down both into the water, both Philip and the eunuch and he went on his way rejoicing."

The Eunuch:

Believed in Christ

Desired to be baptized

Saw water

Went into the water

Was baptized

Came up out of the water and went on his way rejoicing

This practice of baptism has continued until this day.

What is the mode of Baptism?

The Bible clearly teaches how water baptism should be done.

When a candidate is baptized their entire body should be immersed or dipped in water.

Mark 1:9-10

"And it came to pass in those days that Jesus came from Nazareth of Galilee, and was baptized of John.

And straightway **coming up out of the water**, he saw the heavens opened, and the Spirit like a dove descending upon him:"

The whole body of Jesus was immersed in the Jordan River and came up out of the water.

In whose name should we be baptized?

Matthew 28:19

"Go ye therefore, and teach all nations, baptizing them in the **name** of the Father, and of the Son, and of the Holy Ghost:"

The Greek word for **"name"** used here is **"honoma."** It means **authority**.

We are therefore to be baptized in the authority of God the Father, Jesus Christ the Son and the Holy Ghost. The three days that Jesus was buried in the

Tomb, are symbolical of the threefold authority of the Godhead that Believers are baptized into.

1 John 5:7

"For there are three that bear record in heaven, the Father, the Word, and the Holy Ghost: and these three are one."

We should therefore be baptized in the authority of God the Father, Jesus the Son and the Holy Spirit.

Baptism is a command and not an option.

Jesus never requested His Disciples to be baptized.

He commanded them to be baptized.

Matthew 28:19

"Go ye therefore, and teach all nations, baptizing them in the name of the Father, and of the Son, and of the Holy Ghost:"

The Lord's Supper:

The Lord's Supper is also called -

- *Holy Communion* and
- Eucharist.

It finds its roots in the Passover which was kept by Jesus and His disciples over two thousand years ago in the city of Jerusalem.

Before Jesus was crucified He kept the Passover with His Disciples.

He gathered with His Disciples in the upper room in Jerusalem to keep the Passover.

MATTHEW 26:19-30

"And the disciples did as Jesus had appointed them; and they made ready the Passover.

Now when the even was come, he sat down with the twelve.

And as they were eating, Jesus took bread, and blessed it, and brake it, and gave it to the disciples, and said, Take, eat; this is my body.

And he took the cup, and gave thanks, and gave it to them, saying, Drink ye all of it;

For this is my blood of the new testament, which is shed for many for the remission of sins.

But I say unto you, I will not drink henceforth of this fruit of the vine, until that day when I drink it new with you in my Father's kingdom.

And when they had sung an hymn, they went out into the Mount of Olives."

As they participated in this Supper there were two things of significance:

1. Jesus had looked forward to this Supper with His Disciples.

Luke 22:15
"And he said unto them, with desire I have desired to eat this Passover with you before I suffer:"

2. He shared His Cup with them.

Luke 22:17
"And he took the cup, and gave thanks, and said, take this, and divide it among yourselves:"

A Cup of unfermented wine was on the Passover Table. It was called Elijah's Cup.

It was designated only for the Messiah to drink if He should suddenly appear.

Only the Messiah could take it.

At every Passover Meal, the door of the house was left open for the Messiah to be able to enter in.

When Jesus took this cup in His hands, it clearly revealed to the Disciples that He was the Messiah. They were amazed that He shared the Cup with them.

The Disciples continued keeping the Lord's Supper.

After Jesus ascended into Heaven they continued to come together to keep the Lord's Supper.

Acts 20:7

"And upon the first day of the week …the disciples came together to break bread."

Paul's gave special instructions about the Lord's Supper.

He gave detailed instructions on how Christians should keep the Lord's Supper.

1 Corinthians 11:26-33

"For as often as ye eat this bread, and drink this cup, ye do shew the Lord's death till he come.

Whosoever shall eat this bread, and drink this cup of the Lord, unworthily, shall be guilty of the body and blood of the Lord.

Let a man examine himself, and so let him eat of that bread, and drink of that cup.

For he that eateth and drinketh unworthily, eateth and drinketh damnation to himself, not discerning the Lord's body.

For this cause many are weak and sickly among you, and many sleep.

For if we would judge ourselves, we should not be judged.

But when we are judged, we are chastened of the Lord, that we should not be condemned with the world.

Wherefore, my brethren, when ye come together to eat, tarry one for another."

These instructions emphasize six things:

1. Before we eat the Bread or drink the Cup of grape juice, we should examine ourselves to see if there is sin in our lives.

2. If we have sinned against Heaven or someone, we should confess it and ask God to forgive us and cleanse us of sin.

3. We may then participate and break the Bread and eat it in remembrance of the crucified body of Jesus.

4. We may also drink the Cup in remembrance of the precious Blood of Jesus that was shed for us.

5. We should always calmly and patiently give others the time they need to do what is required in order to participate and enjoy the Lord's Supper.

6. Worship and the singing of Hymns is also a part of the Lord's Supper.

More specifically the Lord's Supper involves three important aspects:

1. Confirmation:

The Lord's Supper confirms the existence of -

A New Covenant that has special blessings.

When Jesus was keeping the Passover He confirmed with His Disciples, that through His Blood they would receive a New Testament.

MATTHEW 26:28

"For this is my blood of the new testament, which is shed for many for the remission of sins."

As we partake of the Cup, we affirm that it is by Christ's Blood that we have this New Covenant with Jesus.

EPHESIANS 2:12-13

"That at that time ye were without Christ, being aliens from the covenants of promise, having no hope, and without God in the world:

But now in Christ Jesus ye who sometimes were far off, are made nigh by the blood of Christ."

In this Covenant, all the blessings and benefits of Abraham have been passed on to us.

Galatians 3:14

"That the blessing of Abraham might come on the Gentiles through Jesus Christ;"

David describes the benefits:

Psalm 103:2-5

Bless the Lord, O my soul, and forget not all his benefits;

Who forgiveth all thine iniquities;

who healeth all thy diseases;

Who redeemeth thy life from destruction;

who crowneth thee with lovingkindness and tender mercies;

Who satisfieth thy mouth with good things;

so that thy youth is renewed like the eagles."

There are seven benefits:

1. Forgiveness of sin.
2. Healing of diseases.
3. Redemption from destruction.
4. Being crowned with loving-kindness.

5. Being crowned with tender mercies.

6. Having our mouth filled with good things.

7. Having our youth renewed like an eagle.

2. Examination:

We are told by the Apostle Paul to examine ourselves before we partake of the Lord's Supper.

If we have sinned we should confess our sin and be cleansed through the Blood of Jesus.

1 Corinthians 5:7-8
"Purge out therefore the old leaven, that ye may be a new lump, as ye are unleavened. For even Christ our Passover is sacrificed for us:

Therefore let us keep the feast, not with old leaven, neither with the leaven of malice and wickedness; but with the unleavened bread of sincerity and truth."

We should never participate unworthily of the Lords Supper, because if we do, we will be judged and chastened by the Lord.

1 Corinthians 11:28-32
"But let a man examine himself, and so let him eat of that bread, and drink of that cup.

For he that eateth and drinketh unworthily, eateth and drinketh damnation to himself, not discerning the Lord's body.

For this cause many are weak and sickly among you, and many are dead.

For if we would judge ourselves, we should not be judged.

But when we are judged, we are chastened of the Lord."

If any sin comes to mind while we are about to partake of the Lord's Supper, we should immediately confess it. If we have sinned against another person we must ask their forgiveness. If we know that someone has something against us we should go to them and resolve the issue. This is God's way of making sure that issues are dealt with and sins confessed and forgiven amongst Christians.

We should not refuse to eat the Bread and drink the Cup.

Some Christians reason that because of sin in their life, they should avoid participating in the Lords Supper. That is why they let it pass.

The Lord expects us to participate and emphasizes its importance.

John 6:53

"Then Jesus said unto them, verily, verily, I say unto you, except ye eat the flesh of the Son of man, and drink his blood, ye have no life in you."

It is therefore important for us to frequently share in the Lord's Supper with other Believers so that the Body of Christ (the Church) can remain spiritually clean and healthy.

It is at the Lord's Supper that we are confronted with the issue of sin and the possibility that we have wronged someone.

We must correct things done wrong.

We must participate in the Lord's Supper.

At the Lords Supper -

We may experience forgiveness and cleansing of sin

We may experience healing

The Church is cleansed

We are blessed

3. Celebration:

The Lords Supper is a Victory Celebration and we celebrate three things:

1. We celebrate the event of Christ's victory.

The enemy satan did everything he could to kill and destroy Jesus.

However, Jesus totally destroyed and overcame him and all the forces of hell.

On the Cross, Jesus cried **"It is finished." (John 19:30)**

After Jesus died on the cross, He descended into Hades, took on satan and his kingdom, spoiled and triumphed over them.

Colossians 2:15
"Having spoiled principalities and powers, he made a shew of them openly, triumphing over them."

2. We celebrate Christ's exaltation.

After His resurrection, Jesus ascended into Heaven.

He sat at the Right Hand of God the Father who highly exalted Him.

Ephesians 1:20-22
"Which he wrought in Christ, when he raised him from the dead and set him at his own right hand.

Far above all principality, and power, and might, and dominion, and every name that is named, not only in this world, but also in that which is to come:

And hath put all things under his feet, and gave him to be the head over all things to the church."

Philippians 2:9-11
"Wherefore God also hath highly exalted him, and given him a name which is above every name: That at the name of Jesus every knee should bow, of things in heaven, and things in

earth, and things under the earth; And that every tongue should confess that Jesus Christ is Lord, to the glory of God the Father."

3. We celebrate the effects of Christ's victory.

Jesus gained the following victory for us:

He overcame sin so that we could be made righteous.

2 CORINTHIANS 5:21

"For he hath made him to be sin for us, who knew no sin; that we might be made the righteousness of God in him."

He overcame sickness for our healing.

MARK 16:17-18

"In my name they shall lay hands on the sick, and they shall recover."

He overcame poverty for our prosperity.

2 CORINTHIANS 8:9

"Yet for your sakes he became poor, that ye through his poverty might be rich."

He overcame satan and his principalities for our victory.

Luke 10:19

"Behold, I give unto you power to tread on serpents and scorpions, and over all the power of the enemy: and nothing shall by any means hurt you."

He overcame death and hell so that we could live and go to Heaven.

Revelation 1:18

"I am he that liveth, and was dead; and, behold, I am alive for evermore, Amen; and have the keys of hell and of death."

Christians always should attend church services and partake of the Lord's Supper:

Hebrews 10:25

"Not forsaking the assembling of ourselves together, as the manner of some is;"

Acts 20:7

"And upon the first day of the week, when the disciples came together to break bread, Paul preached unto them."

Christians are told to have Holy Communion as often as they can.

1 Corinthians 11:26

"For as often as ye eat this bread, and drink this cup, ye do shew the Lord's death till he come."

Today Christians continue to enjoy the Lord's Supper.

Hundreds of millions of Christians come together in church or home settings all over the world to partake of the Lord's Supper.

How does the Lords Supper take place?

A Pastor or church leader officiates and leads the proceedings.

Christians are told to prepare themselves to participate, examine themselves and confess any hindering sins.

The leader breaks the bread and passes it to the Christians to eat in remembrance of Christ's crucified body. That it may bring healing to their sick body.

He passes the grape juice to them to drink in remembrance of the Blood of Christ, shed for forgiveness of sin.

He reminds them of the victory of Christ over satan, hell, sin, sickness, death and poverty.

They celebrate and rejoice in the resurrection and Lordship of Christ!

CHAPTER 9

The Gift of the Holy Spirit

John the Baptist prepared the world for a special Holy Spirit experience.

He said that Jesus would baptize people with the Holy Ghost and fire.

Luke 3:16

"John answered, saying unto them all, I indeed baptize you with water; but one mightier than I cometh, the latchet of whose shoes I am not worthy to unloose: he shall baptize you with the Holy Ghost and with fire:"

The Bible reveals three important aspects of the person of the Holy Spirit in the life of Jesus.

1. Jesus received the anointing of the Holy Spirit in the Jordan River.

MATTHEW 3:16
"And Jesus, when he was baptized, went up straightway out of the water: and, lo, the heavens were opened unto him, and he saw the Spirit of God descending like a dove, and lighting upon him:"

2. Jesus demonstrated the power of the Holy Spirit.

ACTS 10:38
"How God anointed Jesus of Nazareth with the Holy Ghost and with power: who went about doing good, and healing all that were oppressed of the devil; for God was with him."

3. Jesus promised His Disciples that they would also receive the Holy Spirit.

JOHN 14:16-17
Even the Spirit of truth; whom the world cannot receive, because it seeth him not, neither knoweth him: but ye know him; for he dwelleth with you, and shall be in you."

Jesus revealed the value of a relationship with the Holy Spirit.

He promised that the Holy Spirit would be with us and in us -

- He would convict us of sin,
- righteousness,
- judgment and
- guide us in all truth.

John 16:7-13

"Nevertheless I tell you the truth; It is expedient for you that I go away: for if I go not away, the Comforter will not come unto you; but if I depart, I will send him unto you.

And when he is come, he will reprove the world of sin, and of righteousness, and of judgment:

Howbeit when he, the Spirit of truth, is come, he will guide you into all truth: for he shall not speak of himself; but whatsoever he shall hear, that shall he speak: and he will shew you things to come."

Jesus promised that the Holy Spirit would empower us.

This power enables us to be effective witnesses for Him.

Acts 1:8

"But ye shall receive power, after that the Holy Ghost is come upon you: and ye shall be witnesses unto me both in Jerusalem, and in all Judaea, and in Samaria, and unto the uttermost part of the earth."

This Holy Spirit Gift and Baptism would empower Christians to go out and do God's work on earth.

They were advised not to go out until they have received this power.

Acts 1:4

"Commanded them that they should not depart from Jerusalem, but wait for the promise of the Father, which, saith he, ye have heard of me."

This supernatural power imparted into our lives would enable us to do mighty things for the Kingdom of God.

This power would heal any sickness, solve any problem and supply any need.

The Gift of the Holy Spirit

MARK 16:17-18

"And these signs shall follow them that believe; In my name shall they cast out devils; they shall speak with new tongues;

They shall take up serpents; and if they drink any deadly thing, it shall not hurt them; they shall lay hands on the sick, and they shall recover."

Jesus assured us that our experience of ministry would be very similar to His:

JOHN 17:18

"As thou hast sent me into the world, even so have I also sent them into the world."

JOHN 14:12

"He that believeth on me, the works that I do shall he do also; and greater works than these shall he do;"

The important aspect of the experience of the baptism of the Holy Spirit

IS RECEIVING POWER!

To understand the Gift of the Holy Spirit in our lives we should consider five things:

1. We need to consider how the Apostles received the Baptism of the Holy Spirit?

Acts 2:1-4
"And when the day of Pentecost was fully come, they were all with one accord in one place. And suddenly there came a sound from heaven as of a rushing mighty wind, and it filled all the house where they were sitting.

And there appeared unto them cloven tongues like as of fire, and it sat upon each of them.

And they were all filled with the Holy Ghost, and began to speak with other tongues, as the Spirit gave them utterance."

There were one hundred and twenty Christians, sitting and waiting for the promise of the Holy Spirit. The heaven opened and God came down. The Holy Spirit entered the room like a rushing wind.

First - *tongues* **of fire** came upon them and anointed them.

Second - they spoke in **Unknown Tongues.**

The Holy Spirit gave them the ability and words to speak.

No one could understand what they were saying.

The Greek word for tongues in **Acts 2:4** is "**glossais** ".

It means **"a Heavenly language"** that does not belong to this world.

Later they spoke foreign dialects that people from different countries visiting Jerusalem could understand.

Acts 2:6
"Now when this was noised abroad, the multitude came together, and were confounded, because that every man heard them speak in his own language."

The Greek word for **"language"** is "**dialekto** ".

It means "**a foreign earthly language."**

Paul clearly teaches that men can speak in both earthly and heavenly tongues.

1 Corinthians 13:1
"Though I speak with the tongues of men and of angels."

The Holy Spirit empowered them and supernaturally used their tongue.

2. We need to consider why the Holy Spirit supernaturally uses our tongue.

He does this for three reasons:

a. Speaking in tongues is a prayer language that only God understands.

No one else including the devil can understand it.

Romans 8:26
"The Spirit itself maketh intercession for us with groanings which cannot be uttered."

1 Corinthians 14:2
"For he that speaketh in an unknown tongue speaketh not unto men, but unto God: for no man understandeth him; howbeit in the spirit he speaketh mysteries."

The Holy Spirit is the source of this heavenly language.

He gives the words of this new language through the human spirit and the mind of the believer to speak out.

These words are not produced by our mind.

They simply pass through the mind and we speak the words as the Holy Spirit gives them to us to speak.

1 Corinthians 14:14
"For if I pray in an unknown tongue, my spirit prayeth, but my understanding is unfruitful."

It is clear that the Holy Spirit gives the language and we speak the words.

Acts 2:4
"And they were all filled with the Holy Ghost, and began to speak with other tongues, as the Spirit gave them utterance."

The words are spoken, one word at a time and sometimes they gush out like a mighty river.

The Gift of the Holy Spirit

John 7:38
"He that believeth on me, as the scripture hath said, out of his belly shall flow rivers of living water."

When someone speaks in Tongues the hearers hear very distinct words and sentences that are unique, beautiful and refreshing.

b. We surrender our tongue to the Holy Ghost and He uses it to direct our lives.

James 3:4-5
"Behold also the ships, which though they be so great, yet are they turned about with a very small helm, whithersoever the governor listeth.

Even so the tongue is a little member."

Proverbs 18:21
"Death and life are in the power of the tongue:"

It is evident that the Bible says that life and death are in the power of the tongue and by using our tongue, the Holy Spirit steers us and directs our life.

c. The Holy Spirit uses our tongue to speak:

Prophecy

Preaching

Teaching

Wisdom and

Knowledge

3. We need to consider what happened after the day of Pentecost?

Thousands who witnessed the outpouring of the Holy Spirit desperately wanted it.

Peter said:

ACTS 2:38
"Then Peter said unto them, repent, and be baptized every one of you in the name of Jesus Christ for the remission of sins, and ye shall receive the gift of the Holy Ghost."

He clearly outlined the two steps people needed to take to receive this Gift of the Holy Ghost.

1. They needed to repent of their sins and be saved.

2. They needed to be baptized by water baptism.

He also clearly said that this promise was to every Christian the Lord Jesus Christ would ever call, including those living in the last days.

ACTS 2:39
"For the promise is unto you, and to your children, and to all that are afar off, even as many as the LORD our God shall call."

Here are examples of Believers receiving the Gift of the Holy Spirit after Pentecost.

The Gift of the Holy Spirit

Acts 10:44-46
"While Peter yet spake these words, the Holy Ghost fell on all them which heard the word.

And they of the circumcision which believed were astonished, as many as came with Peter, because that on the Gentiles also was poured out the gift of the Holy Ghost.

For they heard them speak with tongues, and magnify God."

Acts 19:1-6
"Paul having passed through the upper coasts ... said unto them, have ye received the Holy Ghost since ye believed? And they said unto him, we have not so much as heard whether there be any Holy Ghost.

And when Paul had laid his hands upon them, the Holy Ghost came on them; and they spake with tongues, and prophesied."

4. We need to consider the Gift and Sealing of the Holy Ghost as the assurance of our Inheritance.

Ephesians 1:13-14
"In whom also after that ye believed, ye were sealed with that Holy Spirit of promise which is the earnest of our inheritance."

The word **"earnest"** means **"down payment or security deposit"**.

After this initial experience, Christians may experience many other glorious things the Lord has prepared for them.

1 Corinthians 2:9-10
"But as it is written, Eye hath not seen, nor ear heard, neither have entered into the heart of man, the things which God hath prepared for them that love him.

But God hath revealed them unto us by his Spirit."

5. We need to consider this Gift of the Holy Spirit that causes us to profit in all aspects of life.

1 Corinthians 12:7
"The manifestation of the Spirit is given to every man to **profit withal.**"

Our spirit profits

Our mind profits

Our emotions profit

Our will profits

Our body profits

Our life profits

We are a Temple of the Holy Ghost full of His presence and glory.

The Gift of the Holy Spirit

1 Corinthians 6:19

"What? know ye not that your body is the temple of the Holy Ghost which is in you, which ye have of God, and ye are not your own?"

How does one receive the Gift of the Holy Spirit?

There are six things to consider when preparing to receive this Gift:

1. The gift of the Holy Ghost is promised to us and it cannot be earned.

Acts 2:38-39

"Then Peter said unto them, Repent, and be baptized every one of you in the name of Jesus Christ for the remission of sins, and ye shall receive the gift of the Holy Ghost.

For the promise is unto you."

2. We must have a thirst for this Gift.

John 7:37

"Jesus stood and cried, saying, if any man thirst, let him come unto me, and drink."

3. We must ask God the Father for the Gift.

Luke 11:13

"How much more shall your heavenly Father give the Holy Spirit to them that ask him?

4. We receive this Gift by faith.

GALATIANS 3:5
"He therefore that ministereth to you the Spirit, doeth he it by the works of the law, or by the hearing of faith?"

By faith we believe that God will keep His promise and give us the wonderful Gift of the Holy Ghost.

We inherit all God's promises by faith and patience.

HEBREWS 6:12
"Who through faith and patience inherit the promises."

5. We receive this Gift by the laying on of hands.

ACTS 19:6

"And when Paul had laid his hands upon them, the Holy Ghost came on them;"

This is how it works:

An anointed Servant of God lays hands upon someone who wants to receive.

The Holy Spirit then comes upon them with fire and power.

At times this anointing can be so strong that they fall down.

When we receive this gift we open our mouth and speak a Heavenly Language.

These words come from our spirit, through our mind and we speak the words by faith, even though we don't understand what we are saying.

2 Samuel 23:2

"The Spirit of the LORD spake by me, and his word was in my tongue."

6. We must continue to do three things after receiving this Gift of the Holy Ghost:

a. Value the Gift that we have received and continue to exercise it.

Hebrews 6:4
"Have tasted of the heavenly gift, and were made partakers of the Holy Ghost."

b. Continue to be filled with the Holy Ghost over and over again.

Ephesians 5:18
"And be not drunk with wine, wherein is excess; but be filled with the Spirit;"

Someone who loves drinking wine continues to do so and it eventually may become habit forming and addictive.

The use of lots of wine causes people to become drunk and behave uninhibited.

Likewise we must be filled each day with the new wine of the Holy Spirit and come under His influence.

When people are intoxicated they laugh, are happy and carefree.

That is how the Holy Spirit wants us to be. He fills us with joy.

c. Edify ourselves with this wonderful gift.

1 Corinthians 14:4
"He that speaketh in an unknown tongue edifieth himself."

The Gift of the Holy Ghost edifies and builds us up spiritually.

It strengthens and blesses everyone around us.

It also creates a desire in others to want what they see we have.

Let us remember two things:

1. The Gift of the Holy Spirit causes no confusion and is always decent and orderly.

1 Corinthians 14:39-40
"Wherefore, brethren, covet to prophesy, and forbid not to speak with tongues.

Let all things be done decently and in order."

2. We must never grieve or hinder the Holy Spirit in any way.

Ephesians 4:30
"And grieve not the Holy Spirit of God, whereby ye are sealed unto the day of redemption."

1 Thessalonians 5:19
"Quench not the Spirit."

CHAPTER 10

The Church of Jesus Christ

What is the Church?

Is it a denomination?

Is it a church building?

Is it a religious service?

The word "Church" comes from a Greek word "Ekklesia".

It is mentioned one hundred and twelve times in the New Testament.

It means a body or group of people who are called out and separated from others.

Paul refers to these called out one's as God's Children:

2 Corinthians 6:17-18

"Wherefore come out from among them, and be ye separate, saith the Lord, and touch not the unclean thing; and I will receive you.

And will be a Father unto you, and ye shall be my sons and daughters, saith the Lord Almighty."

These are Christians who are called out from a sinful world and are separated by God unto Himself as His sons and daughters.

Christians are the Church and they come together to worship God in places of worship or their houses.

Romans 16:5

"Likewise greet the church that is in their house."

There were many such Churches in the early church.

Acts 9:31

"Then had the churches rest throughout all Judaea and Galilee and Samaria, and were edified;"

The Church of Jesus Christ

There are ten aspects of the Church that we need to consider:

1. The Church is the bought possession of our Lord Jesus Christ.

It belongs to Him only and He refers to it as His possession.

MATTHEW 16:18
"And I say also unto thee, that thou art Peter, and upon this rock I will build my church;"

We know that Jesus rightfully possesses the Church, because He bought it for a great price, namely His own precious Blood.

1 CORINTHIANS 6:20
"For ye are bought with a price:"

REVELATION 5:9
"For thou wast slain, and hast redeemed us to God by thy blood out of every kindred, and tongue, and people, and nation."

Jesus refers to this transaction of Himself buying this valuable possession in a parable.

MATTHEW 13:46
"Who, when he had found one pearl of great price, went and sold all that he had, and bought it."

MATTHEW 13:44
"Again, the kingdom of heaven is like unto treasure hid in a field; the which when a man hath found, he hideth, and for joy thereof goeth and selleth all that he hath, and buyeth that field."

It was His great love for the church that motivated Jesus to pay this great price for the Church.

EPHESIANS 5:25
"Even as Christ also loved the church, and gave himself for it;"

2. The Church is valuable:

Each individual member is worth more than all the riches of this world.

MATTHEW 16:26
"For what is a man profited, if he shall gain the whole world, and lose his own soul?"

What is the cumulative value of the Saints throughout the ages?

It is impossible to evaluate their worth.

Within the Church there have been so many Saints whom we regard as priceless gems:

Apostles like Peter, Matthew, Mark, Luke, James, John and Paul.

Prophets like Barnabas, Silas and Agabas.

The Church of Jesus Christ

Evangelists like Phillip.

Pastors like Timothy and Titus.

Deacons like Stephen.

Church Fathers like Justin Martyr, Tertullian, Origen, Jerome and Augustine.

Many Early Church Saints who died for the faith.

Brilliant Scholars like John Wycliffe and Erastus who translated the Bible into the everyday language of the people.

Reformer's, like Martin Luther, Zwingli, John Calvin, John Knox and Armenian.

Preachers like John Wesley, George Whitefield, D.L. Moody, and Charles Finney.

Martyrs like Joan of Arc, Dietrich Bonheoffer, Watchman Nee and others.

Modern day Servants of God like John G Lake, William Branham and Billy Graham.

Examples of Love like Mother Teresa, helping millions of destitute people.

Truly, the Church is the most prized possession of the entire Universe.

3. It is a privilege to be a part of the Church, for three reasons:

a. We have been allowed entrance into it.

Entrance into the Church is exclusive, through Jesus Christ alone.

JOHN 10:9
"I am the door: by me if any man enter in, he shall be saved."

All other religious and man-made ways of entrance into the Church are false, misleading and ineffective.

JOHN 10:1
"He that entereth not by the door into the sheepfold, but climbeth up some other way, the same is a thief and a robber."

It is an esteemed privilege to obtain entrance into the Church by invitation only.

JOHN 15:16
"Ye have not chosen me, but I have chosen you, and ordained you."

It is only when the Lord Jesus knocks at our hearts door that we can be saved.

REVELATION 3:20
"Behold, I stand at the door, and knock: if any man hear my voice, and open the door, I will come in to him."

b. Within the Church, we enjoy blessing, protection and many other assurances.

Jesus knows us individually and we know Him.

He loves and protects us and is willing to lay down His life for us.

John 10:14-15
"I am the good shepherd, and know my sheep, and am known of mine.

As the Father knoweth me, even so know I the Father: and I lay down my life for the sheep."

c. The Church is an eternal experience.

The Church of Jesus Christ will never cease and in eternity all Christians will come to participate in the General Assembly of the Church in Heaven.

Hebrews 12:22-24
"But ye are come unto mount Sion, and unto the city of the living God, the heavenly Jerusalem, and to an innumerable company of angels,

To the *general assembly and church* of the first-born, which are written in heaven, and to God the Judge of all, and to the spirits of just men made perfect.

And to Jesus the mediator of the new covenant."

REVELATION 7:9
"After this I beheld, and, lo, a great multitude, which no man could number, of all nations, and kindred's, and people, and tongues, stood before the throne, and before the Lamb, clothed with white robes, and palms in their hands;"

4. The Church is God's dwelling place.

In the Old Testament God commanded Moses to build a Tabernacle.

It became God's dwelling place where He manifested His presence from within the Holy of Holies.

Solomon built a magnificent Temple where God dwelt and also manifested His glorious presence.

In the New Testament God has chosen another building to dwell in.

1 CORINTHIANS 3:9
"For ye are God's building."

This Church Building is made up of Christians that are a Holy Temple of God.

1 PETER 2:5
"Ye also, as lively stones, are built up a spiritual house."

EPHESIANS 2:20-23
"And are built upon the foundation of the apostles and prophets, Jesus Christ himself being the chief corner stone; In whom all the

building fitly framed together groweth unto a holy temple in the Lord:

In whom ye also are builded together for a habitation of God through the Spirit."

We as Christians are precisely, perfectly built upon the foundation of the Apostles and Prophets of which Jesus Christ is the Chief Corner Stone.

God manifests His glorious presence to the world through the Christians of this Temple.

5. The Church is the Body of Christ.

The Church is the Body of Christ made up of many members and Jesus is the Head of the Church.

EPHESIANS **1:22-23**
"And hath put all things under his feet, and gave him to be the head over all things to the church. Which is his body."

EPHESIANS **5:23**
"Even as Christ is the head of the church: and he is the saviour of the body."

This Body is made up of many members,

1 CORINTHIANS **12:12**

"For as the body is one, and hath many members."

1 Corinthians 12:13

"For by one Spirit are we all baptized into one body, whether we be Jews or Gentiles."

One by one, millions of members have been baptized into this Body over the last two thousand years.

6. Every member is of significant importance.

1 Corinthians 12:27
"Now ye are the body of Christ, and members in particular."

1 Corinthians 12:28
"And God hath set some in the church, first apostles, secondarily prophets, thirdly teachers, after that miracles, then gifts of healings, helps, governments, diversities of tongues."

Every member has been specifically and uniquely placed within this Body.

God has called every member, for a specific purpose.

Romans 8:28
"Them that love God, to them who are the called according to his purpose."

Each member of the body fulfills their own unique function and they need each other.

1 Corinthians 12:15

"If the foot shall say, because I am not the hand, I am not of the body; is it therefore not of the body?"

All the members of the Body are joined and banded together.

Colossians 2:19

"And not holding the Head, from which all the body by joints and bands having nourishment ministered, and knit together."

Like hands that are joined to the arms and arms to the shoulders, so we as the church are joined and need each other.

7. The nine Ministries keep the Church together.

They are the mortar between the bricks.

God has joined the bricks of this Building together with tempered mortar.

Tempered mortar is good mortar, which is good Ministry.

1 Corinthians 12:24
"But God hath tempered the body together."

Like in any normal body, we the members help, protect and nourish each other.

The Blood of Jesus also flows through the entire Church body to purify, feed, bring life to it and destroy the enemy coming against it.

8. The two bonds that bind the members together is the **peace** and **love** of God.

Ephesians 4:3
"Endeavoring to keep the unity of the Spirit in the *bond of peace*."

Colossians 3:14
"And above all these things put on *love, which is the bond* of perfectness."

9. God sanctifies the Church and adorns her with His glory.

Ephesians 5:26
"That he might sanctify and cleanse it with the washing of water by the word."

Ephesians 5:27
"That he might present it to himself a glorious church, not having spot, or wrinkle."

10. The Church is not an organization.

It is a living organism to fulfill the Divine mission of God.

It is to restore, purify, beautify and glorify men and woman.

What does the church do and experience?

The Christians of the Church gather together in an Assembly to worship God.

Hebrews 10:25
"Not forsaking the assembling of ourselves together, as the manner of some is; but exhorting one another: and so much the more."

Jesus placed His name over the Assembly of the Saints in the same way that God placed His Name over the Tabernacle and Temple in the Old Testament.

- Christians gather together in an Assembly to praise and worship God.
- They share testimonies of the goodness of the Lord.
- They listen to the reading and preaching of the Word of God.
- They experience the fruits, gifts and ministries of the Holy Spirit.

Matthew 18:20
"For where two or three are gathered together in my name, there am I in the midst of them."

DEUTERONOMY 16:2
"In the place which the LORD shall choose to place his name there."

That is why it is so important for Christians to gather together in the Church under the covering of the Name of Jesus.

Jesus manifests His presence where they gather together.

He is in its midst of the seven Golden Candlesticks, which is the Church.

REVELATION 1:13
"And in the midst of the seven candlesticks one like unto the Son of man, clothed with a garment down to the foot, and girt about the paps with a golden girdle."

Jesus together with the Saints offer oblations of worship to God.

HEBREWS 2:12
"Saying, I will declare thy name unto my brethren, in the midst of the church will I sing praise unto thee."

The Christians of the Church experience the following:

1. Men and women are saved and baptized.
2. They learn and practice the Doctrines of the Apostles.

The Church of Jesus Christ

3. They have Fellowship with each other.

4. They enjoy the Lords Supper together.

5. They gather together to Pray.

6. They give God their tithes and offerings to extend His Kingdom on Earth.

7. They praise and worship God.

8. The Church membership is multiplied.

Acts **2:41-47**
"Then they that gladly received his word were baptized: and the same day there were added unto them about three thousand souls.

And they continued stedfastly in the apostles' doctrine and fellowship, and in breaking of bread, and in prayers.

And fear came upon every soul: and many wonders and signs were done by the apostles.

And all that believed were together, and had all things common;

And sold their possessions and goods, and parted them to all men, as every man had need.

And they, continuing daily with one accord in the temple, and breaking bread from house to house, did eat their meat with gladness and singleness of heart,

Praising God, and having favor with all the people.

The Lord added to the church daily such as should be saved."

Today the Church is made up of millions of Saints.

It is a Universal Church of many local assemblies throughout the world.

It also consists of those who have passed on to be with the Lord.

They are described as our cloud of witnesses.

Hebrews 12:1

"Wherefore seeing we also are compassed about with so great a cloud of witnesses."

As members we have the responsibility to complete the work of the Church on earth.

Those in Heaven are spectators that watch and cheer us on as we do the work.

Let us heed the words of Jude.

Jude 3

"Ye should earnestly contend for the faith ... once delivered unto the saints."

Let us treasure and protect the Church of Jesus Christ!

CHAPTER 11

The Nine Gifts of the Holy Spirit

Every Child of God who has been baptized with the Holy Spirit may know and experience the nine Gifts of the Holy Spirit.

1 Corinthians 12:1

"Now concerning spiritual gifts, brethren, I would not have you ignorant."

Ignorance comes through a lack of knowledge and if we don't know about these gifts, how will we be able to desire and experience them?

1 Corinthians 12:31

"But covet earnestly the best gifts:"

Here the Greek word for gifts is "**charismata** " and means **gifts of grace.**

These nine gifts of the Holy Spirit are given and ministered by the grace of God and cannot be earned:

1 Corinthians 12:8-10

"For to one is given by the Spirit -

the word of wisdom;

to another the word of knowledge.

to another faith;

to another the gifts of healing;

to another the working of miracles;

to another prophecy;

to another discerning of spirits;

to another divers kinds of tongues;

to another the interpretation of tongues:"

These nine gifts are divided into three categories:

The three revelation gifts

    Word of Wisdom

    Word of Knowledge

    Discerning of spirits

The Nine Gifts of the Holy Spirit

The three power gifts
- Faith
- Gifts of healing
- Working of miracles

The three vocal gifts
- Prophecy
- Divers kinds of tongues
- Interpretation of tongues

Every Christian may receive a gift of the Holy Spirit.

1 Peter 4:10

"As every man hath received the gift, even so minister the same one to another, as good stewards of the manifold grace of God."

Paul had the desire to impart to all believers a gift of the Holy Spirit.

Romans 1:11

"For I long to see you, that I may impart unto you some spiritual gift, to the end ye may be established;"

We receive these gifts according to the measure of God's grace given us.

Romans 12:6

"Having then gifts differing according to the grace that is given to us."

Every child of God is a candidate to receive a gift of the Holy Spirit.

It is important that we do not neglect using the gift the Holy Spirit imparts to us.

1 Timothy 4:14

"Neglect not the gift that is in thee."

We should never let this gift lay dormant and unused in our lives.

2 Timothy 1:6

"Wherefore I put thee in remembrance that thou stir up the gift of God, which is in thee by the putting on of my hands."

The gift that is within us will be manifested and shown through us.

1 Corinthians 12:7

"But the manifestation of the Spirit is given to every man to profit withal."

The Nine Gifts of the Holy Spirit

The invisible person of the Holy Spirit manifests himself by these gifts through us.

The Holy Spirit visibly demonstrates His personality, will and purpose through us.

1 Corinthians 2:4

"And my speech and my preaching was not with enticing words of man's wisdom, but in demonstration of the Spirit and of power:"

What is the purpose of these nine Gifts?

Through the nine gifts, the Holy Spirit meets the needs of people:

1. A Word of Wisdom.

There is a significant difference between a Word of Wisdom and a Word of Knowledge.

A Word of Wisdom is a directive and by that we mean that it gives direction.

Ecclesiastes 10:10
"But wisdom is profitable to direct."

Wisdom effectively uses and directs knowledge.

Proverbs 15:2
"The tongue of the wise useth knowledge aright:"

A word of Wisdom is a tiny fragment and portion of God's immeasurable wisdom given at a specific time, for a specific situation. By using this gift, the Holy Spirit supernaturally effects people, situations and things and brings about His desires and purposes.

Here are examples of the use of this gift.

In the Old Testament King Solomon used this gift. **(1 Kings 3:16-28)**

In the New Testament, a word of wisdom by Paul brought confusion to the counsel of those opposing him and saved his life. **(Acts 23:6)**

2. A Word of Knowledge.

The Holy Spirit is omniscient. He knows everything.

A word of Knowledge is a tiny portion of God's Knowledge supernaturally imparted by the Holy Spirit through man.

It is Divine information imparted by God for a specific time and purpose.

This knowledge is spoken out in words to people, to help them.

Here are some biblical examples of this gift in operation:

The Nine Gifts of the Holy Spirit

In the Old Testament:

The prophet Samuel imparts a word of Knowledge to Saul, the soon to be King of Israel, about his lost asses.

1 Samuel 9:20
"And as for thine asses that were lost three days ago, set not thy mind on them; for they are found."

In the New Testament:

Jesus revealed supernatural knowledge to Nathanael.

John 1:47-49
"Jesus saw Nathanael coming to him, and saith of him, Behold an Israelite indeed, in whom is no guile!

Nathanael saith unto him, whence knowest thou me? Jesus answered and said unto him, before that Philip called thee, when thou wast under the fig tree, I saw thee.

Nathanael answered and saith unto him, Rabbi, thou art the Son of God; thou art the King of Israel."

Similarly, Jesus gave a word of Knowledge to a woman of Samaria.

John 4:16-19
"Jesus saith unto her, Go, call thy husband, and come hither.

The woman answered and said, I have no husband. Jesus said unto her, Thou hast well said, I have no husband:

For thou hast had five husbands; and he whom thou now hast is not thy husband: in that saidst thou truly.

The woman saith unto him, Sir, I perceive that thou art a prophet."

The Apostle Peter spoke a Word of Knowledge to Ananias.

Acts 5:1-3
"But a certain man named Ananias, with Sapphira his wife, sold a possession,

And kept back part of the price, his wife also being privy to it, and brought a certain part, and laid it at the apostles' feet.

But Peter said, Ananias, why hath Satan filled thine heart to lie to the Holy Ghost, and to keep back part of the price of the land?"

The five reasons why the Holy Spirit gives a word of Knowledge are:

1. To warn people.
2. To inform people.
3. To expose hidden things.
4. To confirm things. .
5. To reveal Gods power in knowing secrets.

The Nine Gifts of the Holy Spirit

1 Corinthians 14:25
"And thus are the secrets of his heart made manifest; and so falling down on his face he will worship God, and report that God is in you of a truth."

3. Discerning of spirits.

To discern is to recognize or distinguish between certain things.

This gift allows God's servants to recognize or distinguish between good and evil spirits.

It operates in the following ways:

1. To see people as they actually are.

It helps discerning good or evil people and identify an unclean spirit in a person.

It helps to detect demonic activity in the life of a person.

It clearly identifies different positive or negative characteristics of the human spirit.

It discerns a bitter, fearful, depressed, tormented or broken spirit.

2. To be able to distinguish between different spirits namely;

The Holy Spirit

Angels

Fallen angels

Evil spirits and demons

The Human spirit

There are numerous examples of this gift in operation in the Bible:

Jesus discerns the characteristic of Nathanael's spirit.

JOHN 1:47

"Jesus saw Nathanael coming to him, and saith of him, Behold an Israelite indeed, in whom is no guile."

Peter discerns bitterness as the characteristic of Simon's spirit.

ACTS 8:23

"For I perceive that thou art in the gall of bitterness, and in the bond of iniquity."

Paul perceived that the lame man had a spirit of faith.

ACTS 14:9

"The same heard Paul speak: who steadfastly beholding him, and perceiving that he had faith to be healed."

The Nine Gifts of the Holy Spirit

Paul discerned an evil spirit in a woman.

Acts 16:18

"But Paul, being grieved, turned and said to the spirit, I command thee in the name of Jesus Christ to come out of her. And he came out the same hour."

John encourages us to discern all spirits.

1 John 4:1

"Beloved, believe not every spirit, but try the spirits whether they are of God: because many false prophets are gone out into the world."

God's word has the ability to penetrate and discern the deepest depths of a human being.

Hebrews 4:12

"For the word of God is quick, and powerful, and sharper than any two-edged sword, piercing even to the dividing asunder of soul and spirit, and of the joints and marrow, and is a *discerner* of the thoughts and intents of the heart."

4. The gift of Faith.

A Christian may experience different aspects of faith:

Faith to receive salvation

Faith to experience answers to prayer

Faith as a Fruit of the Holy Spirit to bring forth spiritual character

Faith as a Gift of the Holy Spirit for spiritual warfare

Faith as a portion of God's supernatural Faith

Hebrews 11:3

"Through faith we understand that the worlds were framed by the word of God, so that things which are seen were not made of things which do appear."

When this God kind gift of faith operates through us, we can move mountains.

Mark 11:22-23

"And Jesus answering saith unto them, have faith in God.

For verily I say unto you, That whosoever shall say unto this mountain, Be thou removed, and be thou cast into the sea; and shall not doubt in his heart, but shall believe that those things which he saith shall come to pass; he shall have whatsoever he saith."

1 Corinthians 13:2

"And though I have all faith, so that I could remove mountains."

Here are two examples in the Old Testament of this gift in operation:

a. By faith Gideon defeated the Midianites.

Judges 7:19-21
"So Gideon, and the hundred men that were with him, came unto the outside of the camp … blew the trumpets, and brake the pitchers, and held the lamps in their left hands, and they cried, The sword of the LORD, and of Gideon.

And they stood every man in his place round about the camp; and all the host ran, and cried, and fled."

b. By faith David Killed Goliath.

1 Samuel 17:50
"So David prevailed over the Philistine with a sling and with a stone, and smote the Philistine, and slew him; but there was no sword in the hand of David."

In the New Testament we have two examples of the use of this gift:

a. By faith Peter raised the lame man.

ACTS 3:6-7
"Then Peter said, Silver and gold have I none; but such as I have give I thee: In the name of Jesus Christ of Nazareth rise up and walk. And he took him by the right hand, and lifted him up: and immediately his feet and ankle bones received strength."

b. By faith Peter raised Tabitha from the dead.

ACTS 9:40
"But Peter put them all forth, and kneeled down, and prayed; and turning him to the body said, Tabitha, arise. And she opened her eyes: and when she saw Peter, she sat up."

5. The gifts of healing.

The gifts of healing are God's supernatural way of curing all manner of sickness and disease. We know that God is a healer and loves imparting healing to the sick.

God is called Jehovah Rapha which means the Lord our healer.

EXODUS 15:26
"For I am the LORD that healeth thee."

Many healings were imparted to people by Jesus.

Mark 5:30

"And Jesus, immediately knowing in himself that virtue had gone out of him."

Acts 10:38

"How God anointed Jesus of Nazareth with the Holy Ghost and with power: who went about doing good, and healing all that were oppressed of the devil; for God was with him."

The Apostle Paul ministered healing to the father of Publius.

Acts 28:8

"And it came to pass, that the father of Publius lay sick of a fever and of a bloody flux: to whom Paul entered in, and prayed, and laid his hands on him, and healed him."

The gifts of healing destroy viruses and germs in the human body and reverse the damage they've caused bringing total healing and restoration.

6. The Working of Miracles.

A Miracle is supernatural energy flowing from God that causes instantaneous creative change.

This may be in a human body, nature or a specific situation.

It is described as a mighty work.

MATTHEW 13:54
"Whence hath this man this wisdom, and these mighty works?"

Here are examples of this gift being used in the New Testament:

a. Examples of miracles performed by Jesus.

ACTS 2:22
"Jesus of Nazareth, a man approved of God among you by miracles and wonders and signs."

Jesus turned water into wine:

JOHN 2:7-11
"Jesus saith unto them, Fill the water pots with water. And they filled them up to the brim.

And he saith unto them, Draw out now, and bear unto the governor of the feast.

When the ruler of the feast had tasted the water that was made wine called the bridegroom.

And saith unto him; Every man at the beginning doth set forth good wine; and when men have well drunk, then that which is worse: but thou hast kept the good wine until now.

This beginning of miracles did Jesus in Cana of Galilee, and manifested forth his glory; and his disciples believed on him."

The Nine Gifts of the Holy Spirit

Jesus multiplied the loaves and fishes.

JOHN 6:9-11
"There is a lad here, which hath five barley loaves, and two small fishes: but what are they among so many?

And Jesus took the loaves; and when he had given thanks, he distributed to the disciples, and the disciples to them that were set down; and likewise of the fishes as much as they would."

Jesus walked on water.

MATTHEW 14:25
"And in the fourth watch of the night Jesus went unto them, walking on the sea."

b. The Apostles performed many miracles.

ACTS 5:12
"And by the hands of the apostles were many signs and wonders wrought among the people."

ACTS 8:13
"Then Simon himself believed also and wondered, beholding the miracles and signs which were done."

7. Kinds of Tongues.

Every Believer when baptized in the Holy Spirit, may speak with unknown tongues.

It is a mysterious, heavenly prayer language to God, by the Holy Spirit, through us.

1 Corinthians 14:2
"For he that speaketh in an unknown tongue speaketh not unto men, but unto God: for no man understandeth him; howbeit in the spirit he speaketh mysteries."

Romans 8:26
"Likewise the Spirit also helpeth our infirmities: for we know not what we should pray for as we ought: but the Spirit itself maketh intercession for us with groanings which cannot be uttered."

This Gift is called **divers kinds of Tongues**:

The word "**kinds**" is the Greek word "**genes**" ".

It means **various purposes.**

This gift achieves various purposes that are deemed necessary by the Holy Spirit.

There are four kinds of tongues that are manifest:

Exhortation

With this manifestation, the Holy Spirit speaks a message to the Church in words of comfort, edification and encouragement.

This message requires an interpretation by the gift of Interpretation of tongues.

A rebuke

With this manifestation, the Holy Spirit reveals, rebukes and attacks satanic forces at work against the Church or Believers.

Here no interpretation is always required.

Intercession

With this manifestation, the Holy Spirit intercedes on behalf of a person, a situation or Church where prayer is urgently required.

Here no interpretation is always required.

Praise

With this manifestation, the Holy Spirit introduces, directs, effects or harmonizes praise within the Assembly of Believers.

Here no interpretation is necessary.

8. Interpretation of Tongues.

This manifestation only relates to a situation where a message or utterance has previously been given in an Unknown Tongue. Those who speak by the Holy Spirit, speak a Message in an unknown tongue and should pray for the Interpretation and receive it from the Holy Spirit.

1 Corinthians 14:27-28
"If any man speak in an unknown tongue, let it be by two, or at the most by three, and that by course; and let one interpret."

But if there be no interpreter, let him keep silence in the church; and let him speak to himself, and to God."

Messages in Tongues should be by two or three and followed in course by the Interpretation.

If no interpretation is given all the Saints must silently pray to God.

9. The gift of Prophecy.

This manifestation of the Holy Spirit is strongly emphasized and recommended by Paul for the Saints. It is directed at either the whole church or specific individuals.

It is a supernatural utterance in a known tongue.

It has five purposes:

1. It edifies.

It builds, strengthens and makes Christians more effective.

2. It exhorts.

It encourages, motivates and energizes Christians.

3. It comforts.

It cheers up and comforts Christians when they are discouraged or brought under condemnation by satan.

4. It ordains and sends.

By words of prophecy, Christians are given special Gifts, Ministries, Assignments and are sent forth by the Holy Spirit.

1 Timothy 4:14
"Neglect not the gift that is in thee, which was given thee by prophecy."

Acts 13:2
"As they ministered to the Lord, and fasted, the Holy Ghost said, Separate me Barnabas and Saul for the work whereunto I have called them."

5. It ministers to Unbelievers.

When unbelievers are present in the Church, the Holy Spirit may minister to them through Prophecy.

1 Corinthians 14:24
"But if all prophesy, and there come in one that believeth not, or one unlearned, he is convinced of all, he is judged of all:"

All Prophecy should be judged.

1 Corinthians 14:29

"Let the prophets speak two or three, and let the other judge."

In judging Prophecy, one may ask three questions -

1. Is it scriptural?

2. Does it glorify God?

3. Does it fulfill the five purposes of Prophecy?

How do the nine Gifts of the Holy Spirit operate?

The nine Gifts operate:

1. By the anointing of the Holy Spirit.

Acts 10:38
"How God anointed Jesus of Nazareth with the Holy Ghost and with power: who went about doing good, and healing all that were oppressed of the devil; for God was with him."

1 John 2:20
"But ye have an unction from the Holy One, and ye know all things."

2. By being sensitive to hear the voice of the Holy Spirit.

Revelation 3:6
"He that hath an ear, let him hear what the Spirit saith unto the churches."

Romans 8:14
"For as many as are led by the Spirit of God, they are the sons of God."

3. By faith.

GALATIANS 3:5
"He therefore that ministereth to you the Spirit, and worketh miracles among you, doeth he it by the works of the law, or by the hearing of faith?"

4. By love.

Everything we do for God should be packaged in love.

EPHESIANS 4:15
"But speaking the truth in love."

Those who do not operate in love are irritating, noisy workers and are counted as nothing.

1 CORINTHIANS 13:1-2
"Though I speak with the tongues of men and of angels, and have not love, I am become as sounding brass, or a tinkling cymbal.

And though I have the gift of prophecy, and understand all mysteries, and all knowledge; and though I have all faith, so that I could remove mountains, and have not love, I am nothing."

The manifestation of the Gifts of the Holy Spirit should never bring any glory to man. Only God should be glorified.

1 Peter 4:10-11

"As every man hath received the gift, even so minister the same one to another, as good stewards of the manifold grace of God.

If any man speak, let him speak as the oracles of God; if any man minister, let him do it as of the ability which God giveth: that God in all things may be glorified through Jesus Christ, to whom be praise and dominion forever and ever."

Ministering the Gifts of the Holy Spirit we should focus on two things:

1. Edifying the Church and People:

1 Corinthians 14:12
"Even so ye, forasmuch as ye are zealous of spiritual gifts, seek that ye may excel to the edifying of the church."

2. Defeating satan and his kingdom:

Mark 16:17
"And these signs shall follow them that believe; In my name shall they cast out devils; they shall speak with new tongues;"

Paul wanted us to desire, obtain and use the best Gifts.

The Nine Gifts of the Holy Spirit

1 Corinthians 12:1, 30, 31

"Now concerning spiritual gifts, brethren, I would not have you ignorant.

Have all the gifts of healing? Do all speak with tongues? Do all interpret?

But covet earnestly the best gifts."

Those who operate the Gifts of the Holy Spirit should do so in a decent and orderly way.

They should obey the Lords commandments, living a holy and dedicated spiritual life.

1 Corinthians 14:37, 40

"If any man think himself to be a prophet, or spiritual, let him acknowledge that the things that I write unto you are the commandments of the Lord.

Let all things be done decently and in order."

The Gifts of the Holy Spirit are to be continually manifested until the coming of our Lord Jesus Christ.

1 Corinthians 1:7

"So that ye come behind in no gift; waiting for the coming of our Lord Jesus Christ:"

CHAPTER 12

The Nine Fruits of the Holy Spirit

Christians are trees of righteousness that have been planted by the Lord to produce spiritual fruit.

Isaiah 61:3

"That they might be called trees of righteousness, the planting of the LORD, that he might be glorified."

Psalm 92:13

"Those that be planted in the house of the LORD shall flourish in the courts of our God."

Christians are able to produce spiritual fruit in season.

Psalm 1:3

"And he shall be like a tree planted by the rivers of water, that bringeth forth his fruit in his season."

Christians should always produce Good Fruit.

Matthew 7:17

"Even so every good tree bringeth forth good fruit."

Christians should bring forth the nine fruits of the Holy Spirit:

Galatians 5:22-23

"But the fruit of the Spirit is love, joy, peace, longsuffering, gentleness, goodness, faith, Meekness, temperance:"

These are the nine Fruits of the Spirit:

1. Love
2. Joy
3. Peace
4. Patience

The Nine Fruits of the Holy Spirit

5. Gentleness

6. Goodness

7. Faith or Faithfulness

8. Humility

9. Self control

Fruit is produced by a twofold process:

a. Fruit is formulated.

b. Fruit is cultivated.

a. The formulation process.

Fruit is formed when pollen passes in the blossom from the stigma to the pistil.

The pistil experiences a change and becomes the three parts of the fruit namely:

The outer **skin**

The juicy part of the **flesh**

The **seed** to ensure the reproduction of more fruit later

Similarly the Holy Spirit brings forth the nine fruits of the Spirit from the deep area of our spirit and they are manifest within and through the three parts of our Soul:

The **Intellect**

The **Emotions**

The **Will**

These fruits are to be produced and enjoyed.

Because there seed is within them they are reproduced over and over again.

b. The cultivation process.

In the process of cultivating fruit five things are necessary:

1. The blossoms should be protected from hurt or damage.

2. The roots of the tree must be nurtured and fed with nutrients and water.

3. The branches must be pruned to regulate growth and increase fruit production.

4. The fruit must be protected from insect or storm damage.

5. The fruit must be harvested and enjoyed when it is ripe.

To ensure successful spiritual fruit production, Christians need to be totally yielded to God as trees of righteousness.

They must be in total submission to God and the Ministry of the Church.

The Nine Fruits of the Holy Spirit

The Ministry of the Church helps the process of cultivating, protecting, nurturing, producing, increasing and harvesting the wonderful fruits of the Holy Spirit, in the lives of Christians.

EPHESIANS 4:11-12

"And he gave some, apostles; and some, prophets; and some, evangelists; and some, pastors and teachers;

For the perfecting of the saints, for the work of the ministry, for the edifying of the body of Christ:"

The following six things will enhance the quality of spiritual fruit in our lives and prevent corruption:

1. Spending time in God's Word.

2. Spending time in prayer.

3. Spending time in fasting.

4. Submitting to authority and discipline within the Church.

5. Fellowshipping with other Christians, as we rub shoulders daily with them.

6. Allow the Lord to prune our branches to increase our fruit production.

We are like stones that are rubbed against each other in a stream.

This helps to smooth away our rough edges.

Fruits like love, patience and gentleness are produced.

We must be totally committed to producing the Fruits of the Spirit for God.

2 Timothy 2:6

"The husbandman **that** laboureth must be first partaker of the fruits."

The Fruits of the Spirit are manifested in three ways:

Ephesians 5:9

"For the fruit of the Spirit is in all goodness and righteousness and truth:"

In goodness

> We may eat and enjoy these fruits and they will also have a tasteful, healthy and spiritual effect upon others.

The Nine Fruits of the Holy Spirit

In righteousness

> These fruits are of the highest quality, being a God-kind of fruit, bringing forth righteousness in our lives and others.

In truth

> These fruits are of a specific type with their own uniqueness and purpose.
>
> All fruits are produced and harvested in season.

Isaiah 28:4

"And as the hasty fruit before the summer; which when he that looketh upon it seeth, while it is yet in his hand he eateth it up."

The specific seasons of spiritual fruit production are:

In times of well doing.

Galatians 6:9

"And let us not be weary **in well doing** : for in due season we shall reap, if we faint not."

In seasons of trials and temptations

1 Peter 1:6-7

"Wherein ye greatly rejoice, though now **for a season**, if need be, ye are in heaviness through manifold temptations. That the **trial of your faith**, being much more precious than of gold that perisheth."

In times of chastening

HEBREWS 12:11

"Now no **chastening** for the present seemeth to be joyous, but grievous: nevertheless afterward it **yieldeth the peaceable fruit** of righteousness unto them which are exercised thereby."

We are to be prosperous, fruit bearing trees in all times and situations:

In times of fear - we should produce **love**

In times of mourning and sadness - we should produce **joy.**

In times of storm - we should produce **peace.**

In times of adversity - we should produce **patience.**

In times of aggression - we should produce **gentleness**.

In times of evil - we should produce **goodness.**

In times of doubt - we should produce **faith and faithfulness.**

In times of pride - we should produce **meekness.**

The Nine Fruits of the Holy Spirit

In times of over-indulgence - we should produce **temperance.**

The nine Fruits of the Spirit are divided into three groups of three:

Each group of three is manifested in and through one of three areas of our Soul:

In our Emotions

- Love
- Joy
- Peace

In our Intellect

- Patience
- Gentleness
- Goodness

In our Will

- Faith/Faithfulness
- Humility
- Self control

The nine Fruits of the Spirit have three different effects upon our lives and others:

1. They give **enjoyment** - each fruit has its own unique spiritual taste.

2. They give **nourishment** - each fruit produces spiritual food and enrichment.

3. They give **health** - each fruit enhances spiritual life and healing.

That is why we need all the Fruits of the Spirit for ourselves and others.

The fruits of the Spirit reveal what Spirit is within us.

The Fruits of the Spirit reveal the presence of the Holy Spirit in us.

The works of the flesh reveal a fleshly or carnal nature.

By observing the actions of a person, we can know what their nature is:

a. The works of the flesh reveal a carnal nature:

This is a person who is dominated by the flesh.

GALATIANS 5:19-21
"Now the works of the flesh are manifest, which are these; Adultery, fornication, uncleanness,

The Nine Fruits of the Holy Spirit

lasciviousness, Idolatry, witchcraft, hatred, variance, emulations, wrath, strife, seditions, heresies, envyings, murders, drunkenness, revellings."

b. The fruits of the Spirit reveal a Divine nature:

GALATIANS 5:22-23
"But the fruit of the Spirit is love, joy, peace, longsuffering, gentleness, goodness, faith, Meekness, temperance:"

If the actions of a Christian reveal a carnal nature, it can be changed.

This is done by following these six steps:

1. Identify the actions of the flesh

2. Admit and confess that they are carnal and sinful.

3. Declare that they are unwanted.

4. Reckon them dead and mortify them.

5. Put them off. (Putting off the old man)

6. Replace them with new actions from the Holy Spirit. (Putting on the new man)

ROMANS 6:11
"Likewise reckon ye also yourselves to be dead indeed unto sin."

COLOSSIANS 3:9-17
"Seeing that ye have put off the old man with his deeds ...

And have put on the new man, which is renewed in knowledge after the image of him that created him...

And whatsoever ye do in word or deed, do all in the name of the Lord Jesus."

The nine fruits of the Spirit are given to produce new behavior in our lives.

This new behavior is manifest when the fruits of the Spirit become actual deeds of righteousness.

These deeds become the ***Christian's righteous fine linen garment.***

REVELATION 19:8

"And to her was granted that she should be arrayed in fine linen, clean and white: for the fine linen is the righteousness of saints."

There are three important aspects of this garment:

1. It is the garment we are counseled to buy:

Revelation 3:18
"I counsel thee to buy of me white raiment ... that thou mayest be clothed, and that the shame of thy nakedness do not appear;"

2. It is the overcomers garment:

Revelation 3:5
"He that overcometh, the same shall be clothed in white raiment;"

3. It is a garment we should keep unspotted by the flesh:

Revelations 16:15
"Behold, I come as a thief. Blessed is he that watcheth, and keepeth his garments, lest he walk naked, and they see his shame.

James 1:27
"Pure religion and undefiled before God and the Father is this, to keep himself unspotted from the world."

Now let us focus on each of the nine Fruits of the Spirit:

1. Love.

The Greek word for this kind of love is "**agape**".

It means a "**God kind of love.**"

a. It comes from the Holy Spirit.

ROMANS 5:5
"Because the love of God is **shed abroad in our hearts** by the Holy Ghost which is given unto us."

b. It affects our heart and emotions.

1 PETER 1:22
"See that ye love one another with a pure heart fervently:"

c. This love brings stability to our emotions.

EPHESIANS 3:17
"That ye, being rooted and grounded in love."

Paul describes this love:

1 CORINTHIANS 13:4-8
"Charity suffereth long, and is kind; charity envieth not; charity vaunteth not itself, is not puffed up, Doth not behave itself unseemly, seeketh not her own, is not easily provoked, thinketh no evil; Rejoiceth not in iniquity,

but rejoiceth in the truth; Beareth all things, believeth all things, hopeth all things, endureth all things. Charity never faileth:"

This love is:
Patient

Not envious

Humble

Dignified

Unselfish

Doesn't take offence

Thinks good thoughts

It doesn't wish harm on anyone or rejoice in their harm

It rejoices in reality and truth

It is strong, believing, hopeful and enduring

Love should be the foundation of who we are and what we do:

GALATIANS 5:6

"But faith, which worketh by love."

EPHESIANS 4:15

"But speaking the truth in love"

EPHESIANS 3:17-19

That ye being rooted and grounded in love

It should continuously increase in our lives.

1 THESSALONIANS 3:12

"And the Lord make you to increase and abound in love one toward another."

It should always be fervent within us.

1 PETER 1:22

"See that ye love one another fervently:"

It is an anchor that keeps us through difficult times.

JUDE 21

"Keep yourselves in the love of God."

This Love is dynamic in four ways:

1. It never focuses on the negative.

1 PETER 4:8
"For charity shall cover the multitude of sins."

The Nine Fruits of the Holy Spirit

2. It overcomes opposition and obstacles.

MATTHEW 5:44
"Love your enemies, bless them that curse you, do good to them that hate you, and pray for them which despitefully use you, and persecute you."

3. It is compassionate and helps those in need.

1 JOHN 3:17
"But whoso hath this world's good, and seeth his brother have need, and shutteth up his bowels of compassion from him, how dwelleth the love of God in him?"

4. It will meet the ultimate test of Martyrdom.

1 JOHN 3:16
"Hereby perceive we the love of God, because he laid down his life for us: and we ought to lay down our lives for the brethren."

God's love is perfected in us and makes us more like Jesus.

1 JOHN 4:12

"If we love one another, God dwelleth in us, and his love is perfected in us."

2. Joy.

Our bodies are capable of experiencing pleasure.

Our minds and emotions may experience happiness

However it is the *spirit of man* that experiences joy.

Pleasure and happiness occur as a result of **circumstances**.

A child of God experiences joy **in all circumstances.**

Habakkuk 3:17-18

"Although the fig tree shall not blossom, neither shall fruit be in the vines; the labour of the olive shall fail, and the fields shall yield no meat; the flock shall be cut off from the fold, and there shall be no herd in the stalls:

Yet I will rejoice in the LORD, I will joy in the God of my salvation."

God is the source of a Christian's joy.

Psalm 43:4

"Then will I go unto the altar of God, unto God my exceeding joy:"

God anoints us with joy.

Isaiah 61:3

"To appoint unto them that mourn in Zion, to give unto them beauty for ashes, the oil of joy for mourning."

The Nine Fruits of the Holy Spirit

The joy of the Lord is our strength.

Nehemiah 8:10

"For the joy of the LORD is your strength."

It is interesting to note that a pilot flies a plane with **a joystick,** which steers and gives it direction.

Joy always sets the course for Christians and gives them direction.

There are five different degrees of joy namely:

1. We experience it when we receive Gods Word the first time.

It launches us into a new and continuous experience of joy.

Jeremiah 15:16
"And thy word was unto me the joy and rejoicing of mine heart:"

Romans 14:17
"For the kingdom of God is joy in the Holy Ghost.

2. This joy increases and becomes exceeding joy.

1 Peter 4:13
"Ye may be glad also with exceeding joy."

JOHN 17:13
"And these things I speak in the world, that they might have my joy fulfilled in themselves."

3. It becomes unspeakable.

1 PETER 1:8
"Ye rejoice with joy unspeakable and full of glory:"

4. We experience the full measure of joy.

1 JOHN 1:4
"And these things write we unto you, that your joy may be full."

PSALM 16:11
"In thy presence is fullness of joy;"

5. This joy is unending.

ISAIAH 35:10
"Everlasting joy shall be upon their heads:"

2. Peace.

God is a God of peace and He desires that we experience peace.

PHILIPPIANS 4:9
"And the God of peace shall be with you."

1 CORINTHIANS 7:15
"But God hath called us to peace."

The Hebrew word for peace is **"Shalom"** and it means to experience completeness and wholeness, knowing all is well.

There are six things that bring about our peace:

Romans 14:19

"Let us therefore follow after the things which make for peace."

1. Being justified.

Romans 5:1
"Therefore being justified by faith, we have peace with God through our Lord Jesus Christ:"

We have peace because the partition of sin between God and us has been removed.

2. Having fellowship with the Holy Spirit.

Romans 14:17
"For the kingdom of God is peace in the Holy Ghost."

3. A Godly home.

Psalm 122:7
"Peace be within thy walls, and prosperity within thy palaces."

4. Letting peace direct our decisions.

We know that when we make decisions and feel peaceful about them, we are making the right decisions.

COLOSSIANS 3:15
"And let the peace of God rule in your hearts."

5. Enjoying the protection of mental and emotional peace.

PHILIPPIANS 4:7
"And the peace of God, which passeth all understanding, shall keep your hearts and minds through Christ Jesus."

The word "keep" means to "protect'.

6. Experiencing peace wherever we go.

EPHESIANS 6:15
"And your feet shod with the preparation of the gospel of peace;"

We experience this peace in five different degrees:

a. Our peace is like a river.

It is refreshing and continuously flows.

ISAIAH 48:18
"Then had thy peace been as a river."

The Nine Fruits of the Holy Spirit

b. It increases.

1 Peter 1:2
"Peace, be multiplied."

c. It is great.

Isaiah 54:13
"And great shall be the peace of thy children."

d. It is perfect.

Isaiah 26:3
"Thou wilt keep him in perfect peace, whose mind is stayed on thee:"

e. It goes beyond the human mind and natural thinking.

Philippians 4:7
"And the peace of God, which passeth all understanding."

3. Longsuffering.

Longsuffering is also known as **patience**.

The fruit of Patience is the God-given ability to wait for things to come to pass and to endure trouble or adversity.

ROMANS 5:3
"And not only so, but we glory in tribulations also: knowing that tribulation worketh patience;"

A Christian's patience can be recognized by others.

2 TIMOTHY 3:10
"But thou hast fully known my patience."

Patience helps us in five ways:

a. It helps us to effectively prepare for, run and finish our spiritual race.

HEBREWS 12:1
"And let us run with patience the race that is set before us."

b. It helps us endure persecution and receive God's promises.

ACTS 26:6-7
"And now I stand and am judged for the hope of the promise made of God, unto our fathers:"

c. By patience we enter into our spiritual rest.

HEBREWS 4:1
"Let us therefore fear, lest, a promise being left us of entering into his rest, any of you should seem to come short of it."

d. By patience we continue in well doing.

Galatians 6:9
"And let us not be weary in well doing."

e. By patience we complete our work for God.

Galatians 6:9
"For in due season we shall reap, if we faint not."

4. Gentleness.

The Greek word for this gentleness is "**Chrestotes**".

It means **"kindness."**

This kindness manifests in two ways:

a. Kindness is speaking good words to others.

Proverbs 31:26
"And in her tongue is the law of kindness."

b. Kindness is doing good deeds for others.

Matthew 7:11
"If ye then, being evil, know how to give good gifts unto your children."

It treats others the way we wish to be treated.

LUKE 6:31
"And as ye would that men should do to you, do ye also to them likewise."

Christians should always be kind.

COLOSSIANS 3:12
"Put on therefore kindness."

ISAIAH 54:10
"But my kindness shall not depart from thee."

Kindness is at least six things:

1. Feeding the hungry.
2. Clothing the naked.
3. Speaking words of encouragement and comfort to the hurting.
4. Lending to the poor.
5. Taking care of destitute orphans, widows, the aged and the homeless.
6. Sharing someone's workload or burden.

5. Goodness.

Goodness can be defined as excellence of moral character and behavior.

Only the Godhead can measure up to that perfect definition.

The Nine Fruits of the Holy Spirit

Mark 10:18
"And Jesus said unto him, why callest thou me good?

There is none good but one, that is, God."

Exodus 34:6
"The LORD God, abundant in goodness."

God manifests His goodness in three ways:

1. God thinks good thoughts.

Psalm 139:17
"How precious also are thy thoughts unto me, O God!"

2. God makes good decisions.

Genesis 50:20
"But God meant it unto good."

3. God does good things.

Matthew 7:11
"How much more shall your Father which is in heaven give good things to them that ask him?"

God allows us to partake of His goodness.
There are six purposes of goodness:

a. Goodness manifests God because God is good.

Psalm 31:19
"Oh how great is thy goodness."

b. Goodness overcomes evil.

Romans 12:21
"Be not overcome of evil, but overcome evil with good."

c. Goodness enables us to experience the good works of God.

Psalm 145:9-10
"The LORD is good to all: and his tender mercies are over all his works.

All thy works shall praise thee, O LORD; and thy saints shall bless thee.

d. It causes us to delight in God's goodness.

Nehemiah 9:25
"And delighted themselves in thy great goodness."

e. Goodness keeps us motivated and activated.

Psalm 27:13
"I had fainted, unless I had believed to see the goodness of the LORD in the land of the living."

f. Goodness leads people to repentance.

Romans 2:4
"That the goodness of God leadeth thee to repentance?"

6. Faithfulness.

Faith and faithfulness are like two sides of the same coin and are inter-dependant.

A. Faith is total dependence on God.

The Biblical definition of Faith is found in:

Romans 4:21

"And being fully persuaded that, what he had promised, he was able also to perform."

There are at least three different degrees of Faith:

a. Every believer experiences a small measure of faith.

Romans 12:3
"According as God hath dealt to every man the measure of faith."

b. We may grow into greater measures of faith.

ROMANS 1:17
"For therein is the righteousness of God revealed from faith to faith:"

c. We can experience great faith.

MATTHEW 8:10
"I have not found so great faith, no, not in Israel."

B. Faithfulness is different to faith - it is being dependable.

    God can depend on us

    People can depend on us

    We are faithful in all things

LUKE 16:10
"He that is faithful in that which is least is faithful also in much:"

We are to be faithful in:

1. The smallest duties

2. Keeping promises

3. Paying our debts

4. Keeping all commitments

5. Being on time

6. Stewardship of all that God Has given us Moses was an example of faithfulness.

Hebrews 3:2

"Who was faithful to him that appointed him, as also Moses was faithful in all his house."

There are three things we need to know about faithfulness:

1. God examines our hearts for faithfulness.

Nehemiah 9:8
"And foundest his heart faithful before thee."

2. God's eyes are upon the faithful.

Psalm 101:6
"Mine eyes shall be upon the faithful of the land."

3. God rewards those who are faithful.

Luke 16:11
"If therefore ye have not been faithful in the unrighteous mammon, who will commit to your trust the true riches?"

Proverbs 28:20
"A faithful man shall abound with blessings:"

8. Meekness.

The Greek word for meekness is "**praotes**" and means **humility.**

Meekness is not weakness.

It is a demonstration of strength.

Moses was one of God's greatest servants because he was the meekest man upon the face of the earth.

NUMBERS 12:3
"Now the man Moses was very meek, above all the men which were upon the face of the earth."

In humility we experience six things:

a. A broken heart and contrite spirit.

PSALM 51:17
"The sacrifices of God are a broken spirit: a broken and a contrite heart, O God, thou wilt not despise."

b. Bowing in submission to God's sovereignty, authority and discipline.

JAMES 4:10
"Humble yourselves in the sight of the Lord, and he shall lift you up."

c. Following after humility.

1 Timothy 6:11
"But thou, O man of God follow after meekness."

d. Being clothed in humility.

Colossians 3:12
"Put on therefore, as the elect of God, meekness."

e. Walking in humility.

Ephesians 4:1-2
"I therefore, the prisoner of the Lord, beseech you that ye walk with all lowliness and meekness."

f. All aspects of humility.

Titus 3:2
"To be gentle, shewing **all** meekness unto all men."

Christians need to:

Be humble and have a servant attitude.

Think humble thoughts and not be high-minded.

Be willing to do lowly, humble tasks.

9. Temperance.

The word temperance can be better described as **self-control.**

When people over indulge in areas of their lives they desperately need self-control.

1 Peter 4:3
"For the time past of our life when we walked in lasciviousness, lusts, excess of wine, revellings, banquetings:"

Jesus predicted that in the last days, men would live that way.

Luke 17:27
They did eat, they drank."

Self-control is the fruit of the Spirit that protects the Believer from reckless and riotous living.

Proverbs 25:28
"He that hath no rule over his own spirit is like a city that is broken down, and without walls."

Self-control or temperance is like a wall around our soul and spirit.

It controls what goes in and comes out.

The Nine Fruits of the Holy Spirit

Temperance is three things:

1. It **counteracts** excessive living.

2. It is a **management system.**

Paul teaches that by self-control, we clearly know how much we need and thereby we discipline our lives. We are not excessive.

Philippians 4:12-13

"I know both how to be abased, and I know how to abound: everywhere and in all things I am instructed both to be full and to be hungry, both to abound and to suffer need.

I can do all things through Christ who strengtheneth me."

2 Peter 1:6

"And to knowledge temperance;"

The knowledge we receive from God, helps us to exercise self-control in our lives.

3. It is a **striving for mastery.**

1 Corinthians 9:25

"And every man that striveth for the mastery is temperate in all things."

Mastery is the demonstration of self-control in all the areas of our life.

Mastery is the trophy of self-control.

When we produce the fruits of the Spirit we experience a true sense of how valuable they are.

Let us realize how much we desperately need the Fruits of the Spirit.

We are indebted to the Holy Spirit for them.

CHAPTER 13

The Nine Ministries of the Holy Spirit

Jesus Christ is perfect in all the ministries of the Church.

Jesus Christ is the perfect **Apostle**.

He is the perfect **Prophet**

He is the perfect **Teacher**

He is the perfect **Shepherd**

He is the perfect **Evangelist**

HEBREWS 3:1

"Wherefore, holy brethren, partakers of the heavenly calling, consider the Apostle and High Priest of our profession, Christ Jesus;"

All members of the Church are built upon the Ministries.

All the Ministries are built upon Jesus Christ.

1 Corinthians 3:11

"For other foundation can no man lay than that is laid, which is Jesus Christ."

Ephesians 2:19-20

"Now therefore ye are of the household of God;

And are built upon the foundation of the apostles and prophets, Jesus Christ himself being the chief corner stone;"

After Jesus ascended into Heaven, the Holy Spirit assumed the responsibility as Administrator of the Church and appointed Christians, selected by Jesus Christ for a specific ministry.

Ephesians 4:11

"And he gave some, apostles; and some, prophets; and some, evangelists; and some, pastors and teachers;"

The Ministries in the Church have two main functions:

1. To perfect the Saints.

2. To build the Church.

Ephesians 4:12

"For the perfecting of the saints, for the work of the ministry, for the edifying of the body of Christ:"

The Ministries will finally bring about a Church that is united, perfect and in the full stature of Christ.

The ministries are the **mortar** that keeps the bricks (members) together.

They are the **joints** that hold the members of the Body of Christ together.

Ephesians 4:16

"From whom the whole body fitly joined together and compacted by that which every joint supplieth."

These Ministries hold the members together with two different bands:

Love

COLOSSIANS 2:2

"That their hearts might be comforted, being knit together in love."

Peace.

EPHESIANS 4:3

"Endeavoring to keep the unity of the Spirit in the bond of peace."

These nine Ministries are divided into two groups:

Global Church ministries:

Apostles

Prophets

Evangelists

Miracles

Gifts of healing

These Ministries are mobile and are used wherever they are needed.

The Nine Ministries of the Holy Spirit

Local Church ministries:

Bishop (Overseer)

Shepherds (Pastors or Elders)

Teachers

Deacons

Helps

Administrations

The Ordination of Ministries:

All ministries of the Church are selected and ordained by the Holy Spirit.

Church Leaders are directed by the Holy Spirit to lay their hands in prayerful dedication upon the ministry candidates, to ordain them.

Acts **13:2**

"As they ministered to the Lord, and fasted, the Holy Ghost said, Separate me Barnabas and Saul for the work whereunto I have called them."

Let us look at each of these nine Ministries:

1. Apostles:

The word Apostle means "**one sent forth**".

It is also translated "**messenger**".

The names of the first twelve Apostles are:

Peter

Andrew

James

John

Philip

Bartholomew

Thomas

Matthew

James

Lebbaeus

Simon

Judas

MATTHEW 10:2-4

"Now the names of the twelve apostles are these; Simon, who is called Peter, Andrew his brother; James the son of Zebedee, and John his brother;

Philip, and Bartholomew; Thomas, and Matthew the publican; James the son of Alphaeus, and Lebbaeus, whose surname was Thaddaeus; Simon the Canaanite, and Judas Iscariot."

After Judas committed suicide Matthias took his place.

The Nine Ministries of the Holy Spirit

Acts 1:26

"And they gave forth their lots; and the lot fell upon **Matthias**; and he was numbered with the eleven apostles."

After Pentecost an additional twelve Apostles, were appointed by the Holy Spirit, namely:

Paul - Acts13:4

Barnabas - Acts 14:14

Timothy - 1 Thessalonians 1:1

Titus - Titus 1:5

Silas - Acts 15:40

Andronicus - Romans 16:7

Junia - Romans 16:7

James - Galatians 1:18-19

Joses - Matthew 13:55

Silvanus - 1 Thessalonians 1:1

Judas - Jude 1

Apaphroditus - Philippians 2:25

Since that time, the Holy Spirit has appointed others into this office, as He has deemed it necessary.

Apostleship was the highest office appointed in the church.

1 Corinthians 12:28

"And God hath set some in the church, first apostles."

There is no scriptural evidence of Apostolic succession.

No person has ever had the right to claim the office of Apostleship or appoint Apostles.

It is by Divine appointment only.

Acts 13:2

"As they ministered to the Lord, and fasted, the Holy Ghost said, Separate me Barnabas and Saul for the work whereunto I have called them."

There have always been false Apostles.

2 Corinthians 11:13

"For such are false apostles, deceitful workers, transforming themselves into the apostles of Christ."

It is therefore necessary to test the claim of someone, who says that that they are an Apostle.

Revelation 2:2

"And thou hast tried them which say they are apostles, and are not, and hast found them liars:"

There are three things that prove Apostleship:

1. Godly character.
2. Signs that follow an Apostles ministry.
3. Mighty miracles that follow an Apostles ministry.

The Apostles main task:

An Apostles task is to establish and properly organize Churches.

Acts 14:23

"And when they had ordained them elders in every church, and had prayed with fasting, they commended them to the Lord, on whom they believed."

An Apostle is a "Master Builder" who establishes Churches.

1 Corinthians 3:10

"According to the grace of God which is given unto me, as a wise masterbuilder,

I have laid the foundation, and another buildeth thereon."

This is the seal of Apostleship.

1 Corinthians 9:2

"If I be not an apostle unto others, yet doubtless I am to you: for the seal of mine apostleship are ye in the Lord."

There are levels of Apostleship:

Some Apostles have a higher office than others.

2 Corinthians 11:5

"For I suppose I was not a whit behind the very chiefest apostles."

2 Corinthians 12:11

"For in nothing am I behind the very chiefest apostles,"

There are different areas of Apostleship:

Peter was an Apostle to the Jews and Paul to the Gentiles.

Galatians 2:7-8

"But contrariwise, when they saw that the gospel of the uncircumcision was committed unto me, as the gospel of the circumcision was unto Peter:

For he that wrought effectually in Peter to the apostleship of the circumcision, the same was mighty in me toward the Gentiles:"

Apostles worked together in teams:

Acts 8:14-15

"They sent unto them Peter and John who when they were come down, prayed for them, that they might receive the Holy Ghost:"

2. The Prophet.

A prophet is a person who speaks a word from God to man.

There are three things we need to know about Prophets:

1. Prophets stand before God:

1 Kings 17:1

"And Elijah said unto Ahab, As the LORD God of Israel liveth, before whom I stand."

2. Prophets stand in the counsel of God:

JEREMIAH 23:37
"Thus shalt thou say to the prophet, what hath the LORD answered thee? And, what hath the LORD spoken?"

3. God shares His secrets with the Prophets:

AMOS 3:7
"Surely the Lord GOD will do nothing, but he revealeth his secret unto his servants the prophets."

There are eight Prophets mentioned in the book of Acts:

1. Agabas - Acts 11:28

2. Barnabas - Acts 13:1

3. Simeon - Acts 13:1

4. Lucius - Acts 13:1

5. Manean - Acts 13:1

6. Paul - Acts 13:1

7. Judas - Acts 15:32

8. Silas - Acts 15:32

The Nine Ministries of the Holy Spirit

Prophets of God have to meet certain conditions:

JEREMIAH 15:16-19

"Thy words were found, and I did eat them; and thy word was unto me the joy and rejoicing of mine heart: for I am called by thy name, O LORD God of hosts.

I sat not in the assembly of the mockers, nor rejoiced; I sat alone because of thy hand: for thou hast filled me with indignation.

Therefore thus saith the LORD, If thou return, then will I bring thee again, and thou shalt stand before me: and if thou take forth the precious from the vile, thou shalt be as my mouth: let them return unto thee; but return not thou unto them."

These conditions are:

1. They must be called of God.
2. They must love and enjoy being God's mouthpiece.
3. They must be dedicated to God for service:
4. They must be willing to stand alone in doing God's task.
5. They must believe and passionately give God's message.

There is a distinct difference between the Office of Prophet and Gift of Prophecy:

a. Only some are called to the Office of a Prophet.

EPHESIANS 4:11
"And he gave some, apostles; and some, prophets;"

b. All Christians may exercise the Gift of Prophecy.

1 CORINTHIANS 14:31
"For ye may all prophesy one by one."

Members of the Church may judge a prophetic message.

1 CORINTHIANS 14:29
"Let the prophets speak two or three, and let the other judge."

Prophets are beneficial in three ways:

a. Prophets can predict future events and warn God's people of impending danger:

ACTS 11:28
"And there stood up one of them named Agabus, and signified by the Spirit that there should be great dearth throughout all the world: which came to pass in the days of Claudius Caesar."

b. Prophet's edify the Church.

1 Corinthians 14:3-4
"But he that prophesieth speaketh unto men to edification, and exhortation, and comfort. He that speaketh in an unknown tongue edifieth himself; but he that prophesieth edifieth the church."

c. Prophets may minister to unbelievers.

1 Corinthians 14:24
"But if all prophesy, and there come in one that believeth not, or one unlearned, he is convinced of all, he is judged of all:"

3. The Evangelist

The word Evangelist means - **"one who proclaims Good News"**.

It is a noun and is only mentioned three times in the Bible.

The word **"evangelize"** is mentioned fifty times in the Bible and means to do the work of proclaiming the Gospel which is Good News.

The task of the Evangelist is to preach salvation, introducing people to their Savior the Lord Jesus Christ.

Those saved need to be water baptized and receive the Gift of the Holy Spirit.

ACTS 2:38

"Then Peter said unto them, repent, and be baptized every one of you in the name of Jesus Christ for the remission of sins, and ye shall receive the gift of the Holy Ghost."

Evangelism can be to one person or many people:

The Ministry of Phillip the Evangelist is described in **Acts 8:4-40**.

Part of this scripture shows Phillip ministering to crowds of people at Samaria. Thousands were saved, baptized and filled with the Holy Spirit.

It also shows Phillip reaching out to one person, the Eunuch in the Desert and how he was saved and baptized.

An Evangelist Ministry will always be attested:

The ministry of an Evangelist is attested when people receive healings, miracles and deliverance.

Evangelists are commanded by Paul to make full proof of their Ministry.

2 TIMOTHY 4:5

But watch thou in all things, endure afflictions, do the work of an evangelist, make full proof of thy ministry.

Evangelists minister from place to place:

Acts 8:5, 40

"Then Philip went down to the city of Samaria, and preached Christ unto them.

But Philip was found at Azotus: passing through he preached in all the cities, till he came to Caesarea."

The ministry of an Evangelist is directed at lost souls:

This ministry is not to Christians.

It is to unconverted Souls.

It is to create and build local Churches.

4. The Teacher.

A Teacher is a Christian who is called to understand the doctrines of scripture and teach them to others.

There are two areas of teaching:

a. Teaching Christians on a national or international scale.

These teaching Ministries are often linked with Apostles and Prophets.

Acts 13:1
"Now there were in the church that was at Antioch certain prophets and teachers;"

1 Corinthians 3:6
"I have planted, Apollos watered; but God gave the increase."

Apollos was an expositor of the Bible and where the Apostle Paul ministered, Apollos followed with a teaching ministry.

Acts 18:24-28
"And a certain Jew named *Apollos*, born at Alexandria, an eloquent man, and **mighty in the scriptures,** came to Ephesus.

This man was instructed in the way of the Lord; and being fervent in the spirit, he spake and taught diligently the things of the Lord.

And when he was disposed to pass into Achaia, the brethren wrote, exhorting the disciples to receive him: who, when he was come, helped them much which had believed through grace:

For he mightily convinced the Jews, and that publicly, shewing by the scriptures that Jesus was Christ."

b. Teaching Members of a local Church.

1 Timothy 5:17
"Let the elders that rule well be counted worthy of double honour, especially they who labour in the word and doctrine."

2 Timothy 2:2

"And the things that thou hast heard of me among many witnesses, the same commit thou to faithful men, who shall be able to teach others also."

5. The Shepherd.

The word Shepherd is derived from the Greek word **"Poimen"** and means **"Pastor".**

Another word used for a Shepherd is **Elder** and its Greek word is "**Presbyteros**".

These Elders are always referred to in the plural:

There was more than one Elder in each local Church and one of these Elders was recognized as the "Overseer", derived from the Greek word "Episkopos" which means the Head Elder.

1 Peter 5:1

"The elders which are among you I exhort, who am also an elder."

Here Peter refers to his office as Overseer of a local Church.

Shepherds care for God's Flock:

The local Church is the flock of spiritual sheep and the Shepherds have the responsibility of caring for God's Children in the local Church.

They do this in three ways:

1. Taking oversight of them.
2. Feeding and taking care of them.
3. Being brave and protecting them.

Here are other scriptures that refer to the work of a Shepherd:

John 10:1-28

Psalm 23

Ezekiel 34:1-6

When do Shepherds assume responsibility?

When a local Church is set in order by an Apostle, Elders are ordained and appointed to take oversight. Without an Elder, a Church is incomplete.

The qualifications of a Shepherd:

Paul outlines the qualifications of an Elder:

1 Timothy 3:1-7

"This is a true saying, if a man desire the office of a bishop, he desires a good work.

A bishop then must be blameless, the husband of one wife, vigilant, sober, of good behaviour, given to hospitality, apt to teach;

Not given to wine, no striker, not greedy of filthy lucre; but patient, not a brawler, not covetous;

One that ruleth well his own house, having his children in subjection with all gravity;

For if a man know not how to rule his own house, how shall he take care of the church of God?

Not a novice, lest being lifted up with pride he fall into the condemnation of the devil.

Moreover he must have a good report of them which are without; lest he fall into reproach and the snare of the devil."

An Elder must be:

    Blameless

    The Husband of one wife

    Vigilant

    Of good behavior

    Just

    Holy

    Temperate in all things

    Given to hospitality

    Faithful to the Word of God

    Able to teach sound Doctrine

Sober, not consuming alcohol

Gentle

Free of a love for money and covetousness

An effective Ruler of their home

Proven and not a novice

Respected in the Community

One who associates with good people

6. The Deacon.

It is a great honor to be appointed as a Deacon.

It is described as attaining **a Good Degree.**

1 Timothy 3:13
"For they that have used the office of a deacon, well purchase to themselves a good degree, and great boldness in the faith which is in Christ Jesus."

Deacons were appointed by Apostles as the need arose for their specific type of Ministry, in a local church.

Acts 6:1-6
"There arose a murmuring of the Grecians against the Hebrews, because their widows were neglected in the daily ministration.

Then the twelve called the multitude of the disciples unto them, and said; It is not reason that we should leave the word of God, and serve tables.

The Nine Ministries of the Holy Spirit

Wherefore, brethren, look ye out among you seven men of honest report, full of the Holy Ghost and wisdom, whom we may appoint over this business.

But we will give ourselves continually to prayer, and to the ministry of the word.

And the saying pleased the whole multitude: and they chose Stephen, a man full of faith and of the Holy Ghost, and Philip, and Prochorus, and Nicanor, and Timon, and Parmenas, and Nicolas a proselyte of Antioch:

Whom they set before the apostles: and when they had prayed, they laid their hands on them."

A Deacons task:

A Deacons task is to assist the Church Elders in practical matters of daily administration and the material needs of church members.

Their appointment:

After being selected by a local Church, they are appointed by the Elders.

The twelve qualifications of Deacons are -

    To be of honest report

    To be full of the Holy Spirit

    To be full of wisdom

    To be grave (Dignified)

To be sober not using alcohol

To not love money

To be strong of faith

To be pure of conscience

To be blameless

To have only one spouse

To rule their home effectively

Their spouse must have the same qualifications

1 Timothy 3:8-12
"Likewise must the deacons be grave, not double tongued, not given to much wine, not greedy of filthy lucre; Holding the mystery of the faith in a pure conscience.

And let these also first be proved; then let them use the office of a deacon, being found blameless. Even so must their wives be grave, not slanderers, sober, faithful in all things.

Let the deacons be the husbands of one wife, ruling their children and their own houses well."

7. Miracles.

1 Corinthians 12:28
"And God hath set some in the church ... miracles."

There are those members of the Church that the Holy Spirit selects and endues with a special ministry of Miracles.

They demonstrate creative miracles and the resurrection power of Jesus Christ.

8. Gifts of Healing.

1 Corinthians 12:28

"And God hath set some in the church … gifts of healings."

There are specific gifts of healing directed at all sickness.

There are those members of the Church that the Holy Spirit selects to bring healing to Christians and people.

9. Helps.

The Greek word used here for helps is **"Kubernosis".**

It means "**a Shipmaster"** or those who steer a ship.

It keeps the local church functioning correctly and moving in the right direction.

The highest form of helps can be best described as Governments or Administrations.

1 Corinthians 12:28

"And God hath set some in the church helps."

There are different kinds of helps:

1 Corinthians 14:26

"How is it then, brethren? When ye come together, every one of you hath a psalm, hath a doctrine, hath a tongue, hath a revelation, hath an interpretation. Let all things be done unto edifying."

These are seven different kinds of helpers in the Church:

Romans 12:6-8

"Having then gifts differing according to the grace that is given to us, whether prophecy, let us prophesy according to the proportion of faith;

Or ministry let us wait on our ministering: or he that teacheth, on teaching;

Or he that exhorteth, on exhortation: he that giveth, let him do it with simplicity; he that ruleth, with diligence; he that sheweth mercy, with cheerfulness.

Christians may minister in helps by doing the following:

1. Speaking or teaching the Word of God

2. Doing tasks to help others

3. Guiding others
4. Encouraging others
5. Being financial givers to financially support the Church
6. Leading in the Church
7. Showing mercy to others

All Ministries play a vital role in the success of the Church of Jesus Christ.

All Christians are called to excel in their own unique Ministry.

CHAPTER 14

Prayer and Fasting

The most important aspect of prayer and fasting **is doing it.**

A Christian needs to:

1. Understand what prayer and fasting is all about.
2. Select the best time to do it.
3. Actually pray and fast.

Prayer

Prayer needs to be an integral part of the everyday life of a Christian.

Jesus said that men should always pray:

LUKE 18:1

"And he spake a parable unto them to this end, that men ought always to pray, and not to faint;"

Paul teaches that our prayers should continue throughout the day:

1 THESSALONIANS 5:17

"Pray without ceasing."

Prayers are most valuable and are never lost.

They are caught up in Golden Vials in Heaven.

REVELATION 5:8

"And golden vials full of odours, which are the prayers of saints."

Prayer is approaching God.

There are six important things about approaching God:

1. It is a delightful experience to approach God in prayer.

Prayer and Fasting

Isaiah 58:2
"Yet they seek me daily, they take delight in approaching to God."

2. God causes and allows us to approach Him.

Psalm 65:4
"Blessed is the man whom thou choosest, and causest to approach unto thee."

3. We must prepare our hearts to approach God in prayer.

2 Chronicles 19:3
"Nevertheless there are good things found in thee, and hast prepared thine heart to seek God."

When approaching God we must always ensure that we have:

1. Clean hands

2. A pure heart

3. A humble heart

4. A truthful heart

Psalm 24:3-4
"He that hath clean hands, and a pure heart; who hath not lifted up his soul unto vanity, nor sworn deceitfully."

PSALM 51:10
"Create in me a clean heart, O God; and renew a right spirit within me."

JAMES 4:6
"God resisteth the proud, but giveth grace unto the humble."

4. We must know how to prepare our hearts?

We prepare our hearts by examining ourselves and allowing the Holy Spirit to convict us of sin. We then ask God to forgive us and cleanse us of all sin.

1 JOHN 1:9
"If we confess our sins, he is faithful and just to forgive us our sins, and to cleanse us from all unrighteousness."

5. We must approach God boldly.

We can do that if we know that our sins have been washed away by the precious Blood of Jesus.

1 JOHN 1:7
"And the blood of Jesus Christ his Son cleanseth us from all sin."

HEBREWS 10:19
"Having therefore, brethren, boldness to enter into the holiest by the blood of Jesus."

6. We should approach God in confidence.

EPHESIANS 3:12
"In whom we have boldness and access with confidence by the faith of him."

We boldly approach God's Throne **in faith.**

We need to submit to the Holy Spirit when praying and He will help us.

ROMANS 8:26

"Likewise the Spirit also helpeth our infirmities: for we know not what we should pray for as we ought: but the Spirit itself maketh intercession for us with groanings which cannot be uttered."

1 CORINTHIANS 14:14-15

"For if I pray in an unknown tongue, my spirit prayeth, but my understanding is unfruitful.

What is it then? I will pray with the spirit."

When Believers pray in the Spirit, they pray in tongues (their heavenly language) as the Holy Spirit gives them the words to speak.

1 CORINTHIANS 14:2

"For he that speaketh in an unknown tongue speaketh not unto men, but unto God: for no man understandeth him; howbeit in the spirit he speaketh mysteries."

How to leave God's Throne Room:

We need to leave Gods Throne Room as carefully and respectfully as we did when we first approached Him.

We do this in three ways:

1. We express our thankfulness to God for hearing and answering us.

PHILIPPIANS 4:6
"But in everything by prayer and supplication with thanksgiving let your requests be made known unto God."

2. We acknowledge God's authority and our submission to Him and His Kingdom.

MATTHEW 6:13
"For Thine is the kingdom, and the power, and the glory, forever. Amen."

3. We conclude our prayers with the word "amen".

When bowing out of the presence of the King of the Universe we end our prayer with the word **amen.**

It can be accurately described as a conclusive **surrender** to God's will.

The word **"amen"** means - **"so let it be done."**

It is our acknowledgement that we accept things as God would have them to be.

Prayer is our method of communication with God:

There are three reasons why we need to have an open line of communication with God:

1. God is our Heavenly Father.

2. Children need to be able to speak to their Father at any time.

3. As Soldiers we need to have contact with God our Commander in Chief.

This enables us to be effective in the spiritual warfare we are waging against satan and his kingdom.

This is how we receive God's commands and make our needs known to Him.

Prayer blesses us in six ways.

1. It is our key to provision.

PHILIPPIANS 4:6
"Be careful for nothing; but in everything by prayer and supplication with thanksgiving let your requests be made known unto God."

2. It is our key to power.

Isaiah 40:31
"But they that wait upon the LORD shall renew their strength; they shall mount up with wings as eagles; they shall run, and not be weary; and they shall walk, and not faint."

3. It is the key to our desires.

Mark 11:24
"Therefore I say unto you, what things soever ye desire, when ye pray, believe that ye receive them, and ye shall have them."

4. It is a way to give God our cares.

1 Peter 5:7
"Casting all your care upon him; for he careth for you."

5. It is a way of reminding God of His promises.

Isaiah 43:26
"Put me in remembrance: let us plead together."

6. It is a way of finding help in time of need.

Hebrews 4:16
"Let us therefore come boldly unto the throne of grace, that we may obtain mercy, and find grace to help in time of need."

What posture is needed when praying?

There are at least five mentioned in the Bible:

1. We may bow down and kneel in prayer.

Ephesians 3:14
"For this cause I bow my knees unto the Father of our Lord Jesus Christ."

2. We may stand and pray.

Mark 11:25
"And when ye stand praying, forgive."

3. We may sit and pray.

Acts 2:2
"And suddenly there came a sound from heaven as of a rushing mighty wind, and it filled all the house where they were sitting."

4. We may lay upon our face and pray.

Matthew 26:39

"And he went a little farther, and fell on his face, and prayed." Prayer has three important ingredients:

1. It must be fervent. (Fiery, serious and intense)

James 5:16
"The effectual fervent prayer of a righteous man availeth much."

2. It must be done with a righteous heart.

ROMANS 14:17-18
"For the kingdom of God is not meat and drink; but righteousness, and peace, and joy in the Holy Ghost. For he that in these things serveth Christ is acceptable to God, and approved of men."

3. It must be in accordance with God's will.

COLOSSIANS 4:12
"Always labouring fervently for you in prayers, that ye may stand perfect and complete in all the will of God."

LUKE 22:42
"Saying, Father, if thou be willing, remove this cup from me: nevertheless not my will, but thine, be done."

There are six rules of prayer:

1. Prayer should be made in the Name of Jesus Christ.

JOHN 16:23
"And in that day ye shall ask me nothing. Verily, verily, I say unto you, whatsoever ye shall ask the Father in my name, he will give it you."

2. We are to pray in faith.

Matthew 21:21-22
"Jesus answered and said unto them, Verily I say unto you, if ye have faith, and doubt not, ye shall not only do this which is done to the fig tree, but also if ye shall say unto this mountain, be thou removed, and be thou cast into the sea; it shall be done.

And all things, whatsoever ye shall ask in prayer, believing, ye shall receive."

Hebrews 11:6
"But without faith it is impossible to please him: for he that cometh to God must believe that he is, and that he is a rewarder of them that diligently seek him."

3. We need to pray persistently.

Luke 11:5-9
"And he said unto them, which of you shall have a friend, and shall go unto him at midnight, and say unto him, Friend, lend me three loaves;

For a friend of mine in his journey is come to me, and I have nothing to set before him?

And he from within shall answer and say, Trouble me not: the door is now shut, and my children are with me in bed; I cannot rise and give thee.

I say unto you, though he will not rise and give him, because he is his friend, yet because of his importunity he will rise and give him as many as he needeth.

And I say unto you, Ask, and it shall be given you; seek, and ye shall find; knock, and it shall be opened unto you."

4. We need to pray in secret.

MATTHEW 6:6
"But thou, when thou prayest, enter into thy closet, and when thou hast shut thy door, pray to thy Father which is in secret; and thy Father which seeth in secret shall reward thee openly."

5. We need to pray in humility.

LUKE 18:10-14
"Two men went up into the temple to pray; the one a Pharisee, and the other a publican.

The Pharisee stood and prayed thus with himself, God, I thank thee, that I am not as other men are, extortioners, unjust, adulterers, or even as this publican.

I fast twice in the week, I give tithes of all that I possess.

And the publican, standing afar off, would not lift up so much as his eyes unto heaven, but smote upon his breast, saying, God be merciful to me a sinner.

I tell you, this man went down to his house justified rather than the other: for every one that exalteth himself shall be abased; and he that humbleth himself shall be exalted."

6. We need to pray with a forgiving heart.

MATTHEW 6:14-15
"For if ye forgive men their trespasses, your heavenly Father will also forgive you:

But if ye forgive not men their trespasses, neither will your Father forgive your trespasses."

The realm of prayer has six dimensions.

1. It is an emergency hotline to God.

PSALM 3:4
"I cried unto the LORD with my voice, and he heard me out of his holy hill."

2. It takes us into God's immediate and almighty presence.

PSALM 100:4
"Enter into his gates with thanksgiving, and into his courts with praise:"

3. We experience new dimensions of royal protocol and worship.

When approaching a King, it is necessary to follow special royal protocol, which involves presenting him with a gift. When we approach God, one of the gifts we bring Him is worship, which He so richly deserves.

4. We experience petitioning God.

1 John 5:15
"And if we know that he hear us, whatsoever we ask, we know that we have the petitions that we desired of him."

God has made it possible for us to come before His Throne, to speak to Him and present our requests to Him.

Jesus Christ is our Righteous Advocate and Legal Counsel to help us.

He also is our Intercessor and prays on our behalf.

He knows the requirements and Laws of God because He is the Word of God.

He is completely qualified to help us and has the wisdom and knowledge to defend us and rebut satan's accusations against us.

1 John 2:1

"We have an advocate with the Father, Jesus Christ the righteous:"

As we confess and remind God of His promises, Jesus supports us as the High Priest of our confession.

Hebrews 3:1

"Consider the Apostle and High Priest of our profession (confession), Christ Jesus;"

5. We experience God's secret place.

This is a special place that God has prepared in His presence for every one of His children. We can spend time and abide there. It is a place where we can be close to God and experience His warmth, protection and comforting presence.

It is described as being under His wings and in His shadow.

Psalm 91:1
"He that dwelleth in the secret place of the most High shall abide under the shadow of the Almighty."

Song of Solomon 2:3
"I sat down under his shadow with great delight."

It is a secret place of protection.

Psalm 27:5
"For in the time of trouble he shall hide me in his pavilion: in the secret of his tabernacle shall he hide me; he shall set me up upon a rock."

6. It is a place where we experience fullness of joy and pleasure.

Psalm 16:11
"In thy presence is fulness of joy; at thy right hand there are pleasures for evermore."

It is a place where we can dwell and spend as much time as we want.

Psalm 140:13
"The upright shall dwell in thy presence."

There are three Courts in God's presence that we may prayerfully enter:

The Courts of Praise

Here we function as God's Priests, offering up oblations and spiritual sacrifices of praise to God.

1 Peter 2:5

"Ye also are a holy priesthood, to offer up spiritual sacrifices, acceptable to God by Jesus Christ."

Hebrews 13:15

"By him therefore let us offer the sacrifice of praise to God continually, that is, the fruit of our lips giving thanks to his name."

The Courts of Instruction

It is here in prayerful meditation that we can receive instruction and direction from God.

The Courts of banqueting

Song of Solomon 2:4

"He brought me to the banqueting house, and his banner over me was love."

It is here in God's presence that our spiritual senses are satisfied.

Psalm 36:7-9

"Therefore the children of men put their trust under the shadow of thy wings.

They shall be abundantly satisfied with the fatness of thy house; and thou shalt make them drink of the river of thy pleasures. For with thee is the fountain of life."

In God's presence, we taste, smell, see, hear and feel wonderful things:

Our five spiritual senses are satisfied:

Psalm 34:8

"O taste and see that the LORD is good:"

Song of Solomon 2:3

"I sat down under his shadow with great delight, and his fruit was sweet to my taste."

We can enjoy the fragrance of His presence.

Song of Solomon 2:1

"I am the rose of Sharon, and the lily of the valleys."

There are different kinds of prayer that Christian's may pray:

Ephesians 6:18

"Praying always with **all** prayer."

These are the six kinds of prayer:

1. Asking.
2. Agreeing.
3. Binding and Loosing.
4. Praying in the Spirit.
5. Intercession.
6. Seeking Gods face.

1. The prayer of asking.

Eight things are important about the prayer of asking:

a. Our Heavenly Father knows what we need.

Prayer and Fasting

MATTHEW 6:32
"For your heavenly Father knows that ye have need of all these things."

b. The way to receive what we need is to ask God in the Name of Jesus.

MATTHEW 7:7
"Ask, and it shall be given you;"

JOHN 16:23
"Whatsoever ye shall ask the Father in my name, he will give it you."

c. Believers who do not ask do not receive.

JAMES 4:2
"Ye have not, because ye ask not."

d. The scope for asking is unlimited. God can answer every prayer.

GENESIS 18:14
"Is anything too hard for the LORD?"

ISAIAH 45:11
"Concerning the work of my hands command ye me."

e. God wants our asking to be specific.

MATTHEW 7:9-11
"Or what man is there of you, whom if his son ask bread, will he give him a stone?

Or if he ask a fish, will he give him a serpent?

If ye then, being evil, know how to give good gifts unto your children, how much more shall your Father which is in heaven give good things to them that ask him?"

f. God loves supplying our needs.

PHILIPPIANS 4:19
"But my God shall supply all your need according to his riches in glory by Christ Jesus."

g. God gives to us so that our joy can be full.

JOHN 16:24
"And ye shall receive, that your joy may be full."

h. We should ask with the right motive.

JAMES 4:3
"Ye ask, and receive not, because ye ask amiss, that ye may consume it upon your lusts."

2. The prayer of agreeing.

MATTHEW 18:19
"Again I say unto you, that if two of you shall agree on earth as touching any thing that they shall ask, it shall be done for them of my Father which is in heaven."

The prayer of agreement is the simple act of two or more Christians agreeing and making a request to God in the name of Jesus.

3. Binding and loosing.

MATTHEW 18:18
"Verily I say unto you, whatsoever ye shall bind on earth shall be bound in heaven: and whatsoever ye shall loose on earth shall be loosed in heaven."

The word **whatsoever** means **anything.**

The word **bind** is the Greek word **"Desete"**.

It means **to tie up and captivate.**

The word **loose** is **"Losete"**.

It means **to loosen or break the cords.**

With this kind of prayer we can tie up and capture satan's kingdom and emissaries.

We can also break the cords and set free people or situations bound by satan.

4. Praying in the Spirit.

EPHESIANS 6:18
"Praying always with all prayer and supplication in the Spirit."

When we pray in the Spirit we pray in an **unknown tongue**.

1 CORINTHIANS 14:14
"For if I pray in an unknown tongue, my spirit prayeth, but my understanding is unfruitful."

When we pray in an unknown tongue the Holy Spirit intercedes for us and helps us.

ROMANS 8:26
"Likewise the Spirit also helpeth our infirmities: for we know not what we should pray for as we ought: but the Spirit itself maketh intercession for us with groanings which cannot be uttered."

Often we don't know what we need to pray for and the Holy Spirit helps us in a prayer language.

The prayer language we pray is mysterious and cannot be understood by men or satan.

1 CORINTHIANS 14:2
"For he that speaketh in an unknown tongue speaketh not unto men, but unto God: for no man understandeth him; howbeit in the spirit he speaketh mysteries."

When praying in the Spirit we experience a special refreshing and rest in the Lord.

ISAIAH 28:11-12
"For with stammering lips and another tongue will he speak to this people.

To whom he said, this is the rest wherewith ye may cause the weary to rest; and this is the refreshing: yet they would not hear."

By praying in the Spirit we are built up spiritually.

JUDE 20
"But ye, beloved, building up yourselves on your most holy faith, praying in the Holy Ghost."

5. Intercession.

We need to consider six aspects of intercession:

1. Intercession is praying for others:

a. All men.

b. Our leaders.

c. Those who have authority over us.

1 Timothy 2:1-2
"I exhort therefore, that, first of all, supplications, prayers, intercessions, and giving of thanks, be made for all men:

For kings, and for all that are in authority; that we may lead a quiet and peaceable life in all godliness and honesty."

d. We are to pray for our fellow Believers.

Ephesians 1:16
"Cease not to give thanks for you, making mention of you in my prayers;"

Philippians 1:3
"I thank my God upon every remembrance of you."

Colossians 1:9
"For this cause we also, since the day we heard it, do not cease to pray for you."

2. God always looks for intercessors.

EZEKIEL 22:30
"And I sought for a man among them, that should make up the hedge, and stand in the gap before me for the land."

An Old Testament example:

GENESIS 18:20-23

"And the LORD said, because the cry of Sodom and Gomorrah is great, and because their sin is very grievous; but Abraham stood yet before the LORD.

And Abraham drew near, and said, Wilt thou also destroy the righteous with the wicked?"

A New Testament example:

ACTS 12:5

"Peter therefore was kept in prison: but prayer was made without ceasing of the church unto God for him."

3. Intercession is hard work.

COLOSSIANS 4:12
"Epaphras, who is one of you, a servant of Christ, saluteth you, always labouring fervently for you in prayers."

4. Intercession is spiritual warfare and combat.

Ephesians 6:12
"For we wrestle not against flesh and blood, but against principalities, against powers, against the rulers of the darkness of this world, against spiritual wickedness in high places."

The Greek word "**wrestle**" means "**to fight till death**" in combat.

5. It is a spiritual watching in prayer for others, in all things:

1 Peter 4:7
"Watch unto prayer."

2 Timothy 4:5
"But watch thou in all things."

Hebrews 13:17
"For they watch for your souls."

Galatians 4:19
"My little children, of whom I travail in birth again until Christ be formed in you."

6. It is seeking God's face.

Psalm 24:6
"This is the generation of them that seek him, that seek thy face."

There are six important things about seeking God's face:

a. God looks for Christians to seek Him.

PSALM 53:2
"God looked down from heaven upon the children of men, to see if there were any that did understand, that did seek God."

b. God invites us to seek His face.

PSALM 27:8
"When thou saidst, Seek ye my face; my heart said unto thee, Thy face, LORD, will I seek."

c. We may seek the Lord early each day.

ISAIAH 58:2
"Yet they seek me **daily**."

PSALM 63:1
"O God, thou art my God; **early** will I seek thee:"

d. How long do we seek God's face?

DANIEL 9:3
"And I set my face unto the Lord God, to seek by prayer and supplications, with fasting, and sackcloth, and ashes:"

Seeking Gods face means to wait upon Him for shorter or longer periods.

Prayer and Fasting

PSALM 25:5
"On thee do I wait all the day."

e. We wait for God in prayer before His Throne.

PROVERBS 8:34
"Watching daily at my gates, waiting at the posts of my doors."

f. If we wait upon the Lord we will not be ashamed.

ISAIAH 49:23
"For they shall not be ashamed that wait for me."

There are four reasons why some prayers remain unanswered:

1. Because of carnal motives.

JAMES 4:3
"Ye ask, and receive not, because ye ask amiss, that ye may consume it upon your lusts."

2. Because of conscious sin.

JOHN 9:31
"Now we know that God heareth not sinners:"

3. Because of insincere and repetitious words.

MATTHEW 6:7

"But when ye pray, use not vain repetitions, as the heathen do: for they think that they shall be heard for their much speaking."

4. Because of praying out of God's will.

JOHN 15:7

"If ye abide in me, and my words abide in you, ye shall ask what ye will, and it shall be done unto you."

The ultimate purpose of prayer is to minister to God.

ACTS 13:2

"As they ministered to the Lord, and fasted."

Fasting

There are six aspects of fasting that we should consider:

1. Why Christians should fast.

The Bible gives examples of great spiritual men and woman who fasted.

Fasting releases God's explosive spiritual Power and coupled with prayer brings about amazing results.

Here are four examples of those who fasted:

a. Moses fasted for forty days.

Deuteronomy 9:18
"And I fell down before the LORD, as at the first, forty days and forty nights: I did neither eat bread, nor drink water."

b. David fasted.

Psalm 35:13
"I humbled my soul with fasting;"

c. Jesus fasted for forty days.

Matthew 4:2
"And when he had fasted forty days and forty nights, he was afterward a hungered."

d. The Apostles, Prophets and Teachers fasted.

Acts 13:2
"As they ministered to the Lord, and fasted."

2 Corinthians 11:27
"In fastings often"

2. Fasting is unto God and is God centered.

Matthew 6:18
"That thou appear not unto men to fast, but unto thy Father which is in secret:"

3. Fasting is abstaining from eating food.

LUKE 4:2
"Being forty days tempted of the devil. And in those days he did **eat nothing**"

4. When fasting, Christians should drink water.

5. How long should a fast be?

Christians fast for as long as the Holy Spirit leads them to fast.

ROMANS 8:14
"For as many as are led by the Spirit of God, they are the sons of God."

There are many examples in the Bible of Christians fasting for one, three, twenty-one or even forty days.

6. When we fast we are to do so in secret.

MATTHEW 6:16-18
"Moreover when ye fast, be not, as the hypocrites, of a sad countenance: for they disfigure their faces, that they may appear unto men to fast. Verily I say unto you, they have their reward.

But thou, when thou fastest, anoint thine head, and wash thy face;

That thou appear not unto men to fast."

There are five reasons for fasting:

1. As a consecration to God.

Joel 2:12
"Therefore also now, saith the LORD, turn ye even to me with all your heart, and with fasting."

2. To be heard of God.

Ezra 8:23
"So we fasted and besought our God for this: and he was intreated of us."

3. To bring deliverance in any situation.

Isaiah 58:6
"Is not this the fast that I have chosen? To loose the bands of wickedness, to undo the heavy burdens, and to let the oppressed go free, and that ye break every yoke?"

4. For a revelation from God.

Daniel 9:2, 3, 22, 23
"In the first year of his reign I Daniel ... I set my face unto the Lord God,

And he informed me, and talked with me, and said, O Daniel, I am now come forth to give thee skill and understanding.

At the beginning of thy supplications the commandment came forth, and I am come to show thee; for thou art greatly beloved: therefore understand the matter, and consider the vision."

5. For health and healing.

Fasting cleanses the whole body and after its conclusion brings about health, healing and a general sense of well-being.

Believers are challenged to initially fast no more than one day at a time.

After showing progress they can proceed for longer periods, as the Holy Spirit leads them.

Remember to drink lots of water when you fast.

If you have medical problems and are under doctors or medical treatment, be sure to first consult with them before fasting.

How does one break a fast?

It is necessary to cautiously and slowly break a fast.

This can be done with diluted soup first and then baby foods and mashed fruit later.

The stomach must be given time to return to its normal size.

A stomach after fasting is like a baby's stomach.

The digestive organs must also be gently caressed into resuming their activity.

The longer the fast the longer it takes to break a fast.

Here are some closing words about fasting.

From Jesus:

MATTHEW 9:15

"But the days will come, when the bridegroom shall be taken from them, and then shall they fast."

From Paul:

1 CORINTHIANS 7:5

"That ye may give yourselves to fasting."

From personal experience:

Every day of fasting helps a Christian grow spiritually with great success.

It is wise to make the choice of fasting.

ISAIAH 58:6

"Is not this the fast that I have chosen?"

CHAPTER 15

Stewardship

It is important for Christians to learn how to successfully manage their finances.

Most Christians experience debt some time during their life.

It is advisable for them to get out of debt and stay out of debt.

Many people today have been trained with certain skills to be money earners.

Some have increased that ability by developing those skills or changing their vocation.

Very few have been trained on **how to** effectively **spend and manage money**.

Christians should be taught how to biblically and sensibly manage their finances.

Knowing basic fiscal principles will help Christian's to be financially successful.

When becoming a Christian a person experiences three basic changes:

1. A change of status.

We are no longer subject to satan, but are children of the Most High God and citizens of His Kingdom.

2. A change of position.

We are seated together with Jesus Christ in heavenly places.

3. A change of allegiance.

Our allegiance is to God, His Kingdom, its laws, culture and financial system.

It is important for Christians to adapt themselves to this new way of living.

There are nine important things we should understand about true riches, possessions and the things of this world:

1. We should understand the infinite principle of ownership.

Stewardship

It is important to understand that God owns everything.

Psalm 24:1

"The earth is the LORD's, and the fulness thereof; the world, and they that dwell therein."

Haggai 2:8

"The silver is mine, and the gold is mine, saith the LORD of hosts."

God owns everything and can pass its ownership to whomsoever He pleases.

2. We should understand *what* is most important to us?

God and His Kingdom should always be first in our lives above all the things that we desire and possess.

Matthew 6:33
"But seek ye first the kingdom of God, and his righteousness; and all these things shall be added unto you."

3. We should understand what the true focus of our love should be.

We are told to love God and not things.

I John 2:15
"Love not the world, neither the things that are in the world. If any man love the world, the love of the Father is not in him."

We are to set our affection on Him and His things.

Colossians 3:1-2
"If ye then be risen with Christ, seek those things which are above, where Christ sitteth on the right hand of God.

Set your affection on things above, not on things on the earth."

4. We should understand that God is the source of everything we need and desire.

God entrusts possessions and wealth to all of us.

Deuteronomy 8:18

"But thou shalt remember the LORD thy God: for it is he that giveth thee power to get wealth."

God knows what we need, supplies those needs and continuously blesses us.

Stewardship

MATTHEW 6:32

"For your heavenly Father knoweth that ye have need of all these things."

PHILIPPIANS 4:19

"But my God shall supply all your need according to his riches in glory by Christ Jesus."

5. We should understand that God prospers and blesses us in five areas of our life:

1. Financially,
2. Physically,
3. Intellectually,
4. Emotionally,
5. Spiritually.

3 JOHN 2

"Beloved, I wish above all things that thou mayest prosper and be in health, even as thy soul prospereth."

PSALM 1:3

"And he shall be like a tree planted by the rivers of water, that bringeth forth his fruit in his season; his leaf also shall not wither; and *whatsoever he doeth shall prosper.*"

Go wants us to experience total prosperity.

We are to prosper in everything we do.

We are to prosper in Body, Soul and Spirit.

If we are obedient to God and do what he commands us to do, we will experience total prosperity and success.

JOSHUA 1:8

"This book of the law shall not depart out of thy mouth; but thou shalt meditate therein day and night, that thou mayest observe to do according to all that is written therein: for then thou *shalt make thy way prosperous,* and then thou shalt *have good success.*"

6. We should understand that we may receive the things we need, by prayerfully asking God.

MATTHEW 21:22
"And all things, whatsoever ye shall ask in prayer, believing, ye shall receive."

7. We should understand that we must be good stewards of what God gives us.

Stewardship

He requires us to intelligently, responsibly use and invest what He has given us.

God gives:

Abilities

Talents

Health

Wealth

Money

Property

Possessions

Stocks and shares

Valuables

Positions

Honor

Royalty

Many other things

8. We should understand that God requires good stewardship of our talents and abilities!

He wants us to use our talents and develop what He has given us.

Matthew 25:15-21
"And unto one he gave five talents, to another two, and to another one; to every man, according to his several abilities; and straightway took his journey.

After a long time the lord of those servants cometh, and reckoneth with them.

And so he that had received five talents came and brought other five talents, saying, Lord, thou deliveredst unto me five talents: behold, I have gained beside them five talents more.

His lord said unto him, well done, thou good and faithful servant: thou hast been faithful over a few things, I will make thee ruler over many things."

By knowing and practicing the above eight principles, we will be able to experience the ninth principle.

We will be able to move to a higher dimension of receiving from God.

This higher dimension of receiving comes, after God has found us to be faithful good stewards of earthly riches. He then can entrust to us true spiritual riches.

9. We should understand that God requires Good stewardship of spiritual riches.

There is a scriptural connotation between earthly and spiritual riches.

If God cannot trust us with earthly riches, why would He trust us with spiritual riches?

Luke 16:11
"If therefore ye have not been faithful in the unrighteous mammon, who will commit to your trust the true riches?"

There are many Christians who go through life and ignorantly or stubbornly miss this truth.

They never experience the powerful spiritual things of God in their life. How sad!

It is wonderful for those who are good stewards of God's earthly blessings, to then focus their attention on and seek above things.

Colossians 3:1-2
"If ye then be risen with Christ, seek those things which are above, where Christ sitteth on the right hand of God.

Set your affection on things above, not on things on the earth."

Experiencing the financial realm of God's Kingdom

The Kingdom of God is not subject to earthly kingdoms.

Its finances and economy are far above the fiscal principles of this world.

The Kingdom of God is above negatives things such as inflation, depression, recession, loss or lack.

God's Kingdom enjoys an abundance of supply and its wealth is designated for the needs of Christians. Gods Kingdom here on earth, has enjoyed a consistent track record of prosperity and success. This is evident throughout the Bible and history. God wants to bless all of His children as He blessed Abraham in the Old Testament.

GALATIANS 3:14

"That the blessing of Abraham might come on the Gentiles through Jesus Christ;"

Like any other father, God wants heaven and earth to see how He profits and blesses His children.

1 TIMOTHY 4:15

"Meditate upon these things; give thyself wholly to them; that thy profiting may appear to all."

Stewardship

MATTHEW 7:11

"How much more shall your Father which is in heaven give good things to them that ask him?"

God actually causes an exchange of wealth in favor of the righteous.

PROVERBS 13:22

"The wealth of the sinner is laid up for the just.

A new way of thinking will make better stewards of us

This new thinking involves a new value system that has three aspects:

1. How we value ourselves.

PROVERBS 23:7
"For as he thinketh in his heart, so is he:"

Do we think about ourselves, positively or negatively?

We should think of ourselves as Children of the Most High God.

We are citizens of Gods kingdom and of Royal and Kingly stature.

Our body is a Temple of the Holy Ghost.

We need a change and renewal of mind.

Romans 12:2

"But be ye transformed by the renewing of your mind."

God wants us to put away childish thinking and think soberly and maturely.

1 Corinthians 13:11

"When I was a child, I spake as a child, I understood as a child, I thought as a child: but when I became a man, I put away childish things."

We must not harbor thoughts of worry that cause us to take unwise and irresponsible financial decisions.

Matthew 6:31-34

"Therefore take no thought, saying, what shall we eat? Or, what shall we drink? Or, Wherewithal shall we be clothed?

For your heavenly Father knoweth that ye have need of all these things.

Take therefore no thought for the morrow: for the morrow shall take thought for the things of itself."

God doesn't want us to worry.

He wants us to relax, trust Him and enjoy a peaceful nights rest.

Stewardship

Psalm 127:2

"He giveth his beloved sleep."

2. How we value others.

We are to respect, value and love others as we love ourselves.

James 2:8
"If ye fulfill the royal law according to the scripture, Thou shalt love thy neighbour as thyself, ye do well:"

3. How we value things and possessions.

We should appreciate all that God has created on land, in the forests, skies, rivers and oceans. We should love and respect nature.

John 1:3
"All things were made by him; and without him was not anything made that was made."

We should appreciate and value all wealth and possessions that God has entrusted to our care.

Christians should be hardworking and creative.

God abhors idleness and laziness.

Christians should always be hard working and care for their family.

Proverbs 19:15

"An idle soul shall suffer hunger."

Nehemiah 4:6

"For the people had a mind to work."

1 Timothy 5:8

"But if any provide not for his own, and specially for those of his own house, he hath denied the faith, and is worse than an infidel."

God gives Christians special abilities, creative thoughts, inventions and favor.

Proverbs 8:12

"I wisdom dwell with prudence, and find out knowledge of witty inventions."

Philippians 4:13

"I can do all things through Christ which strengtheneth me."

We need to take the challenge and with confidence achieve success.

Hebrews 10:35-36

"Cast not away therefore your confidence, which hath great recompence of reward.

For ye have need of patience, that, after ye have done the will of God, ye might receive the promise."

Galatians 6:9

"And let us not be weary in well doing: for in due season we shall reap, if we faint not."

By perseverance and hard work we will achieve our goals, be successful and prosperous.

Christians are called to be givers.

God is the greatest giver of all time to those who are willing to receive:

He gave us:

Himself

His only begotten Son

The Holy Spirit

Salvation

Eternal life

The Kingdom of God

Heaven

The Angelic Hosts

Creation

Our daily needs

We are God's children, born again of His incorruptible seed and partakers of His Divine Nature.

2 Peter 1:4

"Whereby are given unto us exceeding great and precious promises: that by these ye might be partakers of the divine nature."

By our new nature we should also be givers.

God's example of giving inspires us to be givers.

By giving, we empty our barns and make room for more blessings from God in our lives.

Luke 6:38

"Give, and it shall be given unto you; good measure, pressed down, and shaken together, and running over, shall men give into your bosom. For with the same measure that ye mete withal it shall be measured to you again."

Understanding the Genesis Principle

In the book of genesis, many spiritual principles have been introduced and established.

God meant them to be applied by all generations until the end of time.

Here are seven spiritual principles introduced in Genesis:

Man experienced God's fellowship and love.

Man experienced God's mercy and forgiveness of sin.

Man served and obeyed God.

Man experienced God's provision for every need.

Man prayed and God answered.

Man worshipped God by giving first fruits.

God Covenanted with man.

The giving of first fruits is one of these principles and continues throughout the Bible.

Genesis 4:4

"And Abel, he also brought of the firstlings of his flock and of the fat thereof.

And the LORD had respect unto Abel and to his offering:"

Exodus 23:15-19

"And none shall appear before me empty ... When thou hast gathered in thy labours out of the field ... The first fruits of thy land thou shalt bring into the house of the LORD thy God."

Nehemiah 12:44

"And at that time were some appointed ... for the first fruits, and for the tithes, to gather into them out of the fields."

First fruits are tithes.

Leviticus 27:30

"And all the tithe of the land, whether of the seed of the land, or of the fruit of the tree, is the LORD'S: it is holy unto the LORD."

Malachi 3:10

"Bring ye all the tithes into the storehouse."

Here are five examples:

1. First fruits in the time of Adam.

It is evident from scripture that Adam taught his children to bring their first fruits to God.

Stewardship

GENESIS 4:4
"And Abel, he also brought of the firstlings of his flock and of the fat thereof. And the LORD had respect unto Abel and to his offering:"

HEBREWS 11:4
"By faith Abel offered unto God a more excellent sacrifice than Cain, by which he obtained witness that he was righteous, God testifying of his gifts: and by it he being dead yet speaketh."

Cain brought "some" of his fruit to and God had no respect for it.

GENESIS 4:3
"Cain brought of the fruit of the ground an offering unto the LORD."

2. First fruits during the time of the Patriarchs.

Abraham brought his first fruits (tithes) to the High Priest of the Most High God.

HEBREWS 7:1-2
"For this Melchisedec, king of Salem, priest of the Most High God, who met Abraham returning from the slaughter of the kings, and blessed him:

To whom also Abraham gave a tenth part of all:"

3. First fruits during the time of the Law and Prophets.

Words spoken by Moses:

LEVITICUS 27:30
"And all the tithe of the land, it is holy unto the LORD."

Words spoken by Solomon:

PROVERBS 3:9
"Honour the LORD with thy substance, and with the first fruits of all thine increase:"

Words spoken by the Prophets:

NEHEMIAH 12:44
"And at that time were some appointed over the chambers for the treasures, for the offerings, for the first fruits, and for the tithes."

MALACHI 3:10
"Bring ye all the tithes into the storehouse."

4. During the ministry of Christ.

Jesus gave a parable that relates to first fruit giving.

MARK 12:1-2
"And he began to speak unto them by parables. A certain man planted a vineyard ... and let it out to husbandmen, and went into a far country.

And at the season he sent to the husbandmen a servant that he might receive fruit of the vineyard."

Stewardship

At about the same time of this parable, they asked Him a question about giving to God and He answered them:

Mark 12:15-17
"Shall we give, or shall we not give? ...

And Jesus answering said unto them; Render to God the things that are God's."

He then went to the Temple to watch people giving.

Mark 12:41-44
"And Jesus sat over against the treasury, and beheld how the people cast money into the treasury: and many that were rich cast in much.

And there came a certain poor widow, and she threw in two mites, which make a farthing.

And he called unto him his disciples, and saith unto them, Verily I say unto you, that this poor widow hath cast more in, than all they which have cast into the treasury:

For all they did cast in of their abundance; but she of her want did cast in all that she had, even all her living."

Jesus commended the giving of tithes:

Luke 11:42
"For ye tithe mint and rue and all manner of herbs, these ought ye to have done."

5. In the times of the Apostles:

New Testament Christians give their tithes to their High Priest, Jesus Christ.

HEBREWS 7:8
"And here men that die receive tithes; but there He (Jesus Christ) receiveth them, of whom it is witnessed that he liveth."

1 CORINTHIANS 16:2
"Upon the first day of the week let every one of you lay by him in store, (give) as God hath prospered him."

2 CORINTHIANS 9:7
"Every man according as he purposeth in his heart, so let him give; not grudgingly, or of necessity: for God loveth a cheerful giver."

There are five aspects that show the importance of giving first fruits:

1. Giving first fruits is putting God first.

MATTHEW 6:33
"But seek ye first the kingdom of God, and his righteousness; and all these things shall be added unto you."

It is giving to God before we give to ourselves or anyone else.

2. Giving first fruits is honoring God.

Proverbs 3:9
"Honour the LORD with thy substance, and with the first fruits of all thine increase:"

It is giving God our very best.

Numbers 18:12
"All the best of the oil, and all the best of the wine, and of the wheat, the first fruits of them which they shall offer unto the LORD, them have I given thee.

3. How much is first fruits?

First fruits are synonymous with tithes.

Nehemiah 12:44
"And at that time were some appointed ... for the first fruits, to gather into them out of the fields."

Giving first fruits is giving to God at least a tithe, or one tenth of what we have received.

The Apostle Paul refers to this:

Hebrews 7:2
"To whom also Abraham gave a tenth part of all; first being by interpretation King of righteousness, and after that also King of Salem, which is, King of peace;"

The Hebrew word tithe is **"maser".**

The Greek word tithe is **"dekate".**

It means **a tenth part.**

4. What does first fruits do?

Giving first fruits is for our own benefit.

It does not focus on what we are giving to God.

It focuses on what He is giving to us.

If God had not given us an income in the first place, we would not have first fruits to give to Him.

The first fruits (tithe) we give, sanctifies the nine tenths of income that we have and removes all curses from it.

ROMANS 11:16
"For if the first fruit be holy, the lump is also holy:"

The first fruit is holy and always removes the curse.

When God gave His Son Jesus as the first fruit of His children, Jesus removed the following curses from them:

Sin

Sickness

Poverty

Death and

Hell.

When we give first fruits, we give the first tenth of our income to God.

Stewardship

The remaining nine tenths is ours.

The first fruit sanctifies and blesses the remaining nine tenths.

Without this blessing, our money would remain as ungodly mammon.

Luke 16:11
"If therefore ye have not been faithful in the unrighteous mammon, who will commit to your trust the true riches?"

5. To whom do we give the first fruits?

First fruits are given to the Priesthood.

Hebrews 7:5
"And verily they that are of the sons of Levi, who receive the office of the priesthood, have a commandment to take tithes of the people …"

Abraham brought his first fruits (tithes) to his High Priest Melchisidec.

Hebrews 7:1-2
"For this Melchisedec, king of Salem, priest of the Most High God, who met Abraham returning from the slaughter of the kings, and blessed him: To whom also Abraham gave a tenth part of all; first being by interpretation King of righteousness, and after that also King of Salem, which is, King of peace;"

Paul teaches that Jesus Christ is our High priest and we should give our first fruits to Him:

HEBREWS 7:14-17

"For it is evident that our Lord sprang out of Juda.

And it is yet far more evident: for that after the similitude of Melchisedec there ariseth another priest,

Who is made, not after the law of a carnal commandment, but after the power of an endless life. For he testifieth, Thou art a priest forever, after the order of Melchisedec."

HEBREWS 7:8

"And here men that die receive tithes; but there He (Jesus Christ) receiveth them, of whom it is witnessed that he liveth.

Four facts about Jesus and giving:

a. He received financial gifts from men.
b. He observed and commended people for giving in the Temple.
c. He commanded us to give God the finances that belong to Him.
d. He continues today to receive from us our first fruits (tithes).

Stewardship

Why would the Lord require us to pay tithes?

God has given us everything we have and is entitled to ask us for anything.

Job 1:21

"The LORD gave, and the LORD hath taken away; blessed be the name of the LORD."

The purpose of tithing is fourfold:

1. It is to return to God what belongs to Him.

God has entrusted ten tenths to us. Surely He has the right to test our faithfulness and honesty by expecting us to return a small portion, only one tenth to Him.

Malachi 3:10
"Bring ye all the tithes into the storehouse."

2. It is God's way of financing His Kingdom on earth.

With the tithes received from Christians, the financial needs of the Church are taken care of.

Malachi 3:10
"Bring ye all the tithes into the storehouse, that there may be meat in mine house."

The storehouse is the place where the income is received and dispersed by God's leadership.

Earthly Kingdoms receive taxes from their citizens to finance their economy.

God receives first fruits from His citizens to finance His Kingdom on earth.

EPHESIANS 2:19
"Now therefore ye are no more strangers and foreigners, but fellow citizens with the saints and of the household of God;"

3. It is an opportunity to experience God's faithfulness:

MALACHI 3:10
"Bring ye all the tithes into the storehouse, that there may be meat in mine house, and prove me now herewith, saith the LORD of hosts, if I will not open you the windows of heaven, and pour you out a blessing, that there shall not be room enough to receive it."

4. It is a personal experiment:

The only way to find out if God blesses the giving of first fruits is to personally do it.

2 CORINTHIANS 9:13
"While by the experiment ...your liberal giving unto them, and unto all men;"

What happens if we do not pay our tithes or first fruits to God?

1. We rob God.

MALACHI 3:8
"Will a man rob God? Yet ye have robbed me. But ye say, wherein have we robbed thee? In tithes and offerings."

2. We bring a curse into our lives.

MALACHI 3:9
"Ye are cursed with a curse: for ye have robbed me."

This curse is activated and perpetuated by the "devourer."

MALACHI 3:11
"And I will rebuke the devourer for your sakes, and he shall not destroy the fruits of your ground;"

In our lives we experience either blessings or curses.

1. Experiencing Blessings.

The Blessings of Abraham were spoken over the Israelites.

Deuteronomy 28:2-13

"And all these blessings shall come on thee, and overtake thee, if thou shalt hearken unto the voice of the LORD thy God.

Blessed shalt thou be in the city, and blessed shalt thou be in the field.

Blessed shall be the fruit of thy body, and the fruit of thy ground, and the fruit of thy cattle, the increase of thy kine, and the flocks of thy sheep.

Blessed shall be thy basket and thy store.

Blessed shalt thou be when thou comest in, and blessed shalt thou be when thou goest out.

The LORD shall cause thine enemies that rise up against thee to be smitten before thy face:

The LORD shall command the blessing upon thee in thy storehouses, and in all that thou settest thine hand unto:

The LORD shall open unto thee his good treasure,

And the LORD shall make thee the head, and not the tail:"

These same blessings are spoken over the New Testament Saints:

Galatians 3:14

"That the blessing of Abraham might come on the Gentiles through Jesus Christ;"

Stewardship

2. Experiencing Curses.

DEUTERONOMY 28:15-20
"But it shall come to pass, if thou wilt not hearken unto the voice of the LORD thy God, that all these curses shall come upon thee, and overtake thee:

Cursed shalt thou be in the city, and cursed shalt thou be in the field.

Cursed shall be thy basket and thy store.

Cursed shall be the fruit of thy body, and the fruit of thy land, the increase of thy kine, and the flocks of thy sheep.

Cursed shalt thou be when thou comest in, and cursed shalt thou be when thou goest out.

The LORD shall send upon thee cursing, vexation, and rebuke, in all that thou settest thine hand unto for to do, until thou be destroyed."

Pharaoh and Egypt experienced being cursed.

When God pronounced the curses of the ten plagues on the Egyptians, He was actually reversing the process of blessing.

The normal process is giving one tenth to God, keeping nine tenths and then being blessed.

God cursed Egypt with nine plagues, and the tenth was to take back their firstborn (first fruits) of everything.

How can this curse of not giving first fruits be removed?

There are three things we need to do in order for God to remove this curse:

1. We need to recognize and admit our sin of robbing God of the first fruits (tithes).

2. We need to repent, ask forgiveness and God will forgive our debt of the past unpaid tithes.

MATTHEW 6:9-12
"After this manner pray: Our Father which art in heaven, Hallowed be thy name ... forgive us our debts."

3. We need to give God our first fruits and continue doing so.

Compassionate giving

This charitable giving to help others is called offerings and should be in addition to our first fruits.

1 JOHN 3:16-17

"Hereby perceive we the love of God, because he laid down his life for us: and we ought to lay down our lives for the brethren.

But whoso hath this world's good, and seeth his brother have need, and shutteth up his bowels of compassion from him, how dwelleth the love of God in him?"

Galatians 6:9-10

"And let us not be weary in well doing: for in due season we shall reap, if we faint not.

As we have therefore opportunity, let us do good unto all men, especially unto them who are of the household of faith."

Matthew 25:44-45

"Then shall they also answer him, saying, Lord, when saw we thee an hungered, or athirst, or a stranger, or naked, or sick, or in prison, and did not minister unto thee? Then shall he answer them, saying, Verily I say unto you, Inasmuch as ye did it not to one of the least of these, ye did it not to me."

Giving to those in Ministry

1 Corinthians 9:11-14

"Do ye not know that they which minister about holy things live of the things of the temple? They which wait at the altar are partakers with the altar? Even so hath the Lord ordained that they which preach the gospel should live of the gospel."

Galatians 6:6-7

"Let him that is taught in the word communicate (financially give) unto him that teacheth in all good things.

Be not deceived; God is not mocked: for whatsoever a man soweth, that shall he also reap."

The law of sowing and reaping

The law of sowing and reaping applies to all the principles of life.

It is a perpetual law that has never failed from the beginning of time until now.

It also applies to financial giving.

It is a Biblical principle:

Galatians 6:7

"For whatsoever a man soweth, that shall he also reap."

Paul teaches this truth.

Stewardship

2 Corinthians 9:6-7

"But this I say, he that soweth sparingly shall reap also sparingly; and he, which soweth bountifully, shall reap also bountifully.

Every man according as he purposeth in his heart, so let him give: not grudgingly, or of necessity: for God loveth a cheerful giver."

A financial harvest next year will depend on the financial seed sown this year.

Luke 6:38

"Give, and it shall be given unto you; good measure, pressed down, and shaken together, and running over, shall men give into your bosom. For with the same measure that ye mete withal it shall be measured to you again."

Giving is a cycle that never stops.

As we give to God we empty ourselves. He then blesses us and refills us, so that we can give to him again. This cycle continues without end.

The hundredfold principle

Mark 10:28-30

"Then Peter began to say unto him, Lo, we have left all, and have followed thee.

And Jesus answered and said, Verily I say unto you, there is no man that hath left house, or brethren, or sisters, or father, or mother, or wife, or children, or lands, for my sake, and the gospel's,

But he shall receive an hundredfold now in this time, houses, and brethren, and sisters, and mothers, and children, and lands, with persecutions; and in the world to come eternal life."

Here Jesus specifically mentions four things:

1. There is a special hundredfold promise of increase for our giving.

2. We will receive it now in this time.

3. It includes possessions, family blessings and eternal life.

4. We receive all of this in spite of persecutions.

Paul teaches this also:

2 CORINTHIANS 9:8-10

"And God is able to make all grace abound toward you; that ye, always having all sufficiency in all things, may abound to every good work:

Now he that ministereth seed to the sower both minister bread for your food, and multiply your seed sown, and increase the fruits of your righteousness:"

Stewardship

Giving to God may take on four different forms:

1. Giving first fruits to a Church or Ministry.

2. Giving to the poor.

Proverbs 19:17
"He that hath pity upon the poor lendeth unto the LORD; and that which he hath given will he pay him again."

3. Investing in other Ministries.

Romans 15:26
"For it hath pleased them of Macedonia and Achaia to make a certain contribution for the poor saints which are at Jerusalem."

4. Giving to Christians.

Acts 2:45
"And sold their possessions and goods, and parted them to all men, as every man had need."

Whenever we give to God and for whatever reason, we will be blessed.

Luke 6:38
"Give and it shall be given unto you;"

The principle of vowing

Vowing to God is a special agreement made between a person and God.

When Believers experience a problem or special need in their life, making a vow to God can bring about His special intervention and help.

A person can vow to give a gift or service to God in return for His help.

David did this at God's invitation.

Psalm 50:14-15

"Offer unto God thanksgiving; and pay thy vows unto the most High: And call upon me in the day of trouble: I will deliver thee, and thou shalt glorify me."

When God comes to our aid, it is important to keep the vow we have promised.

Psalm 76:11

"Vow, and pay unto the LORD your God: let all that be round about him bring presents unto him that ought to be feared."

Stewardship

Christians need to be balanced in their giving.

They need to be good stewards of all that the Lord has entrusted to them.

1. They need firstly to give themselves to God.

2 Corinthians 8:5
"But first gave their own selves to the Lord."

2. They need to esteem giving to God as a special privilege and honor.

3. They need to be stable in financial matters.

*Those who are **unstable** in fiscal matters do the following:*

1. They break their promises to pay bills.

2. They often are deceitful.

3. They often are greedy.

4. They often are covetous.

5. They can be resentful of those who are blessed.

6. They worry.

God's children always give with the right attitude.

They give with cheerfulness.

2 Corinthians 9:7

"God loveth a cheerful giver."

They give with forgiveness.

Matthew 5:23-24

"Therefore if thou bring thy gift to the altar, and there rememberest that thy brother hath ought against thee:

Leave there thy gift before the altar, and go thy way: first be reconciled to thy brother, and then come and offer thy gift."

It grieves God if His children are offended.

That is why He demands the reconciliation of His children before they offer gifts to Him.

Christians should not be lovers or servants of money.

Matthew 6:24

"No man can serve two masters: for either he will hate the one, and love the other; or else he will hold to the one, and despise the other. Ye cannot serve God and mammon."

Christians should be content with the things they have.

1 Timothy 6:10

"For the love of money is the root of all evil:"

Proverbs 30:8-9

"Remove far from me vanity and lies: give me neither poverty nor riches; feed me with food convenient for me: Lest I be full, and deny thee, and say, who is the LORD? or lest I be poor, and steal, and take the name of my God in vain."

Philippians 4:11

"For I have learned, in whatsoever state I am, therewith to be content."

Job 31:24-28

"If I have made gold my hope, or have said to the fine gold, Thou art my confidence;

If I rejoiced because my wealth was great, and because mine hand had gotten much;

This also was an iniquity to be punished by the judge: for I should have denied that God is above."

Christians should be thankful for the blessings they receive from God.

Proverbs 10:22

"The blessing of the LORD maketh rich, and he addeth no sorrow with it.

Christians should be liberated from debt.

Our enemy satan tries to control and make our lives unpleasant, destroying us with debt.

Debt robs us of our freedom to do things and go places for God.

It causes unnecessary worry and uncertainty in our lives.

God wants to liberate us from this form of bondage.

Proverbs 22:7

"The rich ruleth over the poor, and the borrower is servant to the lender."

Galatians 5:1

"Stand fast therefore in the liberty wherewith Christ hath made us free, and be not entangled again with the yoke of bondage."

It often takes a miracle to be delivered from debt.

We read of a man that was in trouble because he lost his neighbors axe.

Stewardship

He was indebted to his neighbor and needed a miracle:

2 Kings 6:5-7

"One was felling a beam, the ax head fell into the water: and he cried, Alas, master! For it was borrowed.

And the man of God said, where fell it? And he showed him the place. And he cut down a stick, and cast it in thither; and the iron did swim.

Therefore said he, Take it up to thee. And he put out his hand, and took it."

Peter needed a miracle to pay his taxes.

Matthew 17:24-27

"And when they were come to Capernaum, they that received tribute money came to Peter, and said, Doth not your master pay tribute?

Jesus saith unto him … Notwithstanding, lest we should offend them, go thou to the sea, and cast an hook, and take up the fish that first cometh up; and when thou hast opened his mouth, thou shalt find a piece of money: that take, and give unto them for me and thee."

Eleven steps to a new future without debt and financial bondage:

1. Pay your first fruits and offerings to God before anything else.

2. If you have failed in the past admit it, confess it to God, repent and be faithful to pay first fruits and offerings from today onwards.

3. Never submit yourself to financial bondage and debt again.

4. Develop a budget for managing your income and expenditure.

5. Work out a recovery plan to pay back the debt you owe.

6. Increase your income -

    Get a better job

    Get a second job

    Embark on a money making business venture.

7. Increase your finances by saving on your expenditures:

    Cut your interest rates.

    Buy at cheaper prices.

    Shop around for cheaper payments.

Stewardship

8. Pay off your smaller debts first and then use that extra money to pay off the larger debts.

9. Never buy on the spur of the moment.

10. Live within your means.

11. Walk in the counsel of Godly people for:

Finances

Investments

Purchases

Real Estate

Legal counsel

Health services

All other matters

Memorize these promises of God and apply them in your life:

Philippians 4:19

"But my God shall supply all your need according to his riches in glory by Christ Jesus."

Joshua 1:8

"This book of the law shall not depart out of thy mouth; but thou shalt meditate therein day and night, that thou mayest observe to do according to all that is written therein: for then thou shalt make thy way prosperous, and then thou shalt have good success."

Psalm 35:27

"Let the LORD be magnified, which hath pleasure in the prosperity of his servant."

Jeremiah 29:11

"For I know the thoughts that I think toward you, saith the LORD, thoughts of peace, and not of evil, to give you an expected end."

Psalm 139:17

"How precious also are thy thoughts unto me, O God! how great is the sum of them!"

John 10:10

"I am come that they might have life, and that they might have it more abundantly."

Psalm 116:12

"What shall I render unto the LORD for all his benefits toward me?"

Deuteronomy 8:18

"But thou shalt remember the LORD thy God: for it is he that giveth thee power to get wealth."

Psalm 112:1-3

"Praise ye the LORD. Blessed is the man that feareth the LORD, that delighteth greatly in his commandments.

His seed shall be mighty upon earth: the generation of the upright shall be blessed.

Wealth and riches shall be in his house: and his righteousness endureth for ever."

Christians should never give up on prosperity and success!

Galatians 6:9

"And let us not be weary in well doing: for in due season we shall reap, if we faint not."

CHAPTER 16

Walking by Faith

There is something mysterious about faith.

Paul refers to this mystery:

1 Timothy 3:9

"Holding the **mystery** of the faith in a pure conscience."

The Greek word for "holding" is "**echontas**".

It means **to be told a secret**.

Holding a mystery means to receive, believe and use exclusive information.

We therefore can receive special information about faith and apply it in our life.

All over the world, Believers have an intense desire to find out more about faith.

Many thousands of books and articles have been written on this subject.

What money is to the natural world, faith is to the spiritual world.

Faith is the spiritual currency that obtains things in the spiritual realm.

When believers hear about faith for the first time, they wonder if they have faith.

Paul assures us that every believer has been given faith. (This spiritual currency)

ROMANS 12:3

"According as God hath dealt to every man the measure of faith."

Even if that measure of faith is the size of a little mustard seed, it has the power to remove mountains and do impossibilities.

MATTHEW 17:20

"If ye have faith as a grain of mustard seed, ye shall say unto this mountain, Remove hence to yonder place; and it shall remove; and nothing shall be impossible unto you."

Faith is our God given currency to do anything!

Paul advises us to use faith for our personal benefit.

ROMANS 14:22

"Hast thou faith? have it to thyself before God."

It pleases God when we have faith in Him.

HEBREWS 11:6

"But without faith it is impossible to please him: for he that cometh to God must believe that he is, and that he is a rewarder of them that diligently seek him."

Our Christian life is a life of faith.

ROMANS 1:17

"The just shall live by faith."

A Biblical definition of Faith:

ROMANS 4:21

"And being fully persuaded that, what he had promised, He was able also to perform."

We therefore believe that what God promised us in the Bible, he can and will do.

Faith is therefore taking God at His word.

If we are sick, we believe God's promise to heal us and we claim our healing.

Exodus 15:26

"For I am the LORD that healeth thee."

If we have a financial need, we believe God's promise and claim financial supply.

Philippians 4:19

"But my God shall supply all your need according to his riches in glory by Christ Jesus."

Faith is the substance of all needs:

Hebrews 11:1

"Now faith is the substance of things hoped for, the evidence of things not seen."

The need could be **healing**

The need could be **money**

The need could be **help**

The need could be **deliverance**

Faith is the **underlying substance** of healing, supply, help and deliverance.

The Greek word **"substance"** is **"hypostasis"**

It means **"the essence or basic element that things are made of."**

Faith is therefore the unseen material that our needs are made of.

The moment our faith is released, the invisible substance of our need actually materializes and manifests itself in a visible form:

Faith is that healing.

Faith is that miracle.

Faith is that financial supply.

Faith is that help.

Faith is that deliverance.

The intangible becomes the tangible.

Jesus said -

Mark 5:36

"Be not afraid, only believe."

He really was saying - "Don't be afraid, I will keep my promise, so trust me."

There are three things about faith that are important.

These different levels of faith start with a measure of a little faith.

1. Little faith:

MATTHEW 6:30
"Shall he not much more clothe you, O **ye of little faith**?"

Faith can increase to a greater measure.

2. Great faith:

MATTHEW 8:10
"Verily I say unto you, I have not found **so great faith**, no, not in Israel."

3. God kind of faith:

MARK 11:22
"And Jesus answering saith unto them, have faith in God. (**The God kind of faith**)

It was with the God kind of faith, that God created the Universe.

He called the things that did not exist into existence.

ROMANS 4:17
"God calleth those things which be not as though they were."

Our walk of faith

2 CORINTHIANS 5:7
"For we walk by faith, not by sight:"

Those who walk by sight, walk according to the five physical senses of their body.

When we are born again into God's Kingdom we move into a new dimension.

It is the **dimension of faith** and we obtain and achieve all things by faith.

Romans 1:17
"For therein is the righteousness of God revealed from **faith to faith**:"

The two Greek words for faith used here are **"Pisteo"** and **"Pistin"**.

Pisteo means **"the first experience of faith"**.

Pistin means **"the highest experience of faith"**.

Our walk of faith is a journey from the first experience of faith to the highest experience of faith.

This walk of faith in each situation is made up of seven steps:

1. Clearly identify your need.

Mark 10:36
"And he said unto them, what would ye that I should do for you?"

Faith is the substance of what you need and therefore you must identify your need.

2. Receive God's promise for that specific need.

We are children of promise and were created by God to experience His promises.

Romans 9:8
"But the children of the promise are counted for the seed."

2 Peter 1:4
"Whereby are given unto us exceeding great and precious promises: that by these ye might be partakers of the divine nature."

These promises are priceless and are greater than any need we ever may experience.

How do we receive these promises for our needs?

The Bible is the Word of promise and it reveals a promise for every specific need.

Romans 9:9

"For this is the word of promise."

As we read or hear the Bible, we discover these amazing promises of God for our needs.

If we have a financial need, there is a promise for that need.

Philippians 4:19

"But my God shall supply all your need according to his riches in glory by Christ Jesus."

3. Visualize receiving God's promise for that need.

God helped Abraham by letting him visualize the promise He gave him.

Genesis 15:5
"And He brought him forth abroad, and said, **look now toward heaven**, and tell the stars, if thou be able to number them:

and he said unto him, **so shall thy seed be**."

God promised to give Abraham a son and multiply his descendants as the stars of the heaven. Every night Abraham looked at the sky, he saw the millions of stars and could visualize God's promise to him.

Whatever your need is, visualize your need being supplied.

If you need healing, see yourself being healed and enjoying health.

If you need financial supply, see money in your billfold or being deposited into your bank account.

See yourself getting a raise in salary, a new job or signing a business contract.

See your situation change!

4. Believe God's promise.

By faith we believe God's promise and wait for it.

Hebrews 6:12
"Who through faith and patience inherit the promises."

We know that God cannot lie.

Numbers 23:19
"God is not a man, that he should lie; neither the son of man, that he should repent: hath he said, and shall he not do it? Or hath he spoken, and shall he not make it good?"

We also know that He is able to perform His promise.

Romans 4:21
"And being fully persuaded that, what he had promised, he was able also to perform."

5. We then act upon God's promise.

Faith is a **verb** and not a **noun.** A verb is a **doing word**.

Our faith should be an action, acting upon God's promise.

Hebrews 11:7
"By faith Noah, being warned of God of things not seen as yet, moved with fear, prepared an ark."

Noah believed God would save him and his family from the flood and went to action building an ark.

Peter believed Jesus, climbed over the side of the boat and started walking on the water.

Matthew 14:29
"And he said, come. And when Peter was come down out of the ship, he walked on the water, to go to Jesus."

6. Speak God's promise.

Confess it with your mouth.

Romans 10:10
"For with the heart man believeth unto righteousness; and with the mouth confession is made unto salvation."

We receive God's promises through His Word into our heart.

Within our mind we meditate the promise.

Then we act upon it by confessing and speaking it as reality.

Every time we speak God's promise, our tongue becomes a pen that writes the promise in our hearts.

The more we speak God's promises, the more they are accentuated in our heart.

Psalm 45:1
"My heart is processing a good matter: my tongue is the pen of a ready writer."

2 CORINTHIANS 4:13
"We having the same spirit of faith, according as it is written, I believed, and therefore have I spoken; we also believe, and therefore speak;"

PSALM 35:27
"Let them **say** continually; Let the LORD be magnified, which hath pleasure in the prosperity of his servant.

An example of this is seen in the life of Abraham, when God changed his name.

GENESIS 17:4-5
"As for me, behold, my covenant is with thee, and thou shalt be a father of many nations.

Neither shall thy name any more be called Abram, but thy name shall be Abraham; for a father of many nations have I made thee."

God gave him a new name **Abraham,** which means **"father of a multitude."**

Although he had no children at that time, every time Abraham spoke his name, he was confessing to be a father of a multitude. This was a confession of faith.

It wasn't long after he began doing this, that God fulfilled this promise and gave him a son, Isaac.

Why is it so important to speak God's promises?

It is important because Jesus as our High Priest works with these confessions, to help us to receive from God what we need.

He is the High priest of our profession (confession.)

Hebrews 3:1

"Wherefore, holy brethren, partakers of the heavenly calling, consider the Apostle and High Priest of our profession, Christ Jesus;"

In the Old Testament the High Priest worked with the sacrifices the Israelites brought to God.

In the New Testament Jesus our High Priest works with the confessions of the Saints of God.

Our walk of faith is a spiritual walk of confessions:

We confess sin and receive Jesus Christ as our Savior.

We confess healing and we are healed.

We confess financial supply and our needs are met.

With our mouth we confess what we believe and Jesus Christ our High Priest works with the confessions on our behalf.

7. Obtain God's promise.

The great men of faith are mentioned in Hebrews chapter eleven.

All of them by faith **obtained Gods promises.**

Heb 11:33
"Who through faith subdued kingdoms, wrought righteousness, obtained promises."

They believed God's promises and obtained them.

2 Corinthians 1:20
"For all the promises of God in him are yea, and in him Amen."

Therefore the promises of God in Jesus are **yea** which means **Yes.**

When we confess these promises, God says yes and we obtain them.

Then by faith we say **"Amen."**

The word amen is the closing word of our prayers.

Like a computer, it is our log-off or completion key.

The word amen concludes the promise of God as completed and done.

It is important to understand that faith is a powerful force in action:

Romans 3:27
"By the law of faith."

The Greek word for law is "**Nomon**".

It means **a powerful force in action.**

It is a powerful force of the spoken word completing its full course.

2 Thessalonians 3:1
"Finally, brethren, pray for us, that the **word of the Lord may have free course**, and be glorified, even as it is with you:"

This course could be better described in six parts:

1. A promise of God's Word received in a Christian's heart.
2. The promise meditated upon and understood.
3. A Christian believing God will perform the promise.
4. Acting in faith and confessing the promise.
5. The faith then becomes tangible. It becomes substance. It becomes the thing believed for.
6. The active force of faith brings about the completion and fulfillment of the promise of God.

The test of faith

1 PETER 1:7

"That the trial of your faith, being much more precious than of gold that perisheth, though it be tried with fire, might be found unto praise and honor and glory at the appearing of Jesus Christ:"

There are many situations that arise in our lives to test our faith.

These are situations of sickness, hurt, loss, lack, need, crises, fear and danger.

They are never easy because they burn like fire, but there results are more precious than gold.

Any manufactured product, coming off the production line must undergo a quality test.

Pipes that are welded at the seams must be air pressure tested, to ensure that they do not leak. A leaking pipe is a worthless pipe if it cannot process water, oil or gas pumped through it.

New trucks and cars must be driven and tested before they are sold.

Your faith will be tested!

How can we develop our faith?

There are three ways to develop faith and ensure its growth:

1. We develop our faith by hearing God's word and His promises.

Romans 10:17
"So then faith cometh by hearing, and hearing by the word of God."

As we hear God's word and embrace these promises in our heart our faith is stimulated.

It is important to search the Bible for God's promises and read them over and over again.

If we retain them within our hearts they will be available to use in the time of need.

2. Our faith grows as we see that confessing these promises really works.

We will see results in our own personal life and that of others. We will see healing, deliverance and the supply of needs and our faith will continue to grow.

3. Our faith becomes a natural part of everyday living.

Speaking these promises becomes a part of our conversation.

We will continually experience miracles, healing, supply, answers to prayer and the supernatural.

We walk by faith, never speak or react negatively and only speak positively.

Our faith will be perfected:

HEBREWS 12:2

"Looking unto Jesus the author and finisher of our faith;"

Jesus will complete our faith!

Our Lord Jesus Christ wants our faith to rise up within us and be demonstrated.

He wants our faith to grow from a small measure to a great measure, finally becoming the God kind of faith.

By faith Christians do great exploits:

HEBREWS 11:33-39

"Who through faith subdued kingdoms, wrought righteousness, obtained promises, stopped the mouths of lions. Quenched the violence of fire, escaped the edge of the sword, out of weakness were made strong, waxed valiant in fight, turned to flight the armies of the aliens.

Women received their dead raised to life again: and others were tortured, not accepting deliverance; that they might obtain a better resurrection:

And others had trial of cruel mockings and scourgings, yea, moreover of bonds and imprisonment:

They were stoned, they were sawn asunder, were tempted, were slain with the sword: they wandered about in sheepskins and goatskins; being destitute, afflicted, tormented;

Of whom the world was not worthy: they wandered in deserts, and in mountains, and in dens and caves of the earth. And these all, having obtained a good report through faith."

We are challenged to fight for and keep the faith delivered to the saints:

Jude 3

"That ye should earnestly contend for the faith which was once delivered unto the saints."

Faith is valuable!

It is worth contending for!

CHAPTER 17

Spiritual Warfare

The Apostle Paul addresses the subject of Spiritual Warfare and warns Christians that they are involved in a **Serious Spiritual War.**

EPHESIANS 6:10-13

"Finally, my brethren, be strong in the Lord, and in the power of his might.

Put on the **whole armour of God,** that ye may be able to stand against the wiles of the devil.

For we **wrestle** not against flesh and blood, but against principalities, against powers, against the rulers of the darkness of this world, against spiritual wickedness in high places.

Wherefore take unto you the whole armour of God, that ye may be able to **withstand in the evil day**, and having done all, to stand."

The Greek word for **wrestle** is **"pale"**.

It means **"man to man combat to the death."**

It was used of two Greek wrestlers who fought till one lay dead.

As Children of God, we are involved in a death struggle, with satan and the kingdom of darkness.

The organization of this kingdom is very clearly outlined in the **twelfth verse:**

"For we wrestle not against flesh and blood, but against **principalities**, against **powers,** against the **rulers** of the darkness of this world, against **spiritual wickedness** in high places."

There are four levels of authority within satan's kingdom.

1. **Principalities** (Archas) - Highest ranking evil beings

2. **Powers** (Exousias) - Evil powers of high authority

3. **Rulers** (Kosmokratipis) - World rulers of the spiritual darkness

4. **Spiritual wickedness** (Ponerias) - Wicked spirits

The hierarchy of satan's kingdom:

1. At the top is satan or lucifer, who is in command.

He **was** one of the three Archangels in Heaven.

The other two are Michael, Gabriel.

Each of them commanded a third of the Heavenly Angels.

When lucifer and a third of Angels under his command sinned and rebelled against God, they were cast out of Heaven. **(Ezek 28)**

Michael and Gabriel remained loyal to God and they continue to preside over the other two thirds of the Heavenly Angels.

2. *Then there is **abaddon or appolyon** the king of the underworld who answers to satan.*

Revelation **9:11**
"And they had a king over them, which is the angel of the bottomless pit, whose name in the Hebrew tongue is **Abaddon**, but in the Greek tongue hath his name **Apollyon.**"

3. *There is **belial.***

2 Corinthians **6:15**
"And what concord hath Christ with Belial?"

4. *There is **Beelzebub** and his name means **"lord of the flies"** and is over the hosts of demons.*

MATTHEW 12:24
"But when the Pharisees heard it, they said, this fellow doth not cast out devils, but by Beelzebub the prince."

5. *There are the **high ranking fallen angels**, who are the executive officers of satan.*

6. *There are the **powers of authority** executing the commands and operations.*

7. *There are the **rulers** who are over Continents, Countries, States, Counties, Cities, Subdivisions, Streets and Homes.*

8. *In subjection to them are **demons** that target and destroy people.*

More about demons:

The three aspects of demons:

a. Their nature

Jesus calls them **unclean.**

MATTHEW 10:1
"And when he had called unto him his twelve disciples, he gave them power against **unclean spirits.**"

They are like **frogs.**

Spiritual Warfare

REVELATION 16:13
"And I saw three unclean spirits like **frogs.**

Similar to frogs, demons are creatures of the spiritual night.

They are persistent and keep attempting to jump into people's lives.

b. Their personalities

They have names, speak, show emotions, tremble and manifest themselves.

They hate God the Father, Jesus Christ, the Holy Spirit and every Christian.

They tempt, seduce and strategize against men.

1 TIMOTHY 4:1
"Now the Spirit speaketh expressly, that in the latter times some shall depart from the faith, giving heed to **seducing spirits**."

c. Their purpose

There sole purpose is to oppose and destroy God's Kingdom.

This dark, demonic kingdom exercises its control and influence over the world:

1 John 5:19

"And we know that ... the **whole world lieth in wickedness.**"

The prince of this world is satan who exercises authority over it.

The pleasures, possessions and positions of this world belong to him and are under his control.

The military war machine of satan has had almost six thousand years to practice and perfect warfare upon a defenseless humanity.

The various subtle forms of attack often overcome and destroy people.

2 Corinthians 2:11

"Lest Satan should **get an advantage of us**: for we are not ignorant of his **devices**."

The Greek word for devices is "**methodias**".

It means the **methods and strategies** that satan uses.

We need protection against these methods:

Ephesians 6:11

"Put on the whole armour of God, that ye may be able to stand against the **wiles** of the devil."

The Greek word for "**wiles**" is **"noemata".**

It means the **plans** of the devil.

God's armor will help us stand against satan's plans.

The ten attacks of satan against men:

1. Temptation.

God does not tempt any man, only satan does.

James 1:13-15
"Let no man say when he is tempted, I am tempted of God: for God cannot be tempted with evil, neither tempteth he any man:

But every man is tempted, when he is drawn away of his own lust, and enticed.

Then when lust hath conceived, it bringeth forth sin: and sin, when it is finished, bringeth forth death."

2. Tribulation.

REVELATION 2:10
"The devil shall cast some of you into prison that ye may be tried; and ye shall have tribulation ten days:"

3. Resistance and persecution.

ACTS 26:10-11
"Many of the saints did I shut up in prison, having received authority from the chief priests; and when they were put to death, I gave my voice against them.

And I punished them oft in every synagogue, and compelled them to blaspheme; and being exceedingly mad against them, I persecuted them even unto strange cities."

The kingdom of satan does this by using authorities, earthly organizations and his resources against us.

4. Sickness.

JOB 2:7
"So went Satan forth from the presence of the LORD, and smote Job with sore boils from the sole of his foot unto his crown."

Spiritual Warfare

5. Torment.

HEBREWS 11
"They were … tormented;"

6. Deception.

He changes his appearance or voice to that of an Angel, in order to mislead and deceive people.

2 CORINTHIANS 11:14
"And no marvel; for Satan himself is transformed into an angel of light."

7. Instigation.

He causes enemies to rise up against God's people:

JOHN 13:2
"The devil having now put into the heart of Judas Iscariot, Simon's son, to betray him;"

8. Accusations.

JOB 1:9
"Then Satan answered the LORD, and said, Doth Job fear God for nought?"

9. Negative influences.

MATTHEW 13:27-28
"Sir, didst not thou sow good seed in thy field?

From whence then hath it tares? ... an enemy hath done this."

Strategically satan places sinful and destructive people around us to negatively influence and affect our lives.

10. Hurt and loss.

John 10:10
"The thief cometh not, but for to steal, and to kill, and to destroy:"

His objective is to isolate and cut us off from those who love us.

To single us out, wear us down and take away everything we have, including our dignity.

He wants to oppress us, depress us, take away our self worth and finally kill us.

The attacks of satan are directed at six areas of our life:

1. Our Body.

He wants to destroy our body with sickness and unclean living.

2. Our Soul.

He surrounds us with negative influences from the day of our birth to impact our **mind, emotion** and **will.** He implants bad

Spiritual Warfare

thoughts, experiences and feelings into our mind, imagination, emotions and memory.

He uses people like parents, family, teachers, classmates, friends and associates to do this.

He tricks us into making wrong decisions.

He causes us to be fearful and indecisive, weakening our will.

3. Our spirit or spiritual life.

He will place obstacles in the way of Christians to prevent them from becoming more spiritual.

He wants those who are spiritual to lose spiritual ground.

By neglecting the Word of God, Prayer and going to Church, many Christians backslide and often fall away from the Faith.

4. Our Ministry.

The enemy satan causes Christians to lose sight of the importance and value of their ministry.

Through neglect, inactivity, disobedience, unbelief and fear many fail.

By compromise, sin or fear many promising Ministries are destroyed.

5. Our finances.

We know that he tries to steal everything we have.

We know that he tries to decrease our productivity and financial income.

Often he tries to cut off financial supply lines of blessing coming to us.

Negatively affecting our work, assets and investments are part of his strategy.

By doing this he ultimately affects God's Kingdom.

6. Our close family.

The ultimate goal of satan is to destroy families.

Disrupting the daily program of a home will cause inconvenience, stress and disharmony. Unhappy family relationships will create an unbearable atmosphere within a home and cause the breakup of the family.

Effective soldiers.

God wants us to be successful and effective Soldiers in His Kingdom.

He wants us to war a good spiritual warfare.

2 Corinthians 10:3-4

"For though we walk in the flesh, we do not war after the flesh:

Spiritual Warfare

For the weapons of our warfare are not carnal, but mighty through God to the pulling down of strong holds:"

We need four things to be effective soldiers in spiritual warfare:

We need to be strong in the Lord.

EPHESIANS 6:10

"Finally, my brethren, be strong in the Lord, and in the power of his might."

It would be unwise to send unprepared Christians into spiritual battle to fight against satan and his kingdom.

Those who are spiritually weak, sick or untrained would not be good soldiers.

To become strong in the Lord Christians need:

Spiritual **food**

Spiritual **exercise**

Spiritual **rest**

Spiritual **anointing** of power

We need to be strong in the Word of God, fasting, prayer and spiritual discernment, to overcome the enemy.

We need to endure hardness as good Soldiers of Jesus Christ.

2 Timothy 2:3

"Thou therefore endure hardness, as a good soldier of Jesus Christ."

As good soldiers we need:

To be **enlisted** as a soldier in God's army.

To have **confidence** that we are on the winning side

To be a **good soldier**

To **believe in the cause** of God's army

To be **well trained** and effective in God's army

To **know the details** of our part in God's military plans

To be **dedicated** to God's purpose

To be **loyal** to God's army

To **keep our rank** in God's army

To be **totally prepared** for battle

To **take up** our spiritual weapons

To be **exercised** in using our spiritual weapons

To **have stamina** to endure the heat of battle

Spiritual Warfare

To have killer instinct and **no sympathy** for our enemy

To be **obedient** to our Leaders and the Godhead

We need to be able to discern the enemy.

Any good soldier who goes to battle is taught about warfare.

The instructions include books, videos, classes and on the job training.

We as God's children need to be instructed from God's Word about spiritual warfare. We need to learn about the strategies of our enemy satan.

We need to receive Godly instruction and advice from those who have been successful in spiritual battle.

As we get involved in warfare we will also learn by observation and experience.

God also reveals to us what we need to know by giving us teachings, visions, dreams and revelations.

The Holy Spirit gives us a special gift of Discerning of spirits to help us in spiritual battle.

This Gift enables us to know details about the spirits we are dealing with.

We discover their evil characteristics, activities and areas of activity in the spirit realm.

We are able to discern enemy activity in the spirit realm, countries, cities, cultures, families and people.

The Holy Spirit reveals to us the traps and wiles of the devil.

He teaches us how defeat the enemy and what weapons to use.

He gives us the Gift of Wisdom to help us make the right decisions.

All nine Gifts of the Spirit are at our disposal to give us the victory in battle.

1 Corinthians 12:8-10

"For to one is given by the Spirit the **word of wisdom**; to another the **word of knowledge** by the same Spirit; To another **faith** by the same Spirit; to another the gifts of **healing** by the same Spirit; To another the **working of miracles**; to another **prophecy**; to another **discerning of spirits**; To another **divers kinds of tongues**; To another the **interpretation of tongues**:"

4. We need to take up our protective armor and offensive weapons.

Ephesians 6:11-13
"Put on the **whole armor of God**, that ye may be able to stand against the wiles of the devil.

For we wrestle not against flesh and blood, but against principalities, against powers, against the rulers of the darkness of this world, against spiritual wickedness in high places.

Wherefore **take unto you the whole armor of God,** that ye may be able to withstand in the evil day, and having done all, to stand."

We must put on the five protective pieces of Gods armor:

1. The helmet of salvation
2. The breastplate of righteousness
3. The shield of faith
4. The loins girt about with truth
5. The feet shod with the preparation of the Gospel of peace

Ephesians 6:14-17

"Stand therefore, having your loins girt about with truth, and having on the breastplate of righteousness: And your feet shod with the preparation of the gospel of peace:

Above all, taking the shield of faith, wherewith ye shall be able to quench all the fiery darts of the wicked. And take the helmet of salvation."

We must take up the two offensive weapons:

1. The sword of the Spirit, which is the Word of God.
2. All prayer and supplication in the Spirit.

EPHESIANS 6:17-18

"And the sword of the Spirit, which is the word of God:

Praying always with all prayer and supplication in the Spirit, and watching thereunto with all perseverance and supplication for all saints;"

Now let us consider each of these five pieces of protective armor:

1. The helmet of salvation;

This piece of armor covers the head of a soldier.

In spiritual warfare, satan comes against our mind.

His attacks are directed at our thoughts, feelings and decisions we make.

Without the helmet of salvation we are left unprotected and may receive a deadly spiritual wound.

2 CORINTHIANS 10:4-5

Spiritual Warfare

"For the weapons of our warfare are not carnal, but mighty through God to the pulling down of strong holds; Casting down *imaginations*, and every high thing that exalteth itself against the knowledge of God, and bringing into captivity *every thought* to the obedience of Christ;"

2. The breastplate of righteousness

A breastplate protects vital organs such as the heart and lungs that are necessary for life. Similarly, the breastplate of righteousness protects one of the most vital areas of our spiritual life, namely **righteousness**.

Our enemy satan tries to make us doubt our righteousness in Christ.

He tries to get us to depend on our own righteous deeds.

He tempts us to sin, be defiled and lose our breastplate.

Our breastplate of righteousness is made up of two things:

a. Knowledge that we have been cleansed from all our own unrighteous deeds.

1 John 1:7,9
"But if we walk in the light, as he is in the light, we have fellowship one with another, and the blood of Jesus Christ his Son cleanseth us from all sin.

If we confess our sins, he is faithful and just to forgive us our sins, and to cleanse us from all unrighteousness."

b. Knowledge that we have been clothed with God's righteousness.

PHILIPPIANS 3:9
"And be found in him, not having mine own righteousness, which is of the law, but that which is through the faith of Christ, the righteousness which is of God by faith:"

1 CORINTHIANS 1:30
"But of him are ye in Christ Jesus, who of God is made unto us righteousness."

2 CORINTHIANS 5:21
"That we might be made the righteousness of God in him."

When satan comes knocking at our door to accuse us, we send Jesus who is our righteousness to answer the door.

3. The shield of faith.

When satan shoots a fiery dart at us, we are able to block or fend it off with the shield of faith.

He sends these darts against different areas of our life:

Against our health

Spiritual Warfare

Against our finances

Against our obedience to follow God's commands

Against our abilities

When under attack, by **faith** we speak God's Word and our shield of faith stops the incoming fiery dart.

For example we may use any of the following scriptures:

GENESIS 18:14
"Is anything too hard for the LORD?"

LUKE 1:37
"For with God nothing shall be impossible."

ISAIAH 53:5
"And by his stripes I am healed."

PHILIPPIANS 4:19
"But my God shall supply all my needs according to his riches in glory by Christ Jesus."

4. Our loins girded with truth.

To experience this protection in our lives we:

a. Walk in truth.

3 JOHN 3
"For I rejoiced greatly, when the brethren came and testified of the truth that is in thee, even as thou walkest in the truth."

God wants us at all times to be genuine, having our own true personality and identity, just as he made us.

He wants us to be who we are and not try to be someone else.

b. Speak the truth.

EPHESIANS 4:15
"But speaking the truth in love."

We need to have integrity, be of truthful character, reliable and trustworthy.

c. Be **unmovable** in truth.

2 PETER 1:12
"And be established in the present truth."

By truth in our lives, we will overcome an enemy attack against us.

We will not -

- Be untruthful
- Pretend to be what we are not
- Do something that is questionable
- Be deceitful

Spiritual Warfare

5. Our feet covered with the preparation of the Gospel of peace.

As Christians we prepare for the spreading of the Gospel.

First we read and study God's Word.

2 Tim 2:15
"**Study** to shew thyself approved unto God, a workman that needeth not to be ashamed, rightly dividing the word of truth."

Then we apply God's Word in our lives and it enables us to experience peace.

Then we can **spread it** wherever we go in a **peaceful way** and bring **peace.**

Now let us consider the two offensive weapons:

1. The sword of the Spirit, the Word of God

Jesus clearly used this weapon against satan.

When satan attacked Him, He spoke the Word of God and defeated satan.

Matt 4:4
"But **he answered** and said, **it is written**,

Man shall not live by bread alone, but by every word that proceedeth out of the mouth of God."

In the book of Revelation John sees Jesus with this weapon proceeding out of His mouth.

Rev 1:16
"And out of his mouth went a sharp two-edged sword:"

There are two words in the Greek used for Word of God.

Logos - The living written Word of God.

Rhema -The spoken Word of God.

The Word of God entering our heart is "**Logos**"

The Word of God spoken out of our mouth is "**Rhema** "

The Rhema Word is a mighty sword of God that goes out of our mouth.

It is powerful defeating satan and the demonic forces of darkness.

Isaiah 55:11

"So shall my **word** be that goeth forth **out of my mouth**: it shall not return unto me void, but **it shall accomplish** that which I please, and it **shall prosper** in the thing whereto I sent it."

2. All prayer and supplication in the Spirit.

To defeat the enemy, we are to use every avenue of prayer available to us and at all times pray in the Spirit.

Spiritual Warfare

There are five kinds of prayer:

1. The prayer of asking

2. The prayer of agreeing

3. The prayer of binding and loosing

4. The prayer of intercession

5. The prayer of tongues (Heavenly languages)

As soldiers of Jesus Christ we need to strive for mastery in using these kinds of prayer.

2 Timothy 2:5

"And if a man also **strive for masteries**, yet is he not crowned, except he strive lawfully."

Our Kingly authority:

Jesus has made us Kings within His Kingdom.

Revelation 5:10

"And hast made us unto our God, **kings**"

As Christians, we have taken up our position with Him in heavenly places and are seated together with Him on His Throne.

Ephesians 2:6

"And hath raised us up together, and made us **sit together** in heavenly places in Christ Jesus:"

In ChristJesus we are to exercise our Kingly authority:

As Kings our authority is vested in the authority of Jesus.

He has all authority.

MATT 28:18

"And Jesus came and spake unto them, saying, all **power** (authority) is given unto me in heaven and in earth."

As Kings we decree things in His Name.

In the Name of Jesus, we execute judgement upon the demons and forces of hell.

PSALM 149:5-9

"Let the saints be joyful in glory: let them sing aloud upon their beds.

Let the high praises of God be in their mouth, and a two-edged sword in their hand:

To execute vengeance upon the heathen, and punishments upon the people;

To bind their kings with chains, and their nobles with fetters of iron;

To execute upon them the judgment written:

This honor have all his saints."

We have been given authority over demons:

Jesus specifically gave us power and authority over demons.

Luke 10:19

"Behold, I give unto you power to tread on serpents and scorpions, and over all the power of the enemy: and nothing shall by any means hurt you."

Newly saved Christians, (babes in Christ) have power and authority over satan, his kingdom and demons.

Ps 8:2

"Out of the mouth of **babes and suckling** hast thou ordained strength because of thane enemies, that thou mightiest still the enemy and the avenger."

Mark 16:17

"And these signs shall follow them that believe:

In my name shall they cast out devils:"

Demons

The four different gates demons use to enter people:

1. Willful sin

When people willfully sin they open themselves to demons.

2. Occult entanglement

When people engage in witchcraft, consult psychics, fortunetellers and practice satanism, they open themselves to demon possession. Demonic activity within families can be generational, being passed on from parents to children.

EXODUS **20:5**
"Visiting the iniquity of the fathers upon the children **unto the third and fourth generation** of them that hate me;"

3. Addiction

Anything that weakens, neutralizes or shuts down the will of a person, opens the door to demon possession. This includes hypnoses.

4. Traumatic experiences.

Experiences like abuse, abandonment, shock or severe trauma can bring about demon possession in people's lives.

The place that demons occupy in men:

EPHESIANS 4:27

"Neither give **place** to the devil."

Demons do not reside in the human spirit.

They reside in the sub-conscious.

Here they hide, retreat and lay low until they manifest themselves through the persons mind, emotion or will.

When demons manifest they may be seen in the eyes of the person.

There is an infrastructure that demons set up in person when they enter.

There is normally more than one demon in a demon possessed person.

LUKE 8:30

"And Jesus asked him, saying, what is thy name? And he said, Legion: because **many devils** were entered into him."

These demons have a hierarchy with a chain of command.

The leader is the strongman and must be cast out first.

Casting out demons

There are ten things to consider:

1. To be delivered from demons, a person must first renounce the demonic presence in their life.
2. They must openly confess their desire to be set free.
3. They must repent of any sin they may have committed, and anything they may have done that caused them to be demon possessed.
4. God's servant must address and bind the controlling demon in the person, in the Name of Jesus Christ and command it to go.
5. If necessary, interrogate the demons for information needed.
6. Dismantle their hierarchy as the demons are cast out.
7. Totally ignore demonic conversation like:
   - Refusing to go
   - Bargaining
   - Threatening
   - Begging
8. Be sure that the person is **totally free** from demon possession, being able to confess that Jesus Christ is Lord.

Spiritual Warfare

9. Be sure that the delivered person becomes **filled with the Holy Spirit.**

10. Be sure that **restoration takes place** in the life of the delivered person and that complete healing has occurred.

Ministers of deliverance

Only Gods anointed children can cast out demons and minister deliverance in the Name of Jesus Christ.

Scripture aids for those ministering deliverance.

Christians are secure because Jesus Christ is always with them:

MATTHEW 28:20

"Lo, I am with you always, even unto the end of the world."

Jesus has overcome satan and all demons:

PHILIPPIANS 2:9-10

"Wherefore **God also hath highly exalted him**, and given him a name which is above every name:

That at the name of Jesus **every knee should bow**, of things **in heaven**, and things **in earth,** and things **under the earth;**

COLOSSIANS 2:15

"And having **spoiled principalities and powers**, he made a shew of them openly, **triumphing over them** in it."

1 JOHN 3:8

"For this purpose the **Son of God** was manifested, that he might **destroy the works of the devil.**"

REVELATION 1:18

"I am he that liveth, and was dead; and, behold, I am alive for evermore, Amen; and **have the keys of hell** and of death."

JAMES 2:19

"The devils also believe, and tremble."

Jesus gave Christians power over demons:

LUKE 10:19

"Behold, **I give unto you power** to tread on serpents and scorpions, and **over all the power of the enemy**: and nothing shall by any means hurt you."

Matthew 18:18

"Verily I say unto you, **whatsoever ye shall bind** on earth **shall be bound** in heaven:"

James 4:7

"Submit yourselves therefore to God. Resist the devil, and he will flee from you."

The Blood of Jesus within a Christian overcomes satan.

1 John 1:7

"And the **blood of Jesus Christ** his Son cleanseth us from all sin."

Revelation 12:11

"They overcame him by the blood of the Lamb."

Romans 8:1

"There is therefore now **no condemnation** to them which are in Christ Jesus."

God's Angels protect Christians.

Psalm 34:7

"The **angel of the LORD** encampeth round about them that fear him, and delivereth them."

The end-time Army of the Lord

1. It is a great army.

JOEL 2:11
"And the LORD shall utter his voice before his army: **for his camp is very great**:"

2. The soldiers are mighty.

JOEL 2:7
"They shall run like mighty men; they shall climb the wall like men of war; and they shall march everyone on his ways, and they shall not break their ranks:"

3. All spiritual battles are recorded in God's war book.

At the final Judgment we read that "Books" will be opened.

REVELATION 20:12
"And the **books were opened**."

One of these books in Heaven is Gods "**war book**" where all the wars fought by God's soldiers are recorded.

NUMBERS 21:14
"Wherefore it is said in the **book of the wars** of the LORD."

All exploits and victories of God's soldiers are recorded in this **book of wars.**

May you enjoy great victories for the Kingdom of God.

They are recorded in Heaven and will always be remembered.

Like Paul you will be able to say:

2 Tim 4:7-8

"I have fought a good fight, I have finished my course, I have kept the faith: Henceforth there is laid up for me a crown of righteousness which the Lord, the righteous judge, shall give me at that day: and not to me only, but unto all them also that love his appearing."

CHAPTER 18

Thanksgiving, Praise and Worship

The greatest honor of the citizens of any kingdom is to meet with their King.

To receive this invitation and great honor, would be a once in a lifetime experience.

They would arrive on time and be appropriately dressed.

They would carefully and graciously approach the Kings throne.

They would bow before him and honor him.

They would humbly present him with a special gift.

They would express their thankfulness and gratitude to him.

They would follow all royal protocol towards him.

They would behave with dignity and respect.

They would address the King with words like "Your Royal Highness."

They would then wisely listen to what the King said and carefully answer him.

One of the greatest Kings that ever lived was King Solomon.

He built a magnificent Palace and when the Queen of Sheba saw it, it took her breath away.

The Bible describes his Throne Room:

2 Chronicles 9:17-20

"Moreover the king made a great throne of ivory, and overlaid it with pure gold.

And there were six steps to the throne, with a footstool of gold, which were fastened to the throne, and stays on each side of the sitting place, and two lions standing by the stays:

And twelve lions stood there on the one side and on the other upon the six steps.

There was not the like made in any kingdom."

We must remember that Solomon's throne cannot compare with -

The Magnificent Throne of the God of Heaven and Earth, JEHOVAH.

Coming before God's Throne:

Christians are children of the Most High God and citizens of His Kingdom.

They have been given the esteemed right to approach His supreme Throne.

How much more should they render Him respect, honor and obeisance.

It is a priceless privilege to carefully and appropriately come before Him and enjoy His awesome presence!

The Bible describes the heavenly domain of the Great King of the Universe.

It is greater in size than the immeasurable universe.

Isaiah 66:1

"Thus saith the LORD, The heaven is my throne, and the earth is my footstool:"

24 Doctrines of the Bible

There are five things to consider about Gods Throne:

1. God's Throne is magnificent.

REVELATION 4:2-6
"A Throne was set in heaven, and one sat on the throne. And he that sat was to look upon like a jasper and a sardine stone: and there was a rainbow round about the throne, in sight like unto an emerald. And before the throne there was a sea of glass like unto crystal:"

REVELATION 4:5
"There were seven lamps of fire burning before the throne, which are the seven Spirits of God.

Take a moment and imagine God's Throne Room.

Gods Throne rises up bigger than the Universe.

It shines so brightly that no human eye can look upon it.

Around the Throne there is an **emerald green rainbow.**

In front of His Throne is a **crystal sea** bigger than all the oceans of the world.

Huge **Seraphim** are around and protect the Throne crying with thunderous voices,

Holy, Holy, Holy is the Lord of Hosts.

Seven fire burning lamps are before God's Throne.

Thanksgiving, Praise and Worship

The mist of God's presence permeates and glorifies everything in Heaven.

2. An indescribable power proceeds from God's Throne.

REVELATION 4:5
"And out of the throne proceeded lightnings and thunderings and voices:"

Awesome power sustaining the life of every creature and atom in the Universe proceeds from God's throne.

His decrees control the universe, earth and all of creation.

Millions of prayers reach God's Throne every second and are answered.

3. God's Throne is surrounded by many Celebrities:

Cherubim and Seraphim worship God.

Archangels Michael and Gabriel await to perform God's commands.

Myriads of Angelic hosts come and go doing God's bidding.

Patriarchs like Abraham, Isaac, and Jacob grace the Heavenly Palace.

Hero's like Moses, Samuel, David, Daniel, Peter, Paul, John, Mary and many others come before God's Throne to worship Him.

4. God who sits upon His Throne is beyond description.

He is:

Ancient of days

Elohim - Creator of Heaven and Earth

El-eljon - God Most High

El-shaddai - God Almighty

Yahweh - Jehovah

Isaiah and David saw God upon His Throne and were amazed.

ISAIAH 6:1-5

"I saw also the LORD sitting upon a throne, high and lifted up, and his train filled the temple.

Above it stood the seraphim's: each one had six wings; with twain he covered his face, and with twain he covered his feet, and with twain he did fly.

And one cried unto another, and said, Holy, holy, holy, is the LORD of hosts: the whole earth is full of his glory.

And the posts of the door moved at the voice of him that cried, and the house was filled with smoke.

Then said I, Woe is me! for I am undone; because I am a man of unclean lips, and I dwell in the midst of a people of unclean lips: for mine eyes have seen the King, the LORD of hosts."

Psalm 18:6-10

"I cried unto my God: he heard my voice out of his temple,

Then the earth shook and trembled; the foundations also of the hills moved and were shaken, because he was wrath. There went up a smoke out of his nostrils, and fire out of his mouth devoured: coals were kindled by it.

He bowed the heavens also, and came down: and darkness was under his feet.

And he rode upon a cherub, and did fly: yea, he did fly upon the wings of the wind."

5. How do we approach this awesome God?

We come before God with reverence and greatly praise Him.

This is what David said.

Psalm 138:2-5
"I will worship toward thy holy temple ...for thou hast magnified thy word above all thy name.

All the kings of the earth shall praise thee, O LORD, when they hear the words of thy mouth.

Yea, they shall sing in the ways of the LORD: for great is the glory of the LORD."

Psalm 104:1-2

"Bless the LORD, O my soul. O LORD my God, thou art very great; thou art clothed with honour and majesty. Who coverest thyself with light as with a garment:"

What is the appropriate way of approaching God?

We need to be clean.

When we come before God we ask Him to cleanse us from all sin and sanctify us with the precious Blood of Jesus.

Psalm 24:3-4

"Who shall ascend into the hill of the LORD? or who shall stand in his holy place?

He that hath clean hands, and a pure heart."

Matthew 6:9-12

"Our Father which art in heaven, Hallowed be thy name. Thy kingdom come, Thy will be done in earth, as it is in heaven ... forgive us our sins."

I John 1:7

"And the blood of Jesus Christ his Son cleanseth us from all sin."

Thanksgiving, Praise and Worship

Once we have been sanctified we do three things:

a. We Thank Him.

b. We Praise Him.

c. We Worship Him.

Our thanksgiving, praise and worship is directed toward God the Father, Jesus Christ the Son and the Holy Spirit.

Thanksgiving

The word thanksgiving means an expression of gratitude to God.

(Saying thanks to God)

We thank Him for all the things that He has done for us and others.

Thank you God:

For giving Yourself to be my God

For being my Heavenly Father

For giving Jesus Christ as my Savior

For giving me the Holy Spirit

For giving me the Word of God

For saving me

For writing my name in the Book of Life

For giving me everlasting life

For delivering me from sinful habits

For restoring my soul

For healing me

For supplying all my needs

For your Divine Nature of love, mercy, kindness, truth, justice, life, peace, joy.

For all your provisions and blessings

For all the many other things You do for me.

Praise

To praise God means to extol and glorify Him.

To extol Him for His attributes, deeds and who He is.

Praising God can be done privately in our home or openly before people.

It can also be done together with other Christians with prayers or songs of praise.

There are five different utterances of praise:

1. Words of praise.
2. Statements of praise.
3. Songs of praise.
4. Scriptures of praise.
5. Prayers of praise.

Thanksgiving, Praise and Worship

There are four important aspects of praise we need to know:

1. Praise is a powerful weapon.

Acts 16:25-26
"And at midnight Paul and Silas prayed, and sang praises unto God: and the prisoners heard them.

And suddenly there was a great earthquake, so that the foundations of the prison were shaken: and immediately all the doors were opened, and every one's bands were loosed."

2 Chronicles 20:22
"And when they began to sing and to praise, the LORD set ambushments against the children of Ammon, Moab, and mount Seir, which were come against Judah; and they were smitten."

Praise is a powerful weapon that brings about the defeat of our enemies.

2. We praise God for who He is.

We praise Him for His:

Greatness

Excellence

Omnipotence

Omniscience

Omnipresence

Eternal existence

Divine Nature

There are many other things to praise God for.

His praise should be continually within our mouth.

PSALM 34:1
"I will bless the LORD at all times: his praise shall continually be in my mouth."

3. Praise is a way of entry into God's Courts.

PSALM 100:4
"Enter into his gates with thanksgiving, and into his courts with praise."

It is with praise that we are allowed entrance into these exclusive Heavenly Courts.

There we experience more of God and the things of God.

It is there that we are clothed with a special garment of praise.

ISAIAH 61:3
"To give unto them … the garment of praise."

4. God is to be praised continually and in all circumstances.

Psalm 71:8
"Let my mouth be filled with thy praise and with thy honour all the day."

Hebrews 13:15
"By him therefore let us offer the sacrifice of praise to God continually."

We can praise God in difficult times because we know that all things we experience are for our good.

Romans 8:28
"And we know that all things work together for good to them that love God."

Children normally enjoy a close relationship with their parents.

A child may sit on a father's knee, look into his eyes and experience a special closeness to him.

There is something special in this relationship of sharing intimate feelings and words of love.

This loving relationship of God's children and their Heavenly Father is wonderful.

In these moments of worship we are and feel close to God.

Similarly we also experience precious moments in worshiping our lord Jesus Christ and the Holy Spirit.

Worshiping God

The word worship means to be devoted to, honor, respect and adore someone of Divinity.

Worshiping God is a deep spiritual experience and may be expressed in four ways:

1. Our worship may be expressed outwardly with words and gifts to God.

We have the example of Mary Magdalene worshiping Jesus with a gift in the company of others.

LUKE 7:37-38
"And, behold, a woman in the city, which was a sinner, when she knew that Jesus sat at meat in the Pharisee's house, brought an alabaster box of ointment,

And stood at his feet behind him weeping, and began to wash his feet with tears, and did wipe them with the hairs of her head, and kissed his feet, and anointed them with the ointment."

2. Worship can also be very intimate.

When we are alone with God we can share our deep innermost secrets and warm feelings of love for Him.

Thanksgiving, Praise and Worship

3. We may also worship God as Priests, in our Priestly Office.

As Children of God, Jesus has appointed us to be a Royal Priesthood unto God.

REVELATION 5:10
"And hast made us unto our God… priests"

1 PETER 2:9
"But ye are a chosen generation, a royal priesthood."

It is our Priestly responsibility to offer up praise and worship to Him.

2 PETER 2:5
"A royal priesthood… that ye should shew forth the praises of him;"

HEBREWS 13:15
"By him therefore let us offer the sacrifice of praise to God continually, that is, the fruit of our lips giving thanks to his name."

As Priests we may spend time in God's presence bringing Him our sacrifices of worship.

Our sacrifices ascend before His Throne as holy incense and are:

a. Sacrifices of our lips.

b. Sacrifices of our body. (This could be suffering through persecution or fasting.)

ROMANS 12:1
"I beseech you therefore, brethren, by the mercies of God, that ye present your bodies a living sacrifice, holy, acceptable unto God, which is your reasonable service."

4. Worship is a Ministry of excellence in the Temple.

The worship in Solomon's Temple was a wonderful example of excellence.

Four thousand people praised God.

1 CHRONICLES 23:5

"Four thousand praised the LORD with the instruments which I made, said David, to praise therewith."

Thanksgiving, Praise and Worship

One hundred and twenty Priests played trumpets.

2 Chronicles 5:12

"Being arrayed in white linen, having cymbals and psalteries and harps, stood at the east end of the altar, and with them an hundred and twenty priests sounding with trumpets:"

Twenty-four choirs sang with one hundred and fifty members in each choir.

Each ministered unto the Lord for periods of two weeks in the Temple.

They came to Jerusalem from all over Israel.

Once a year four thousand came together in one mass choir and sang for two weeks during the main Feast. All things were done excellently unto the Lord.

Josephus the historian said that the music and singing during this time could be heard echoing for miles over the mountains near Jerusalem.

The priestly activities of the Old Testament Tabernacle are symbolical of our New Testament priestly activities.

This Tabernacle in the wilderness consisted of an outer court, a holy place and a holy of holies.

We are the Temples of the Holy Spirit in this New Testament dispensation.

We consist of three parts:

A body

A soul

A spirit

1 Corinthians 6:19

"Your body is the temple of the Holy Ghost which is in you."

The Outer Court of the Old Testament Tabernacle is symbolical of our human body where physical sacrifices are made to God.

With our bodies we kneel, speak, sing and lift up our hands.

The Holy Place is symbolical of the human soul and here from our emotion, mind and will we offer the incense of praise and worship to God.

These are our thoughts, feelings and decisions of praise and worship.

The Holy of Holies is symbolical of the human spirit where God is present.

Our worship of God knows three dimensions:

1. Worshiping God with our physical Body.
2. Worshiping God with our Soul.
3. Worshiping God with our Spirit.

Worshiping God is the highest ultimate experience of heaven, earth and creation.

Revelation 4:8-11

"And the four beasts … rest not day and night, saying, Holy, holy, holy, LORD God Almighty, which was, and is, and is to come.

The four and twenty elders fall down before him that sat on the throne, and worship him that liveth forever and ever, and cast their crowns before the throne, saying,

Thou art worthy, O Lord, to receive glory and honour and power: for thou hast created all things, and for thy pleasure they are and were created."

We are called to worship God in Spirit:

John 4:23

"True worshippers ... worship the Father in spirit and in truth: for the Father seeketh such to worship him."

Spiritual worship is deeper than physical or intellectual worship.

It comes from the realm of the spirit.

Genuine true spirit worship pleases God more than all other forms of worship.

It is the most important activity of our spiritual lives.

It may take place at all times, in all circumstances and all situations.

Ephesians 5:20

"Giving thanks always for all things unto God and the Father in the name of our Lord Jesus Christ;"

In times of desperate need, worshiping God takes precedence over our need.

We first worship God and then He will take care of our needs.

Thanksgiving, Praise and Worship

Mark 7:25

"For a certain woman, whose young daughter had an unclean spirit, heard of him, and came and fell at his feet:"

After she fell at Jesus feet and worshipped Him, He took care of her need.

There are three kinds of worship:

1. Strange worship.

Leviticus 10:1
"And Nadab and Abihu, the sons of Aaron, took either of them his censer, and put fire therein, and put incense thereon, and offered strange fire before the LORD, which he commanded them not."

2. Ignorant worship.

Manmade forms of liturgical or traditional worship are not pleasing to God.

Jesus said:

Matthew 15:9
"But in vain they do worship me, teaching for doctrines the commandments of men."

Paul speaks of people who worship God in ignorance.

Acts 17:23
"To the unknown God. Whom therefore ye ignorantly worship."

We should not be ignorant in worship.

The Bible clearly teaches us what we have to do.

3. True worship.

This kind of worship costs something and God demands our best.

1 Chronicles 16:29
"Give unto the LORD the glory due unto his name: bring an offering, and come before him: worship the LORD in the beauty of holiness."

Malachi 1:6-8
"Where is mine honour? Where is my fear? saith the LORD of hosts unto you, O priests, that despise my name. Ye offer polluted bread upon mine altar;

And if ye offer the blind for sacrifice, is it not evil? And if ye offer the lame and sick, is it not evil? Offer it now unto thy governor; will he be pleased with thee, or accept thy person? saith the LORD of hosts."

When David worshipped the Lord God, it cost him a great price.

Thanksgiving, Praise and Worship

1 Chronicles 21:23-24

"And Ornan said unto David, Take it to thee, and let my lord the king do that which is good in his eyes: lo, I give thee the oxen also for burnt offerings, and the threshing instruments for wood, and the wheat for the meat offering; I give it all.

And king David said to Ornan, Nay; but I will verily buy it for the full price: for I will not take that which is thine for the LORD, nor offer burnt offerings without cost."

There is a definite way of approaching God:

Psalm 100:4

"Enter into his gates with thanksgiving, and into his courts with praise: be thankful unto him, and bless his name."

It is threefold:

1. We firstly enter the gates of God's presence with thanksgiving.

2. We then enter His courts with praise.

Here we are drawn closer to God because He inhabits our praises.

PSALM 22:3
"But thou art holy, O thou that inhabits the praises of Israel."

The Hebrew word for inhabit is "yashab" and means to sit or dwell with.

3. We love and worship God.

Understanding the Hebrew words relating to thanksgiving, praise and worship.

Here are eight words that are used:

1. Hallal.

This word occurs eighty-eight times in the New Testament and means to celebrate or boast in the Lord.

When we boast about God, everyone knows how we feel about Him.

He is exalted as the greatest!

We call all our family and friends together to celebrate Him.

He is our celebration!

2. Hilluwi.

It means to say thanks for what God has given.

3. Tehillah.

It means to sing or boast in the Lord.

4. Shabach.

It means to shout in triumph when experiencing victory.

5. Yadah.

It means to lift up and extend our hands in adoration towards God.

6. Barak.

It means to kneel before God in adoration.

7. Towdah.

It means to lift up and extend our hands in thanksgiving to God.

8. Zamar.

It means to touch and play the strings of a musical instrument with great rejoicing and praise.

God wants us to experience and enjoy all forms of praise and worship.

There is a definite measuring scale of thanksgiving, praise and worship.

It ranges from the lowest to the highest level of praise:

1. Natures praise is the lowest form.

Luke 19:37-40
"And when he was come nigh, even now at the descent of the mount of Olives, the whole multitude of the disciples began to rejoice and praise God with a loud voice for all the mighty works that they had seen;

Saying, Blessed be the King that cometh in the name of the Lord: peace in heaven, and glory in the highest.

And he answered and said unto them, I tell you that, if these should hold their peace, **the stones would immediately cry out.**"

This is a praise that ascends to God from all of nature.

2. Babes and sucklings.

This praise is higher than that of creation.

Matthew 21:16
"Have ye never read, Out of the mouth of babes and suckling's thou hast perfected praise?"

3. Spirit Praise.

This is the highest form of praise and worship.

1 Corinthians 14:15
"What is it then? **I will pray with the spirit,** and I will pray with the understanding also: **I will sing with the spirit."**

This is speaking and singing to God with our human spirit by the Holy Spirit.

It is speaking and singing in tongues **"glossais"** which is **"heavenly languages".**

That's what happened to Paul and Silas in **Acts 16:25.**

Their praises became the high praises of God and caused an earthquake that shook the foundations of the prison and brought about their deliverance.

David refers to this kind of praise.

Psalm 149:6-9
"Let the high praises of God be in their mouth, and a two-edged sword in their hand:

To execute vengeance upon the heathen, and punishments upon the people;

To bind their kings with chains, and their nobles with fetters of iron;

To execute upon them the judgment written: This honour have all his saints. Praise ye the LORD."

*This is a **God kind of praise and worship.***

What is incorrect or incomplete thanksgiving, praise and worship?

Thanksgiving, praise and worship to God often needs to be corrected or perfected:

Incorrect praise is:

In ignorance

With pride

Incomplete

Traditional

It may need correcting, adjusting or perfecting.

The Holy Spirit perfects the praise and worship of Christians.

Acts 2:11-17

"We do hear them speak in our tongues the wonderful works of God.

And they were all amazed, and were in doubt, saying one to another, what meaneth this?

But Peter, standing up with the eleven, lifted up his voice, and said unto them,

This is that which was spoken by the prophet Joel:

And it shall come to pass in the last days, saith God, I will pour out of my Spirit upon all flesh:"

Thanksgiving, Praise and Worship

Thanksgiving, praise and worship is very important for end-time Christians.

We know that the Holy Spirit is restoring the end-time Church of Jesus Christ.

Christians are being enlarged in their spiritual understanding.

Their intentions and expressions of thanksgiving, praise and worship are being purified.

We have been given a prophetic word about this.

Acts 15:16

"After this I will return, and will build again the tabernacle of David, which is fallen down; and I will build again the ruins thereof, and I will set it up:"

David built this Tabernacle for the Ark of the Covenant.

It was there where he came before the Lord in worship.

It was a place where God manifested His presence and glory.

When the Temple of Solomon was built, the Tabernacle of David was broken down.

We understand that true and glorious worship of God will be fully restored in the end-time.

David exhorts us to praise God in his last recorded Psalm:

Psalm 150:1-6

"Praise ye the LORD. Praise God in his sanctuary: praise him in the firmament of his power.

Praise him for his mighty acts: praise him according to his excellent greatness.

Praise him with the sound of the trumpet: praise him with the psaltery and harp.

Praise him with the timbrel and dance: praise him with stringed instruments and organs.

Praise him upon the loud cymbals: praise him upon the high sounding cymbals.

Let everything that hath breath praise the LORD. Praise ye the LORD."

CHAPTER 19

The Purposes of God

God is eternal and has eternal plans and purposes:

EPHESIANS 3:11

"According to the eternal purpose which God purposed in Christ Jesus our Lord:"

In the eternal past, God created Heaven and all its glorious Creatures.

He created:

Seraphim and Cherubim

Michael, Gabriel and Lucifer the three Archangels

Myriads of Angels divided in three groups, each under an Archangel

It was during this time that lucifer instigated a rebellion against God.

He persuaded the third of the Angels under his authority to rebel with him against God.

Because of their rebellion God cast these rebels out of Heaven.

Ezekiel 28:13-15

"Thou hast been in Eden the garden of God; every precious stone was thy covering, the sardius, topaz, and the diamond, the beryl, the onyx, and the jasper, the sapphire, the emerald, and the carbuncle, and gold: the workmanship of thy tabrets and of thy pipes was prepared in thee in the day that thou wast created.

Thou art the anointed cherub that covereth; and I have set thee so: thou wast upon the holy mountain of God; thou hast walked up and down in the midst of the stones of fire.

Thou wast perfect in thy ways from the day that thou wast created, till iniquity was found in thee."

Isaiah 14:12-15

"How art thou fallen from heaven, O Lucifer, son of the morning! how art thou cut down to the ground, For thou hast said in thine heart, I will ascend into heaven, I will exalt my throne above the stars of

God: I will sit also upon the mount of the congregation, in the sides of the north:

I will ascend above the heights of the clouds; I will be like the most High.

Yet thou shalt be brought down to hell, to the sides of the pit."

This rebellion of lucifer brought contamination to the Heavens and the Earth.

The two Archangels Michael and Gabriel together with two thirds of the Angelic hosts remain loyal to God until this day.

Yet there remains a need for cleansing and restoration because of satan.

God planned and decreed by His purposes to bring about total restoration to the Heavens and the Earth.

The plans and purposes of God have been mysterious.

Ephesians 1:9-10

"Having made known unto us the mystery of his will, according to his good pleasure which he hath purposed in himself:

That in the dispensation of the fulness of times he might gather together in one all things in Christ, both which are in heaven, and which are on earth; even in him:"

In God's program everything is timed with perfect precision.

ECCLESIASTES 3:1

"To everything there is a season, and a time to every purpose under the heaven:"

JOB 24:1

"Why, seeing times are not hidden from the Almighty."

Eternity existed before God created time.

Time is related to the universe.

Time was created by God with a beginning and an end.

The Bible mentions the beginning and the end of time.

GENESIS 1:1

"In the beginning God created the heaven and the earth."

REVELATION 10:6

"That there should be time no longer:"

The Bible teaches that there are numerous ages.

EPHESIANS 3:21

"Throughout **all age's** world without end."

There are three age periods:

1. Past Age's

These past ages existed before the Garden of Eden.

2. The present Age

This present age was from Eden to the end of the Millennial reign of Jesus Christ.

3. Future Age's

These are future eternal ages.

The future age's are after the Millennium reign of Christ.

EPHESIANS 2:7

"That in the **ages to come** he might shew the exceeding riches of his grace."

Now let us look at these ages in more detail.

The Past Ages

These are pre-edenic ages existing before the creation of the Garden of Eden.

Very little information is given in the Bible of the past ages.

This Present Age

It begins when God created the Heavens and the Earth.

Genesis 1

"In the beginning God created the heaven and the earth."

The Bible refers to this age as **sundry times.** (Different times.)

Hebrews 1:1

"God, who at sundry times and in divers manners spake unto the fathers by the prophets."

This present Age covers a period of seven thousand years, from Adam to the end of the Millennium.

The seven creation days in **Genesis 1** are symbolical of the seven thousand years of this present age.

The six days symbolize the six thousand years of man on earth.

The seventh day of rest (the Sabbath) symbolizes the Millennium, which is one thousand years of Christ's Kingdom on earth.

One day, prophetically spoken, is symbolical of a thousand years in scripture.

2 Peter 3:8

"But, beloved, be not ignorant of this one thing, that one day is with the Lord as a thousand years, and a thousand years as one day."

Each of the 7 days represented a thousand years in this present age.

These seven thousand years are made up of dispensations.

A Dispensation is a period of time during which God deals with man in a specific way.

Each of these dispensations introduce and complete God's purposes for man for that specific time.

Ephesians 1:10

"That in the dispensation of the fullness of times he might gather together in one all things in Christ."

Each time that God changes His global way of dealing with man, a new Dispensation begins.

This present Age is made up of seven dispensations:

1. The Dispensation of Innocence
2. The Dispensation of Conscience
3. The Dispensation of Nations
4. The Dispensation of Patriarchs
5. The Dispensation of Law
6. The Dispensation of Grace
7. The Messianic Dispensation

Let us look at each of these dispensations:

1. The Dispensation of Innocence.

In Genesis chapters one and two we read that God created everything in an atmosphere of innocence. There was a total absence of sin and man had no knowledge or experience of sin.

Adam and Eve lived in the Garden of Eden in absolute innocence of sin.

This dispensation of innocence ended when they sinned.

God changed His dealings with humanity because of their experience of sin.

The Purposes of God

Genesis 3:6
"And when the woman saw that the tree was good for food, and that it was pleasant to the eyes, and a tree to be desired to make one wise, she took of the fruit thereof, and did eat, and gave also unto her husband with her; and he did eat."

Verses 22-23
"And the LORD God said, Behold, the man is become as one of us, to know good and evil: Therefore the LORD God sent him forth from the Garden of Eden."

2. The Dispensation of Conscience.

Adam, Eve and their offspring now directed what they did by their conscience.

They and their descendents had the choice of serving God or the devil.

Abel pleased God and his offering was accepted.

In his bloodline people like Seth, Enoch, Methuselah, Lamech and Noah chose to serve God.

Cain displeased God and his offering was rejected.

His descendents multiplied and were exceedingly ungodly.

Genesis 6:11-13
"The earth also was corrupt before God, and the earth was filled with violence.

And God said unto Noah, The end of all flesh is come before me; for the earth is filled with violence through them; and, behold, I will destroy them with the earth."

Noah found grace in the eyes of God. God commanded him to build an ark and prepare for the great flood that would destroy the whole earth. After the flood subsided the only survivors were Noah and his family.

This brought about the end of the dispensation of conscience and the beginning of the new dispensation of Nations.

3. The Dispensation of Nations.

Noah, his three sons, Shem, Ham, Japheth and their families went out from the Ark. As they multiplied their children and descendents filled the earth.

Initially, God dealt with all mankind as one people.

They became united in a rebellion against God.

They built the Tower of Babel and God had to change His dealings with them.

God caused them to speak different languages, separated them from one another and they became different nations.

GENESIS 11:1-9
"And the whole earth was of one language, and of one speech.

And they said, Go to, let us build us a city and a tower, whose top may reach unto heaven; and let us make us a name, lest we be scattered abroad upon the face of the whole earth.

And the LORD said, Behold, the people is one, and they have all one language and now nothing will be restrained from them, which they have imagined to do.

Go to, let us go down, and there confound their language, that they may not understand one another's speech. So the LORD scattered them abroad from thence upon the face of all the earth: and they left off to build the city.

Therefore is the name of it called Babel:"

It was in this dispensation that God scattered men and defined the boundaries of the nations.

Acts 17:26
"And hath made of one blood all nations of men for to dwell on all the face of the earth, and hath determined the times before appointed, and the bounds of their habitation;"

Kingdoms and Governments were established and God began to deal with individual nations separately.

From the lineage of Shem, we have the Semitic nations that are Syrian, Asiatic and Jewish.

From Ham's lineage we have the Hametic Nations that are Arabic and African.

From Japheth's lineage, we have the Japhetic Nations that are European.

All nations take their lineage from these roots.

4. The Dispensation of Patriarchs.

This dispensation began when God called out one of the nations for Himself.

It extends from the call of Abraham to the giving of the Ten Commandments on Mt Sinai.

It includes the four hundred years of captivity of the Israelites in Egypt.

This dispensation relates to Gods dealings with the three Patriarchs:

1. Abraham

2. Isaac

3. Jacob

In this dispensation God called and established the nation of Israel.

He called Abraham to be its progenitor.

GENESIS 12:1
"Now the LORD had said unto Abram, Get thee out of thy country, and from thy kindred, and from thy father's house, unto a land that I will shew thee:"

The Purposes of God

God promised to bless Abraham, making his descendents a great nation and gave them a land for their eternal possession.

He made a Covenant with Abraham and instituted the circumcision of all the newborn eight-day-old males of Israel.

This made them different from other nations.

When Abraham died, God called his son Isaac to continue with his father's legacy.

He continued God's covenant, circumcision and sacrificial worship.

When Isaac died God continued His covenant with Jacob.

Jacob wrestled with an Angel and received a special blessing from God.

His name was changed to Israel and it became the name of God's chosen Nation.

The twelve sons of Jacob became the progenitors of the twelve tribes of Israel.

Exodus 1:1-5
"Now these are the names of the children of Israel, which came into Egypt; every man and his household came with Jacob.

Reuben, Simeon, Levi, and Judah,

Issachar, Zebulun, and Benjamin,

Dan, and Naphtali, Gad, and Asher.

And all the souls that came out of the loins of Jacob were seventy souls: for Joseph was in Egypt already."

In Egypt, Israel multiplied from seventy souls to over two million souls within four hundred years.

It was the time of waiting for the next dispensation.

It was during this dispensation of Patriarchs that Israel was severely tested in Egypt, to prepare her for the next dispensation. She experienced a mighty demonstration of God's power in defeating Pharaoh and being delivered.

5. The Dispensation of the Law.

This dispensation begins at Mt Sinai and ends at the death of our Lord Jesus Christ.

God used Moses as His instrument to give His moral, civil and health laws to Israel and ultimately the whole world.

He anointed and empowered Moses to lead Israel through the wilderness and commanded him to build a Tabernacle.

It was here that God manifested His presence and shekinah glory.

Animals were sacrificed by High Priests and Priests.

The shedding of animal blood covered the sins of the people in God's sight.

Other deliverers followed Moses, like Joshua, Gideon, Deborah and Samson.

The Purposes of God

Then God gave Israel a Prophet called Samuel and his ministry paved the way for many other Prophets to follow.

These were prophets like Elijah, Elisha, Isaiah, Jeremiah, Ezekiel and Daniel.

Then at Israel's request God made Israel a kingdom and gave her Kings.

Saul, David and Solomon each reigned for forty years.

Israel was then divided into a Northern and Southern Kingdom under many different Kings.

The northern kingdom was taken captive by Assyria and the southern kingdom by Babylon.

Under the leadership of Ezra and Nehemiah the Israelites returned from captivity to the land of Israel.

For four hundred years under Maccabean rule, Israel awaited the coming of their Messiah.

Jesus Christ made His appearance toward the end of this dispensation.

Jesus was the only begotten Son of God and God's gift to mankind.

He was the perfect sacrificial Lamb of God to be sacrificed for the sin of mankind.

He was the promised Messiah.

John 1:29

"The next day John seeth Jesus coming unto him, and saith, Behold the Lamb of God, which taketh away the sin of the world."

Jesus lived a perfect sinless life and fulfilled all the prescriptions of the Torah.

He is the perfect Prophet, Priest and King.

When He was sacrificed on the Cross of Calvary, He shed his precious Blood to pay the price, procuring redemption, salvation, spiritual cleansing and healing for all who believed in Him.

Matthew 27:31

"And after that they had mocked him, they took the robe off from him, and put his own raiment on him, and led him away to crucify him."

Isaiah 53:5

"But he was wounded for our transgressions, he was bruised for our iniquities: the chastisement of our peace was upon him; and with his stripes we are healed."

6. The Dispensation of Grace.

The death and resurrection of Jesus Christ instituted this dispensation.

This dispensation brought about salvation in a new way.

It was by God's grace.

The Purposes of God

Ephesians 2:8
"For by grace are ye saved through faith; and that not of yourselves: it is the gift of God:"

This dispensation begins at the resurrection of Jesus Christ and continues to His Second Coming.

It introduced salvation and remission of sin, by faith in God.

It dispels all fears of failing to keep the law and introduces new hope of forgiveness of sin.

1 Corinthians 15:14-17
"And if Christ be not risen, then is our preaching vain, and your faith is also vain.

And if Christ be not raised, your faith is vain; ye are yet in your sins."

In this new dispensation Believers experience the following:

Salvation

Water baptism

The baptism of the Holy Spirit

The Fruits, Gifts and Ministries of the Holy Spirit

Overcoming by Grace

The dispensation of Grace covers a period of approximately two thousand years and is divided into seven Church periods.

REVELATION 1:13, 20
"And in the midst of the seven candlesticks one like unto the Son of man.

The seven candlesticks which thou sawest are the seven churches."

John the Apostle saw Jesus standing in the midst of the Seven Churches.

They are symbolical of the seven church periods or the seven kinds of churches during the dispensation of Grace. **(Rev 2 & 3)**

These seven churches or church periods are:

1. Ephesus
2. Smyrna
3. Pergamos
4. Thyatira
5. Sardis
6. Philadelphia
7. Laodicea

There were many churches in Asia when John wrote the book of Revelation.

It is clear that the Lord chose the seven churches to represent **seven church periods** or **seven kinds of churches** in this dispensation.

- *Each church is assigned an Angel to help the church.*

The Purposes of God

REVELATION 1:20

"The seven stars are the angels of the seven churches:"

- *Each church receives a portion of the Holy Spirits power and blessing.*

REVELATION 5:6

"The seven Spirits of God sent forth into all the earth."

REVELATION 2:7

"Let him hear what the Spirit saith unto the churches;"

- *The spiritual condition of each of these seven churches is revealed.*

The Seven Church periods:

1. The Ephesus Church (From the time of the Apostles to the Church Fathers)

REVELATION 2:1-7
This was the first dynamic Apostolic Church of the book of Acts.

Christians experienced and continued in the power of God and holiness.

False leaders arose and the church began to backslide, losing her first love.

Paul warned the church of this.

ACTS 20:29-30
"For I know this, that after my departing shall grievous wolves enter in among you, not sparing the flock.

Also of your own selves shall men arise, speaking perverse things, to draw away disciples after them."

2. *The Smyrna Church* (From the Church Fathers to the Dark Ages)

REVELATION 2:8-11
Great spiritual leaders arose to continue contending for the faith delivered to them by the Apostles.

In Church History they were referred to as Church Fathers.

These were men like Polycarp, a spiritual son of the Apostle John.

Justin Martyr whose writings defended Christianity.

Ignatius who encouraged and gave counsel to the elders of the Church.

The church of this period experienced much tribulation and persecution.

3. *The Pergamos Church* (From the Dark Ages to Martin Luther)

Revelation 2:12-17
This church continued to experience persecution.

It was a church misled by false prophets being subjected to many heresies and false teachings.

It encountered a dark spiritual period.

The priests had Bibles but the people did not.

During this time the church lost most of the basic teachings of the Apostles.

4. *The Thyatira Church* (From Martin Luther to John Wesley)

Revelation 2:18-29
It was during this time that there arose men like William Tyndale, Miles Coverdale and John Rogers.

They translated the Bible from the original languages into the language of the common people.

Then God raised up a man called Martin Luther who realized the importance of faith. Against great opposition he preached that just men should live by faith.

Those who were servants of God during this church period could truly be described as ministers of love, service, faith, patience and good works.

5. *The Sardis Church* (From John Wesley to Azusa Street)

REVELATION 3:1-6
When John Wesley began to preach repentance of sin and salvation, he ushered in a new era.

Throughout the world, people began to turn to God in repentance.

Great spiritual leaders arose like Charles Finney, George Whitefield, D L Moody and others, and many people were saved and baptized.

6. The Philadelphia Church (From Azusa Street to the end time Church)

REVELATION 3:7-13
During a service held at the Apostolic Faith Mission in Azusa Street, Los Angeles, people were baptized in the Holy Spirit and began to speak in tongues.

This was the beginning of a great end time Holy Spirit outpouring and it spread across the world to every continent. It was a God given open door that no person or organization could shut. This Holy Spirit experience is still enjoyed today by millions of Christians worldwide.

The Purposes of God

7. *The Laodicea Church.* (The end time Church)

Revelation 3:14-22
This describes the end time church today which is a lukewarm church.

A church that thinks she is rich, clothed with righteousness and has spiritual vision.

This church is ignorant of the fact that she is poor, naked and spiritually blind.

The Lord Jesus Christ stands on the outside of the church knocking at the door, wanting to come in.

For those who open to Him, He will come in and bring great restoration, refreshing and anointing.

At the end of this dispensation Jesus Christ will return to Rapture His Church.

Matthew 24:39-42
"So shall also the coming of the Son of man be.

Then shall two be in the field; the one shall be taken, and the other left.

Two women shall be grinding at the mill; the one shall be taken, and the other left. Watch therefore: for ye know not what hour your Lord doth come."

1 Thessalonians 4:16-17
"For the Lord himself shall descend from heaven with a shout, with the voice of the archangel, and with the trump of God: and the dead in Christ shall rise first:

Then we, which are alive and remain shall be caught up together with them in the clouds, to meet the Lord in the air: and so shall we ever be with the Lord."

Before Jesus returns two things will happen:

1. There will be a falling away from the faith of many Christians.

2. *The antichrist, the son of perdition will be revealed.*

2 Thessalonians 2:1-3
"Now we beseech you, brethren, by the coming of our Lord Jesus Christ, and by our gathering together unto him,

Let no man deceive you by any means: for that day shall not come, except there come a falling away first, and that man of sin be revealed, the son of perdition;"

This man of sin the antichrist, will reign over the earth and he will sign a seven-year contract with Israel.

He will force all people on earth to receive the Mark of the Beast.

Revelation 13:16-18

"And he causeth all, both small and great, rich and poor, free and bond, to receive a mark in their right hand, or in their foreheads:

No man might buy or sell, save he that had the mark, or the name of the beast, or the number of his name.

Here is wisdom. Let him that hath understanding count the number of the beast: for it is the number of a man; and his number is Six hundred threescore and six."

He will severely and cruelly persecute the Saints.

Revelation 13:7

"And it was given unto him to make war with the saints, and to overcome them:"

Daniel 8:24

"And his power shall be mighty... and shall destroy the mighty and the holy people."

Revelation 20:4

"I saw the souls of them that were beheaded for the witness of Jesus, and for the word of God, and which had not worshipped the beast, neither his image, neither had received his mark upon their foreheads, or in their hands;"

After three and a half years the antichrist will enter the newly built Temple in Jerusalem and demand to be worshipped as god, but will be rejected by Israel.

He will then break his seven-year contract with Israel and persecute her.

During these seven years there will be great tribulation in this world as never seen before. More than half of mankind will die by war, disease or catastrophe.

A third of vegetation and animals will be destroyed.

The heavens will be shaken and the earth destroyed by earthquakes, disasters and meteorites.

Here are some scriptures that describe this holocaust:

Luke 21:25-26

"And there shall be signs in the sun, and in the moon, and in the stars; and upon the earth distress of nations, with perplexity; the sea and the waves roaring;

Men's hearts failing them for fear, and for looking after those things which are coming on the earth: for the powers of heaven shall be shaken."

Revelation 16:18-21

"And there were voices, and thunders, and lightnings; and there was a great earthquake, such as was not since men were upon the earth, so mighty an earthquake, and so great.

And every island fled away, and the mountains were not found.

And there fell upon men a great hail out of heaven, every stone about the weight of a talent: and men blasphemed God because of the plague of the hail; for the plague thereof was exceeding great."

Revelation 6:4-8

"And there went out another horse that was red: and power was given to him that sat thereon to take peace from the earth, and that they should kill one another:

And I looked, and behold a pale horse: and his name that sat on him was Death, and Hell followed with him. And power was given unto them over the fourth part of the earth, to kill with sword, and with hunger, and with death, and with the beasts of the earth."

Revelation 8:7

"The first angel sounded, and there followed hail and fire mingled with blood, and they were cast upon the earth: and the third part of trees was burnt up, and all green grass was burnt up."

The Bible declares that God will shorten this time in order to save mankind from total annihilation.

Matthew 24:22

"And except those days should be shortened, there should no flesh be saved:"

7. The Messianic Dispensation.

This one thousand year dispensation begins at Christ's Second Coming.

The Lord's second coming is described in:

Zechariah 14:1-4

"Behold, the day of the LORD cometh.

And his feet shall stand in that day upon the Mount of Olives, which is before Jerusalem on the east, and the Mount of Olives shall cleave in the midst thereof toward the east and toward the west."

Then Israel will then realize that Jesus Christ is their Messiah.

They will be sorrowful and grieve for their past rejection of Him.

They will accept and welcome Him.

Zechariah 12:10

"And they shall look upon me whom they have pierced, and they shall mourn ... as one mourneth for his only son."

Jesus Christ will reign over all the Earth and there will be peace.

ZECHARIAH 14:9

"And the LORD shall be king over all the earth: in that day shall there be one LORD, and his name one."

VERSE 16

"And it shall come to pass, that every one that is left of all the nations which came against Jerusalem shall even go up from year to year to worship the King, the LORD of hosts, and to keep the feast of tabernacles."

MICAH 4:2-3

"And many nations shall come, and say, Come, and let us go up to the mountain of the LORD, and to the house of the God of Jacob; and he will teach us of his ways, and we will walk in his paths: for the law shall go forth of Zion, and the word of the LORD from Jerusalem. And he shall judge among many people, and rebuke strong nations afar off; and they shall beat their swords into plowshares, and their spears into pruning hooks: nation shall not lift up a sword against nation, neither shall they learn war anymore."

During this dispensation, satan will be bound in the bottomless pit.

REVELATION 20:2-3

"And he laid hold on the dragon, that old serpent, which is the Devil, and Satan, and bound him a thousand years, And cast him into the bottomless pit."

The antichrist and the false prophet will be cast into the lake of fire.

REVELATION 19:20

"And the beast was taken, and with him the false prophet that wrought miracles before him, with which he deceived them that had received the mark of the beast, and them that worshipped his image. These both were cast alive into a lake of fire burning with brimstone."

At the end of this dispensation satan will be loosed and will try to deceive the nations once again.

He will be defeated, cast into the lake of fire and punished forever.

REVELATION 20:7-10

"And when the thousand years are expired, Satan shall be loosed out of his prison,

And shall go out to deceive the nations.

And the devil that deceived them was cast into the lake of fire and brimstone, where the beast and the false prophet are, and shall be tormented day and night forever and ever."

The White Throne Judgment

At the end of the Messianic dispensation, the White Throne Judgment will take place and all of mankind that ever lived will be judged.

Revelation 20:11-15

"And I saw a great white throne, and him that sat on it, from whose face the earth and the heaven fled away; and there was found no place for them.

And I saw the dead, small and great, stand before God; and the books were opened: and another book was opened, which is the book of life: and the dead were judged out of those things which were written in the books, according to their works.

And the sea gave up the dead which were in it; and death and hell delivered up the dead which were in them: and they were judged every man according to their works.

And whosoever was not found written in the book of life was cast into the lake of fire."

All sinners and the followers of satan will be removed from the heavens and the earth and cast into hell.

This present age will then come to an end and time will be no more.

All Christians will then enter into the future eternal ages with a New Heaven and Earth.

2 Peter 3:13

"Nevertheless we, according to his promise, look for new heavens and a new earth, wherein dwelleth righteousness."

In the ages to come our future will be secure and we have the great assurance that we will always be with the Lord:

1 Thessalonians 4:17

"And so shall we ever be with the Lord."

It will be an everlasting experience of joy and happiness.

Revelation 21:2-4

"And I John saw the holy city, new Jerusalem, coming down from God out of heaven, prepared as a bride adorned for her husband.

And I heard a great voice out of heaven saying, Behold, the tabernacle of God is with men, and he will dwell with them, and they shall be his people, and God himself shall be with them, and be their God.

And God shall wipe away all tears from their eyes; and there shall be no more death, neither sorrow, nor crying, neither shall there be any more pain: for the former things are passed away."

All the Saints are a part of God's wonderful family.

Ephesians **2:19**

"Now therefore ye are no more strangers and foreigners, but fellow citizens with the saints, and of the household of God:"

Because we are living at the very end of the Dispensation of Grace we know that Jesus Christ is about to return to the Earth.

Let me challenge you to find your place in the plans and purposes of God right now, because you have an important role to play.

Patiently and fervently complete the assignment God has given you.

Hebrews **12:1**

"Let us run with patience the race that is set before us."

Romans 8:28

"And we know that all things work together for good to them that love God, to them who are the called according to his purpose."

Psalm 31:15

"My times are in thy hand:"

I trust that you will complete your life's mission with the words of Paul:

2 Timothy 4:7

"I have fought a good fight, I have finished my course, I have kept the faith:"

CHAPTER 20

Heaven and Hell

Heaven is a wonderful place and most people would like to go there.

Hell is just the opposite.

Heaven

There are three heavens mentioned in the Bible and they are:

1. The Atmosphere.
2. Outer Space.
3. Heaven – where God's Throne is.

1. The atmosphere or firmament.

It extends from the earth's surface to approximately a hundred and twenty miles above the earth.

It is referred to in the Bible as the place where birds fly.

Genesis 1:20
"And God said, let the waters bring forth abundantly the moving creature that hath life, and fowl that may fly above the earth in the open firmament of heaven."

2. Outer Space.

It extends beyond the earth's atmosphere and is where God placed the sun, moon and stars. God called it the firmament of heaven.

Genesis 1:16-17
"And God made two great lights; the greater light to rule the day, and the lesser light to rule the night: he made the stars also. And God set them in the firmament of the heaven to give light upon the earth."

3. Heaven

It is the place where God has set His Throne and Heavenly Kingdom.

Paul refers to this place as Paradise or the third Heaven and it is beyond the universe.

2 Corinthians 12:2-4
"I knew a man in Christ above fourteen years ago, such a one caught up to the third heaven. Caught up into Paradise."

Isaiah 14:13
"I will ascend into heaven, I will exalt my throne above the stars of God: I will sit also upon the mount of the congregation, in the sides of the north:"

It is described as a place that is somewhere in the north beyond the first and second heaven.

Psalm 75:6
"For promotion cometh neither from the east, nor from the west, nor from the south."

This could be a symbolical reason why the compass always points to the north.

It is this Heaven that God inhabits.

Psalm 68:33
"To Him that rideth upon the heavens of heavens."

Heaven is God's dwelling place.

There are six things about Heaven we should know:

1. The focal point of Heaven is the Throne of God.

This is what Isaiah saw:

Isaiah 6:1-5
"I saw also the LORD sitting upon a throne, high and lifted up, and his train filled the temple.

Above it stood the seraphim's: And one cried unto another, and said, Holy, holy, holy, is the LORD of hosts: the whole earth is full of his glory. And the posts of the door moved at the voice of him that cried, and the house was filled with smoke.

Then said I, Woe is me! for I am undone; because I am a man of unclean lips, and I dwell in the midst of a people of unclean lips: for mine eyes have seen the King, the LORD of hosts."

God's awesome presence emanates from His Throne.

John the revelator describes this.

Revelation 4:2-6

"Behold, a throne was set in heaven, and one sat on the throne.

And he that sat was to look upon like a jasper and a sardine stone: and there was a rainbow round about the throne, in sight like unto an emerald.

And round about the throne were four and twenty seats: and upon the seats I saw four and twenty elders sitting, clothed in white raiment; and they had on their heads crowns of gold.

And out of the throne proceeded lightnings and thunderings and voices: and there were seven lamps of fire burning before the throne, which are the seven Spirits of God.

And before the throne there was a sea of glass like unto crystal: and in the midst of the throne, and round about the throne, were four beasts full of eyes before and behind."

God's Throne has eternal dimensions and is surrounded by breathtaking beauty.

These boundless Heavenly domains include Palaces, Temples, Celebration Places, Banquet Halls and indescribably beautiful Mansions.

There are beautiful restful meadows, fountains, streams and lush green fields.

The sweet smelling forests are filled with the playful sounds of chirping birds, critters, friendly animals and the abundance of delicious fruits and berries.

Heaven is an abode beyond description, for the eternal pleasure and enjoyment of the Saints.

2. Heaven has a magnificent Temple:

REVELATION 11:19
"And the temple of God was opened in heaven, and there was seen in his temple the ark of his testament:"

Jesus our High Priest entered into this Temple to offer His precious blood for the remission and cleansing of all sin.

HEBREWS 9:24
"For Christ is not entered into the holy places made with hands, which are the figures of the true; but into heaven itself, now to appear in the presence of God for us:"

It is here where all overcoming Christians will live.

REVELATION 3:12

"Him that overcometh will I make a pillar in the temple of my God, and he shall go no more out:"

It is here where the Saints of God will eternally participate in holy Priesthood.

REVELATION 5:10

"And hast made us unto our God ... priests:"

3. There is also a Judgment Hall or Courtroom in Heaven.

In this Courtroom God litigates and executes His judgment.

It is here where satan comes to accuse Christians.

Job 1:6
"Now there was a day when the sons of God came to present themselves before the LORD, and Satan came also among them."

It is in this Heavenly Courtroom that Jesus Christ the righteous Advocate appears on behalf and in defense of all Christians.

1 John 2:1
"And if any man sin, we have an advocate with the Father, Jesus Christ the righteous:"

Jesus is fully qualified and capable of successfully defending every Christian.

The basis of all of God's judgments are upon the Word of God and Righteousness.

Jesus is the "Word of God" and "total righteousness."

4. There are beautiful Mansions in Heaven for Christians.

JOHN 14:2
"In my Father's house are many mansions: if it were not so, I would have told you. I go to prepare a place for you."

John describes this magnificent city and its buildings.

REVELATION 21:18-21
"And the building of the wall of it was of jasper: and the city was pure gold, like unto clear glass.

And the foundations of the wall of the city were garnished with all manner of precious stones. The first foundation was jasper; the second, sapphire; the third, a chalcedony; the fourth, an emerald;

The fifth, sardonyx; the sixth, sardius; the seventh, chrysolyte; the eighth, beryl; the ninth, a topaz; the tenth, a chrysoprasus; the eleventh, a jacinth; the twelfth, an amethyst.

And the twelve gates were twelve pearls: every several gate was of one pearl: and the street of the city was pure gold, as it were transparent glass."

These mansions by far exceed all our expectations in their design, construction, furnishings, decorations, creativity, comfort and exclusive tastes.

5. The culture of Heaven is of noblest order.

God's children are part of the Heavenly Family. There is a restful and peaceful atmosphere there.

Joy and happiness never ends.

Everything is pure and perfect.

All needs and desires are satisfied.

Feasts and Celebrations are unforgettable events.

The presence of Jesus is always longed for and sought after by the Saints.

Whenever Jesus appears there is much excitement and He also makes available personal time with every Saint.

The Saints attend events dressed in their pure white garments and wear their glorious crowns.

1 Corinthians 2:9
"But as it is written, Eye hath not seen, nor ear heard, neither have entered into the heart of man, the things which God hath prepared for them that love Him."

This Heavenly glory will never end.

6. Heaven is an after death destination for those who are children of God.

2 Corinthians 5:1-8
"For we know that if our earthly house of this tabernacle were dissolved, we have a building of

God, an house not made with hands, eternal in the heavens.

We are confident, I say, and willing rather to be absent from the body, and to be present with the Lord."

Entrance into Heaven, is by invitation of Jesus Christ only.

MATTHEW 25:21
"His lord said unto him; Well done, thou good and faithful servant: enter thou into the joy of thy lord."

Hell

There are three Hell's mentioned in the Bible and they are:

1. Sheol / Hades
2. Tartarus
3. Gehenna

1. Sheol / Hades:

The word *"Sheol"* in Hebrew is equivalent to *"Hades"* in Greek.

It means the place where the *souls of the dead are kept* after death.

Acts 2:27

"Because thou wilt not leave my soul in hell, neither wilt thou suffer thine Holy One to see corruption."

In the Old Testament, when someone died, they went to Sheol/Hades to be kept until the day of Judgment. This place is divided into two compartments and separated by a gulf or bottomless pit. It is in the heart of the earth. On the one side the righteous were kept and on the other side the unrighteous.

Jesus told a true story of two men that were kept in Sheol.

Luke 16: 20-26

"And there was a certain beggar named Lazarus, which was laid at his gate, full of sores,

And it came to pass, that the beggar died, and was carried by the angels into Abraham's bosom: the rich man also died, and was buried;

And in hell he lift up his eyes, being in torments, and seeth Abraham afar off, and Lazarus in his bosom.

And he cried and said, Father Abraham, have mercy on me, and send Lazarus, that he may dip the tip of his finger in water, and cool my tongue; for I am tormented in this flame.

But Abraham said, Son, remember that thou in thy lifetime receivedst thy good things, and likewise

Lazarus evil things: but now he is comforted, and thou art tormented.

And beside all this, between us and you there is a great gulf fixed: so that they which would pass from hence to you cannot; neither can they pass to us."

After Jesus died on the cross he descended into Sheol/Hades.

EPHESIANS 4:9-10

"Now that he ascended, what is it but that he also descended first into the lower parts of the earth?

He that descended is the same also that ascended up far above all heavens, that he might fill all things."

Sheol is within the earth and Jesus descended to it.

Jesus actually preached to everyone in Sheol.

These were the souls of those who had died up until that point in time.

They were held captive by satan.

1 PETER 3:18-19

"For Christ also hath once suffered for sins, the just for the unjust, that he might bring us to God, being put to death in the flesh, but quickened by the Spirit:

By which also he went and preached unto the spirits in prison;"

Here Jesus actually overcame and defeated satan and his kingdom, taking the keys of death and hell from him.

Revelation 1:18

"I am he that liveth, and was dead; and, behold, I am alive for evermore, Amen; and have the keys of hell and of death."

Colossians 2:15

"And having spoiled principalities and powers, he made a shew of them openly, triumphing over them in it."

At the Resurrection of Jesus all the Old Testament Saints were resurrected with Him.

Matthew 27:52-53

"And the graves were opened; and many bodies of the saints which slept arose,

And came out of the graves after his resurrection, and went into the holy city, and appeared unto many."

These resurrected Saints were taken to Heaven by Jesus.

EPHESIANS 4:8-10

"Wherefore he saith, When he ascended up on high, he led captivity captive, and gave gifts unto men.

Now that he ascended, what is it but that he also descended first into the lower parts of the earth?

He that descended is the same also that ascended up far above all heavens, that he might fill all things."

Since the time of Christ's resurrection, all saints who die go directly to Heaven.

2 CORINTHIANS 5:8

"We are confident, I say, and willing rather to be absent from the body, and to be present with the Lord."

Until this day, all the ungodly who die go down to Sheol.

They are kept there until the Day of Judgment.

When they die on earth they open their eyes in Sheol.

LUKE 16:23

"And in hell he lift up his eyes, being in torments."

2. Tartarus.

This is a place where Angels that have sinned are kept until the time of their Judgment.

2 Peter 2:4
"For if God spared not the angels that sinned, but cast them down to hell, and delivered them into chains of darkness, to be reserved unto judgment;"

The Greek word "hell" mentioned here is *"Tartarus"*.

It means the *place of keeping of fallen angels.*

Jude 6
"And the angels which kept not their first estate, but left their own habitation, he hath reserved in everlasting chains under darkness unto the judgment of the great day."

3. Gehenna.

This place is the lake of fire that is mentioned in the Bible.

Revelation 21:8
"But the fearful, and unbelieving, and the abominable, and murderers, and whoremongers, and sorcerers, and idolaters, and all liars, shall have their part in the lake which burneth with fire and brimstone: which is the second death."

Jesus mentions Gehenna twenty-two times in the Gospels.

He does not debate its existence. He confirms it.

MATTHEW 18:9
"And if thine eye offend thee, pluck it out, and cast it from thee: it is better for thee to enter into life with one eye, rather than having two eyes to be cast into hell fire."

MATTHEW 5:22
"But I say unto you, that whosoever is angry with his brother without a cause shall be in danger of the judgment: and whosoever shall say to his brother, Raca, shall be in danger of the council: but whosoever shall say, Thou fool, shall be in danger of hell fire."

The Greek word for "fire" is "Puros" and means real burning fire.

It is a sulphuric, brimstone type of fire and is much more intense in heat, than regular fire. It is like the fire that fell down on Sodom and Gomorrah.

Sheol is beneath the earth's crust at the volcanic lava-boiling center of the earth.

Gehenna is much worse. It is the lake of fire that is called the second death.

Revelation 21:8

"The lake which burneth with fire and brimstone: which is the second death."

Hell is a place of intense pain, suffering, gross darkness and eternal isolation from God.

Matthew 8:12

"But the children of the kingdom shall be cast out into outer darkness: there shall be weeping and gnashing of teeth."

It is an everlasting experience of rotting, smelling flesh, worms gnawing and penetrating the body.

Isaiah describes this:

Isaiah 66:24

"And they shall go forth, and look upon the carcasses of the men that have transgressed against me: for their worm shall not die, neither shall their fire be quenched; and they shall be an abhorring unto all flesh."

Those whose names are not found written in the Book of life are destined for Gehenna.

At the White Throne Judgment of God they will be cast into Gehenna.

Revelation 20:11-15

"And I saw a great white throne, and him that sat on it, from whose face the earth and the heaven fled away; and there was found no place for them.

And I saw the dead, small and great, stand before God; and the books were opened: and another book was opened, which is the book of life: and the dead were judged out of those things which were written in the books, according to their works.

And whosoever was not found written in the book of life was cast into the lake of fire."

These are those whose lives are contaminated with sin.

Men and women who reject the gentle conviction of the Holy Spirit to save them.

Those who have refused to receive Jesus Christ as their Lord and Savior.

Those who continue serving satan.

The devil and all those who follow him will be cast into the lake of fire and they will be tormented forever.

Revelation 20:10

"And the devil that deceived them was cast into the lake of fire and brimstone, where the beast and the false prophet are, and shall be tormented day and night forever and ever."

Be sure to escape this future horrific judgment upon all sinners.

Try to help your Family and Friends to escape this Hell experience.

If possible try to rescue all those that are heading for the lake of fire.

Jude 23

"And others save with fear, pulling them out of the fire; hating even the garment spotted by the flesh."

John 3:16

"For God so loved the world, that he gave his only begotten Son, that whosoever believeth in him should not perish."

CHAPTER 21

False Doctrines, Prophets and Lying Wonders

There are over two thousand Religions in the world today.

They have many variations and forms.

The Apostle Paul warns that people living in the last days will have a form of godliness.

2 Timothy 3:1-5

"This know also, that in the last days perilous times shall come...

For men shall have a form of godliness."

Many church goers can be described as religious.

Their religion has become a form of godliness to them.

They have substituted religion for a true spiritual experience with God.

Unfortunately many churches have become places that cater for the religious tastes of people.

Some people are offended when the sensitive and sinful issues in their lives are addressed. Many only want nice things to be said to them that do not confront sin.

Therefore they are often subjected to false doctrines.

False Doctrines:

2 Timothy 4:3

"For the time will come when they will not endure sound doctrine; but after their own lusts shall they heap to themselves teachers, having itching ears;"

We read in the Bible that there is only one true doctrine that Jesus Christ commanded us to teach.

Matthew 28:20

"Teaching them to observe all things whatsoever I have commanded you:"

The Apostles taught the people what they had learnt from Christ.

False Doctrines, Prophets and Lying Wonders

His doctrine became the doctrine of Christianity.

Acts 2:42

"And they continued stedfastly in the apostles doctrine."

It has been passed on to the generations of Christians until today.

It is to this doctrine that we must remain faithful and true.

Jude 3

"It was needful for me to write unto you, and exhort you that ye should earnestly contend for the faith which was once delivered unto the saints."

We are living in the last days.

Unfortunately people are being subjected to different forms of religion.

They accept and follow a religion and are labeled by it.

They are religious but have no power with God.

2 Timothy 3:5

"Having a form of godliness, but denying the power thereof:"

If we do not have and abide in the true doctrine of Christ, we risk the danger of moving into the realm of false doctrines.

2 John 9

"Whosoever transgresseth, and abideth not in the doctrine of Christ, hath not God. He that abideth in the doctrine of Christ, he hath both the Father and the Son."

Unfortunately many are deceived and move away from Christ's true doctrine.

They move into error following false teaching.

1 Timothy 1:3-4

"That thou mightest charge some that they teach no other doctrine,

Neither give heed to fables and endless genealogies, which minister questions, rather than godly edifying, which is in faith:"

People often believe fables, which are false teachings not based on fact.

False Doctrines, Prophets and Lying Wonders

2 Timothy 4:4

"They shall turn away their ears from the truth, and shall be turned unto fables."

It is this non-factual, incorrect, idle-talk that causes people to stray from the truth.

1 Timothy 6:20-21

"O Timothy, keep that which is committed to thy trust, avoiding profane and vain babblings, and oppositions of science falsely so called: Which some professing have erred concerning the faith."

There are seven verbal actions that bring about error and false doctrine:

1. Meaningless conversations and idle talk.
2. Irrelevant questions.
3. Uncorroborated theories.
4. Inaccurate statements.
5. Unsubstantiated reports and stories.
6. Deluded imaginations of the mind.
7. Demonic deception causing error and false doctrine.

1 Timothy 4:1

"Now the Spirit speaketh expressly, that in the latter times some shall depart from the faith, giving heed to seducing spirits and doctrines of devils;"

People are initially **diverted very slightly** from the truth and end in false doctrine.

Eventually they find that they have strayed far away from the truth.

There are three types of doctrinal and religious error:

- **A.** Minor Christian doctrinal error
- **B.** Major Christian doctrinal error
- **C.** Major non-Christian doctrinal error

A. Minor doctrinal error.

There are different religious doctrines that can be described as in minor error.

They have deviated in some way from the doctrine of Christ.

Here are four examples:

1. Religions not requiring Christians, to be water baptized by immersion.

2. Religions that do not teach and practice the Baptism of the Holy Spirit.

3. Religions that distort the doctrine of the Godhead.

4. Religions that frustrate Gods grace by holding to legalism.
These enforce the keeping of the Sabbath, the Ten Commandments and traditions of men.

B. Major doctrinal error.

There are three religions that have major doctrinal errors:

1. Mormonism.

The founder of this worldwide religion was Joseph Smith born on December 23, 1805, in Sharon, Vermont. In the year 1820 he claimed that he had received a vision in which God the Father and Jesus appeared to him. He was told that all churches were an abomination to God. In 1823, a so-called angel moroni appeared to him and told him of some golden plates which he would later find and translate. In 1830 he published the translations known today as the book of mormon. They say that it is on a higher plain than the Bible.

Here is an example of some of their major doctrinal error:

Mormonism denies salvation by faith in Jesus Christ.

It teaches that works obtain salvation progressively.

It teaches that Jesus Christ is the spirit brother of lucifer.

2. Jehovah Witnesses.

The founder of this religion was Charles T Russell. Initially he was involved in the teachings of the Seven Day Adventists. He came into disagreement with them and then launched a magazine called Zion's Watchtower and Herald of Christ's Presence.

Five years later he founded the Zion's Watchtower Tract Society.

In 1896 it was renamed the Watchtower Bible and Tract Society.

Their teachings deny or distort many significant Biblical truths.

Here is an example of some of their major doctrinal error:

They deny the unity and status of the three Persons of the Godhead.

They deny the deity of the Holy Spirit.

They deny the virgin birth of Jesus Christ.

They deny Jesus' Resurrection.

They deny Jesus' immanent second coming.

They deny Jesus' finished work on the Cross.

They deny the complete work of salvation.

They deny the reality of hell.

They have their own Bible translation, rejecting all others.

They teach that the 144,000 spoken of in Revelation 14:1 are Jehovah Witnesses.

They fail to report that these are actually Jews. (Rev 7:4-8)

3. Christian Science.

The founder of christian science was Mary Baker Eddie and was influenced by the so-called Dr P. H. Quimby. He was influenced by a mesmerist named Charles Poiyen. Charles had developed a theory of healing called the science of health, or christian science.

At the beginning of the nineteen hundreds, over 200,000 people followed Mary Baker Eddie. They regarded her as equal to and a successor to Christ. She made the same claims about herself. Although the Bible is used during their services, the real source of authority is the work of Mary Baker Eddie.

This book repudiates every important Biblical Teaching.

Here are some of their major doctrinal errors:

They deny the deity or Godhead of Jesus Christ.

They describe sin, evil, sickness and death, as allusions of the mind.

C. Major Non-Christian religious error

1. Hinduism

Most Hindus are found in India. Hinduism takes its roots back almost 3000 years, to the Indis Valley in Northern India. It is a polytheistic religion which worships many gods. Their worship takes on an idolatrous form and abounds in immoral practices of superstition, fear, occultism, demon worship and demon possession. They practice the cast system in society that places people at different levels.

Hinduism is a religion that is rigid, unjust, cruel and based on a works system.

Here are some of the peculiarities of their religion:

Hinduism teaches reincarnation.

It teaches that every person has many lives and after death are reborn into another body. This process continues until they reach a state of perfection.

False Doctrines, Prophets and Lying Wonders

They believe in the law of Karma, teaching that man will pay for today's sins in future reincarnated lives.

They deny the deity of Jesus Christ.

They deny Jesus Christ as the only way to God and salvation.

2. Buddhism.

Sidhartha Gitama was born about 560 B.C and founded this religion. Within a period of 45 years, he gathered many disciples in the northern part of India. His disciples knew him as "Buddha". At the age of 80 he died of food poisoning.

The peculiarities of this teaching:

They believe that suffering is caused by mans desire and thirst for pleasure.

They believe that by eliminating these cravings, man will overcome suffering.

They totally deny doctrines of Jesus Christ such as sin, salvation, healing, heaven, hell, and the Godhead.

Buddhists are polytheistic, pantheistic or atheistic.

3. Confucianism.

Confucius established Confucianism in 551 B.C. His real name was Chu Kung and he changed it to Confucius. He taught that man needs no help beyond himself. He taught that because man is not sinful, he doesn't need a savior. He believed and taught that by wisdom men would behave ethically. The popular religion of confucianism in China today is a combination of ancestral worship, animism and social traditions. Many confucianists are also buddhists.

4. Shintoism.

It is an indigenous religion of Japan and has been greatly influenced by buddhism and confucianism. It is made up of two Chinese words, namely:

"Shin" - which means spirit

"Tao" - which means way

These teachings made their appearance about 720 A.D.

In 1882 they were officially made the state religion of Japan.

The teachings of Shintoism include polytheism and the worship of nature.

It rejects the true God of the Bible and minimizes the idea of sin and moral guilt.

It has many social rules and unlike the Bible it is based on fables.

5. Islam

The word islam means to surrender or be brought into submission to the will of allah. The word

False Doctrines, Prophets and Lying Wonders

Moslem or muslim is related to this word and means one who submits.

Mohammad was the founder of islam.

He was born in 570 A.D. in Mecca, which is near the southwest coast of the Arabian Peninsula.

Islam combines some of the elements, of Judaism, Christianity and the native Arabian religion of that time. It contradicts many of the teachings of the Bible.

The book of islam is the koran. The muslims believe it is uncreated, eternal and supersedes the Bible. They do not believe in the Godhead, the Father, Jesus and the Holy Spirit. They reject the Biblical teachings of the crucifixion of Christ and His resurrection. Although they concede that Jesus was God's sinless prophet, they do not believe that He was the Son of God. The god allah who they worship is not merciful and compassionate. Unlike Jehovah, allah has not done anything for man that has cost him anything. Islam makes no Godly provision for forgiving and removing sin. It teaches that salvation is never certain, because it is based on mans works.

6. Occult religions.

There are six teachings that focus on certain aspects of occult activity namely:

1. Transcendental meditation.

Mahesh Warma the founder was born in India in 1918. He taught that after years of practice, a person may pass from transcendental consciousness to higher plains of cosmic consciousness and attain god consciousness. It is far removed from the teachings of the Bible. Its true objective is Hinduism.

2. The unification church.

It was founded by Sun Moon in North Korea.

In 1957 he published his book called "divine principle" and is the authoritive bases of his teachings. It is better described as monism.

He claims to be the only one who can decode the message of the Bible.

He teaches a self-type of salvation based on the human spirit and rejects salvation by grace in Jesus Christ.

Thousands follow Sun Moon and believe he is the Messiah.

3. The New Age movement.

These teachings contain a wide variety and assortment of beliefs.

Their concepts are made up of old and new mysticism.

These are presented in different wrappings that are attractive and deceiving.

In many ways it is a modern version of Hinduism.

They teach that new age enlightenment brings people to the knowledge and experience of being gods.

They actually believe in achieving the dream of being divine human masters of the universe.

To them, man has no moral responsibility to the Creator and therefore redemption and salvation are unnecessary.

They condemn Christianity for preaching the evil concept of sin, arguing that it produces negative thoughts and low self-esteem.

They reject the Divinity of Jesus and relegate Him to the position of other teachers such as buddha and mohammad.

4. Spiritualism.

It is the oldest occult religion in existence.

In civilization spiritualism has been practiced in one degree or another.

Mediums and familiar spirits are mentioned in many ancient writings and sources of the Egyptians, Babylonians and Chinese.

Because they claim to communicate with the spirits of deceased humans, mediums are used to communicate with the dead.

The Bible clearly warns against this:

LEVITICUS 19:31

"Regard not them that have familiar spirits, neither seek after wizards, to be defiled by them: I am the LORD your God."

The Bible pronounces judgment on those who practice as mediums or wizards.

LEVITICUS 20:27

"A man also or woman that hath a familiar spirit, or that is a wizard, shall surely be put to death: they shall stone them with stones: their blood shall be upon them."

5. Satanism.

It goes back to the beginning of time.

The best known modern satanist is Anton Lavey who founded the first church of satan in San Francisco.

He is the author of the satanic bible.

In satanism, satan is worshipped as god and demands that fallen angels, demons and humans worship him. The followers of satan pray to him and work miracles through his powers. Those who participate in satanism become demon possessed.

There are many evil religions around the world today that practice witchcraft.

One of them is *Voodoo*.

There are also religions that *worship the spirits of their forefathers* and practice the *worship of idols.*

False prophets and lying wonders

Jesus spoke of false prophets appearing in the last days.

Matthew 24:11

"And many false prophets shall rise, and shall deceive many."

Peter makes mention of the same.

2 Peter 2:1

"But there were false prophets also among the people, even as there shall be false teachers among you, who privily shall bring in damnable heresies, even denying the Lord that bought them, and bring upon themselves swift destruction."

It is evident that these false prophets prophesy falsely in the Name of Jesus Christ and deceive many people.

Paul warns Timothy of this.

1 Timothy 4:1

"Now the Spirit speaketh expressly, that in the latter times some shall depart from the faith, giving heed to seducing spirits, and doctrines of devils;"

In these last days we are seeing this deception on every hand.

2 John 7

"For many deceivers are entered into the world, who confess not that Jesus Christ is come in the flesh. This is a deceiver and an antichrist."

2 Timothy 3:13

"But evil men and seducers shall wax worse and worse, deceiving, and being deceived."

There are various kinds of deception:

1. Magic
2. Divination
3. Psychic phenomena
4. Astrology
5. Witchcraft
6. Demonic manifestations

False Doctrines, Prophets and Lying Wonders

These deceptions are leading the way to the greatest deception of all time.

It is the coming of the false prophet and the antichrist.

2 Thessalonians 2:8-9

"And then shall that Wicked be revealed, whom the Lord shall consume with the spirit of his mouth, and shall destroy with the brightness of his coming:

Even him, whose coming is after the working of Satan with all power and signs and lying wonders."

Revelation 13:13

"And he doeth great wonders, so that he maketh fire come down from heaven on the earth in the sight of men."

Jesus warns of deception.

He warns of the appearance of false christs and prophets who will do great miracles, signs and lying wonders in the last days.

Matthew 24:24

"For there shall arise false Christ's, and false prophets, and shall shew great signs and wonders; insomuch that, if it were possible, they shall deceive the very elect."

This deception will be so subtle; that many Christians will be deceived and depart from the faith.

1 Timothy 4:1

"Some shall depart from the faith."

A final deception that will have a global effect.

It is that of Alien Creatures and UFO deception.

UFOs are not only a modern-day phenomenon.

Sightings around the globe have been the substance of legend, as well as documented historical records, for thousands of years.

There are drawings of UFOs found in caves that date back thousands of years.

There have been many recent documented sightings and reports.

Who are they?

It is clear that they are satanic forces that will be brought down to the earth from space during the time of the tribulation.

We will not try to speculate their origin.

However this deception will be used by satan to deceive the world and many Christians.

REVELATION 12:3-4

And there appeared another wonder in heaven; and behold a great red dragon.

And his tail drew the third part of the stars of heaven, (satanic forces) and did cast them to the earth:

They will have a very deceptive message to man namely:

1. That they created the DNA of man and all of creation
2. The miracles of the Bible were their handiwork
3. Jesus Christ, Budha and Mohommad were created by them
4. The translations of Elijah and Jesus into heaven were by UFO
5. They have always been watching over mankind
6. The crop circle signs were their communications with humanity
7. They will save man from impending danger and destruction
8. They have new impressive ideas and technologies to help man
9. They want to educate and enlighten humanity.

The results:

The antichrist will embrace them.

Mankind will reject the Bible, Christianity and believe their lies.

Mankind will worship satan, the antichrist and the false prophet.

Many Christians will be deceived and fall away from the faith.

REVELATION 18:23

"For by thy sorceries were all nations deceived."

Five things that Christians should do to safeguard themselves from deception:

1. Become spiritually mature.

HEBREWS 5:14
"To them that are of full age, even those who by reason of use have their senses exercised to discern both good and evil."

2. Be prayerful, sober and spiritually alert.

1 PETER 4:7
"But the end of all things is at hand: be ye therefore sober, and watch unto prayer."

False Doctrines, Prophets and Lying Wonders

3. Be watchful.

2 Timothy 4:5
"But watch thou in all things."

We are to watch for the things our spiritual leaders warn us about.

Heb 13:17
"Obey them that have the rule over you, and submit yourselves: for they watch for your souls."

4. We should discern and know the people we are dealing with.

1 John 4:1
"Beloved, believe not every spirit, but try the spirits whether they are of God: because many false prophets are gone out into the world."

5. We should identify and avoid those who are false or seem suspect.

Romans 16:17
"Now I beseech you, brethren, mark them which cause divisions and offences contrary to the doctrine which ye have learned; and avoid them."

We can and must overcome this deception in the following way:

- By giving heed to the warning of its coming
- By preparing ourselves, becoming strong in the Lord and the power of His might.
- By continuing to be very cautious and warning others of any deception.
- By enduring to the end

Matthew 24:11-13

"And many false prophets shall rise, and shall deceive many.

But he that shall endure unto the end, the same shall be saved."

CHAPTER 22

Gods Restoration Program

God wants to restore wholeness, happiness, peace and joy to mankind.

There are five areas in God's Restoration Program:

1. The restoration of the Earth
2. The restoration of Israel
3. The restoration of the Church
4. The restoration of the Family
5. The restoration of the Christian

1. The restoration of the Earth.

God created the Heavens and the Earth perfectly.

When He finished creation after six days, God saw that everything He created was good - very good!

Genesis 1:31

"And God saw everything that he had made, and, behold, it was very good."

After creating Adam and Eve God placed them in the beautiful Garden of Eden. They were placed in total authority over it and told to have children and multiply.

Almost six thousand years have passed since then.

There are now over 7 billion people in the world.

In many ways man has failed to properly take care of what God has given him.

There has been a slow and constant deterioration of the earth.

It has been a natural aging of the planet.

It has also been a reckless manmade destruction of the earth.

Its resources have been wasted and depleted.

Much of the damage is due to scientific experiments, war and irresponsible human behavior. Nuclear and Industrial Contamination have caused much destruction.

This world has been shaken about like a rag doll and has become like an old faded garment. The earth is destined for a final shaking.

Isaiah 13:13

"Therefore I will shake the heavens, and the earth shall remove out of her place, in the wrath of the LORD of hosts, and in the day of his fierce anger."

Isaiah describes the earth's final disposition.

Isaiah 24:19

"The earth is utterly broken down, the earth is clean dissolved, the earth is moved exceedingly."

The damage is beyond repair and requires a rescue mission.

Our only hope is in Jesus Christ.

He will totally restore the earth when he returns again.

He will also create a new Heaven the Earth at the end of the Millennium.

2 Peter 3:12-13

"Looking for and hasting unto the coming of the day of God, wherein the heavens being on fire shall be dissolved, and the elements shall melt with fervent heat?

Nevertheless we, according to his promise, look for new heavens and a new earth, wherein dwelleth righteousness."

2. The restoration of Israel.

It is a historical fact that Israel was taken into captivity by Syria and Babylon.

By 536 B.C. she had returned again to the Holy Land.

After 600 years in 70 A.D. Israel again was dispersed amongst the nations.

God has promised that in the end-time He will be merciful to Israel and she will again be restored as a nation.

ZECHARIAH 1:16, 2:4
"Therefore thus saith the LORD; I am returned to Jerusalem with mercies: my house shall be built in it, saith the LORD of hosts, and a line shall be stretched forth upon Jerusalem."

"Jerusalem shall be inhabited as towns without walls for the multitude of men and cattle therein:"

EZEKIEL 36: 24-26
"For I will take you from among the heathen, and gather you out of all countries, and will bring you into your own land.

Then will I sprinkle clean water upon you, and ye shall be clean: from all your filthiness, and from all your idols, will I cleanse you.

A new heart also will I give you, and a new spirit will I put within you:"

Gods Restoration Program

JOEL 2:26-28

"And ye shall eat in plenty, and be satisfied, and praise the name of the LORD your God, that hath dealt wondrously with you: and my people shall never be ashamed.

And ye shall know that I am in the midst of Israel and that I am the LORD your

God, and none else: and my people shall never be ashamed.

And it shall come to pass afterward, that I will pour out my spirit upon all flesh; and your sons and your daughters shall prophesy, your old men shall dream dreams, your young men shall see visions:"

This miraculous restoration has been unfolding before our eyes since 1948.

Israel will experience total restoration:

- Jerusalem will be restored.
- The Temple will be restored.
- The Cities of Israel will be restored.
- The Population will be restored.
- Agriculture and the Industries will be restored.

Israel will be cleansed from uncleanness and idolatry.

Israel will receive a New Spirit.

The Holy Spirit will be poured out upon the Israelites.

Israel will have supernatural experiences.

God will be in the midst of Israel.

Israel shall never be ashamed again.

Israel's only hope of complete restoration is God.

She will receive and accept her Messiah.

3. The restoration of the Church.

The New Testament book of Acts Church was a powerful and glorious Church.

The Christians received a mighty empowering of the Holy Spirit at Pentecost.

They did many signs, wonders and experienced unprecedented growth.

The Gospel reached most of the then civilized world by 70 AD.

At the height of this experience the Apostle Paul gave the Church a serious warning.

ACTS 20:29-30
"For I know this that after my departing shall grievous wolves enter in among you, not sparing the flock. Also of your own selves shall men arise, speaking perverse things, to draw away disciples after them."

Gods Restoration Program

Paul warned that satan would attack the Church step by step:

- The Glory of God diminished from the Church.
- The Church lost most of the Ministries, Gifts and Power of the Holy Spirit.
- The Church no longer practiced Baptism by immersion in water.
- Repentance of sin unto salvation rarely occurred in the Church.
- Christians lost their Faith trusting the arm of the flesh and works.
- The Word of God was lost to the Christians and only made available to the Clergy.

During this time there was gross spiritual darkness all over the world.

It seemed that the Church was doomed for total destruction.

Fortunately Jesus had given the Church a promise of restoration.

Matthew 16:18

"And I say also unto thee, that thou art Peter, and upon this rock I will build my church; and the gates of hell shall not prevail against it."

The counsels, strategies and attacks of hell against the Church would inevitably fail.

God launched the restoration program of the Church:

1. He raised John Wycliffe and others to print and provide the Bible for people.
2. He then called Martin Luther to proclaim the message of Faith.
3. God then raised up John Wesley to preach Repentance of sin unto salvation.
4. God opened the eyes of Christians to understand and experience Water Baptism.
5. The nineteenth century brought about a fresh outpouring of the Holy Spirit.
6. The end-time restoration of the Church is now taking place.

This will reveal a new and special manifestation of the Glory of God.

ISAIAH 4:5

"And the LORD will create upon every dwelling place of mount Zion, and upon her assemblies, a cloud and smoke by day, and the shining of a flaming fire by night: for upon all the glory shall be a defence."

Mount Zion is the end-time Church.

Heb 12:22-23

"But ye are come unto mount Sion, and unto the city of the living God, the heavenly Jerusalem, and to an innumerable company of angels,

To the general assembly and church of the firstborn, which are written in heaven."

This end-time Church will experience a greater portion of the glory of God than the Book of Acts Church.

Haggai 2:9

"The glory of this latter house shall be greater than of the former, saith the LORD of hosts:"

God will complete the restoration of the Church and present her as a glorious Bride to Jesus Christ, the Heavenly Bridegroom.

Ephesians 5:27

"That he might present it to himself a glorious church, not having spot, or wrinkle, or any such thing; but that it should be holy and without blemish."

4. The restoration of the family.

The family was God's idea.

He created Adam and Eve and commanded them to have children.

They were God's masterpiece.

He wanted a man and woman to love each other and have a happy marriage.

Out of this loving relationship beautiful children would be born.

Within the family many kinds of wonderful relationships exist such as:

Parents

Children

Brothers and Sisters

Grandparents

Uncles, Aunts, Cousins

The extended Family

Throughout the years these have proved to be family relationships of great importance and blessing.

There are four things satan does to destroy relationships:

1. He viciously attacks families.

He causes marriage separations and divorce

He causes child abuse

He causes children to rebel against their parents

He causes disunity, anger and violence between family members

To achieve his goal he uses everything at his disposal including:

- People
- Printed, audio and visual material.

2. He promotes harmful alternative lifestyles such as:

- Couples living together outside of marriage
- Same sex relationships

3. He attacks Parenthood.

The enemy satan causes Parents to neglect their parental responsibilities.

Many fail to lead by example or provide discipline.

Society and the Government then have to assume these tasks.

One parent or same sex parent situations create difficult family circumstances.

The concept of the global village is promoted as a substitute for the role of parents.

Parental responsibilities are passed on to other people in the community.

4. He affects discipline within the family.

The Biblical approach to discipline has been criticized as old fashioned, ineffective and harmful.

A more modern approach eliminates the Biblical principles of discipline and punishment.

The Bible warns against this.

PROVERBS 13:24
"He that spareth his rod hateth his son: but he that loveth him chasteneth him betimes."

PROVERBS 19:18
"Chasten thy son while there is hope, and let not thy soul spare for his crying."

PROVERBS 23:13
"Withhold not correction from the child: for if thou beatest him with the rod, he shall not die."

Because parents today do not set the right example for their children to follow, we have undisciplined and rebellious children within our Society.

God has provided a restoration program for the family!

God promises that Married Couples who follow Biblical principles will be blessed:

1. They will experience a successful, loving marriage.

Ephesians **5:24-25**
"Therefore as the church is subject unto Christ, so let the wives be to their own husbands in everything.

Husbands, love your wives, even as Christ also loved the church, and gave himself for it:"

2. They will enjoy successful Parenting.

They do this by teaching and training their children in the right way.

Deuteronomy **6:7**

"And thou shalt teach them diligently unto thy children, and shalt talk of them when thou sittest in thine house, and when thou walkest by the way, and when thou liest down, and when thou risest up."

PROVERBS 22:6

"Train up a child in the way he should go: and when he is old, he will not depart from it."

They identify the needs of their children, nurture and provide for them.

2 CORINTHIANS 12:14

"For the children ought not to lay up for the parents, but the parents for the children."

EPHESIANS 6:4

"And ye fathers, provoke not your children to wrath: but bring them up in the nurture and admonition of the Lord."

They prayerfully, carefully and lovingly discipline their children.

1 TIMOTHY 3:4

"One that ruleth well his own house, having his children in subjection with all gravity;"

TITUS 2:4

"That they may teach the young women to love their children."

3. Children will be restored to their parents.

These are children who are turned towards God and serve Him.

Ecclesiastes 12:1
"Remember now thy Creator in the days of thy youth."

Malachi 4:6
"And he shall turn the heart of the fathers to the children, and the heart of the children to their fathers."

Ephesians 6:1
"Children, obey your parents in the Lord: for this is right."

5. The restoration of Christians.

God wants His children to be restored and enjoy total prosperity.

3 John 2
"Beloved, I wish above all things that thou mayest prosper and be in health, even as thy soul prospereth."

A Christian may experience restoration in three areas:

1. Body
2. Soul
3. Spirit

1. Restoration of the Body.

Our body is the Temple of the Holy Ghost and needs to be in perfect health.

1 Corinthians 6:19
"What? Know ye not that your body is the temple of the Holy Ghost which is in you, which ye have of God, and ye are not your own?"

If there is a sickness in our body, God wants us to be healed and restored.

He has provided this as a special benefit that Christians are entitled to.

Psalm 103:2-3

"Bless the LORD, O my soul, who healeth all thy diseases;"

God has provided a way for our bodies to be healed and restored.

James 5:14-15

"Is any sick among you? Let him call for the elders of the church; and let them pray over him, anointing him with oil in the name of the Lord:

And the prayer of faith shall save the sick, and the Lord shall raise him up:"

2. Restoration of the Soul.

Psalm 23:3
"He restoreth my soul:"

The Soul of a person is made up of:

- The Mind
- The Emotions
- The Will

From the moment a person is born into this world, satan attacks these three parts.

He tries to destroy mans mind by:

- Contaminating it with negative, evil and filthy thoughts
- Undermining it with destructive, confusing and foolish thoughts
- Limiting it with negative and unproductive thoughts

God restores the mind.

This takes place after a person receives Jesus Christ as their Savior and Lord.

They read the Bible and its words wash and continually refresh their mind.

EPHESIANS 5:26

That he might sanctify and cleanse it with the washing of water by the word.

Once renewed, the mind experiences three things:

1. It sees and perceives things clearly
2. It reasons and understands things wisely
3. It thinks pure and creative thoughts

PHILIPPIANS 4:8

"Finally, brethren, whatsoever things are true, whatsoever things are honest, whatsoever things are just, whatsoever things are pure, whatsoever things are lovely, whatsoever things are of good report; if there be any virtue, and if there be any praise, think on these things."

God renews and gives us a sound mind.

ROMANS 12:2

"But be ye transformed by the renewing of your mind."

Ephesians 4:23

"And be renewed in the spirit of your mind;

God restores the emotions.

The emotions of people need restoring because of experiencing the following:

- Fear
- Hurt
- Disappointment
- Grief and Sorrow
- Inferiority

God does four things to restore the emotions:

1. God fills us with His love and casts out all fear
2. He heals our hurts, grief and dries away our tears
3. He fills us with joy and happiness
4. He gives us a secure place and a destiny in this world and His Kingdom

God restores the Will.

Under satanic attack a person's will eventually becomes passive and weak.

God restores us by giving our will a spirit of Power.

2 Timothy 1:7

"For God hath not given us the spirit of fear; but of power."

He enables us **to say "yes" to things that are right** and **to say "no" to things that are wrong.**

3. Restoration or renewal of the Spirit.

In this process, God takes away our old spirit and gives us a New Spirit.

Ezekiel 36:26
"A new heart also will I give you, and a new spirit will I put within you:"

When we become a Christian, we enter God's Kingdom and our spirit is born again.

John 3:5

"Jesus answered, Verily, verily, I say unto thee, except a man be born of water and of the Spirit, he cannot enter into the kingdom of God."

The ultimate goal of a successful Christian is:

- To be totally sanctified
- To be restored in Spirit, Soul and Body.

This restoration gives us the hope of becoming God's perfect man.

I Thessalonians 5:23

"And the very God of peace sanctify you wholly; and I pray God your whole spirit and soul and body be preserved blameless unto the coming of our Lord Jesus Christ."

Ephesians 4:13

"Till we all come in the unity of the faith, and of the knowledge of the Son of God, unto a perfect man, unto the measure of the stature of the fullness of Christ:"

Let us therefore fully understand and enjoy God's restoration.

CHAPTER 23

The Three Dimensions of Man

The Bible clearly reveals that a person consists of three parts:

- Spirit
- Soul
- Body

1 Thessalonians 5:23

"And the very God of peace sanctify you wholly; and I pray God your whole spirit and soul and body be preserved blameless unto the coming of our Lord Jesus Christ."

Man is also described as a Tabernacle or a Temple.

2 Corinthians 5:1

"For we know that if our earthly house of this tabernacle were dissolved, we have a building of God, an house not made with hands, eternal in the heavens."

1 Corinthians 6:19-20

"What? Know ye not that your body is the temple of the Holy Ghost which is in you."

Both the Tabernacle of Israel and the Temple of Solomon had three parts:

1. The Outer Court where the sacrifices were made.
2. The Holy Place where the Priests served God.
3. The Holy of Holies where God's Presence and Glory were manifested.

Similarly man also has three parts:

1. A body which may be presented to God as a living sacrifice.

Romans 12:1
"I beseech you therefore, brethren, by the mercies of God, that ye present your bodies a

living sacrifice, holy, acceptable unto God, which is your reasonable service."

2. A Soul that worships God with mind, emotions and will.

3. A Spirit where God's presence and glory is manifested.

Let us deal with these three parts of man in greater depth:

1. The Body.

The body is the physical part of man that consists of three parts:

- Flesh
- Bone
- Blood

David describes the miraculous human body.

PSALM 139:14
"I will praise thee; for I am fearfully and wonderfully made:"

In the body there are five Physical Senses and they are:

1. Sight through the eyes

2. Hearing through the ears

3. Tasting through the tongue

4. Smell through the nose

5. Feeling through the nerves

Through these five physical senses man has **world consciousness** and is able to communicate with the world.

The Body has different parts and its parts do either deeds of righteousness or unrighteousness.

The body is temporal, perishable and corruptible and will return to dust again.

GENESIS 3:19
"Till thou return unto the ground; for out of it wast thou taken: for dust thou art, and unto dust shalt thou return."

2. The Soul.

It consists of three parts:

- Mind
- Emotions
- Will

The Soul is the part through which we have **self-consciousness.**

Our Soul is an eternal being that lives and continues after the death, either in Heaven or Hell.

It is located between the Body and the Spirit.

The Three Dimensions of Man

It has contact with the world through the body.

It has contact with the spirit realm through the spirit.

World < body <------ **Soul** ------ > spirit > Spirit realm

The Soul is very much like a Balance or Scale that weighs things.

The two parts that hold weights on either side are symbolical of the mind and emotions.

The part in the middle that balances the two sides is the will.

Mind   - **Will** -   **Emotions**

The will is that part of the Soul that makes all the decisions.

We are and become what our decisions are.

If we decide and do good things, we are good.

If we decide and do evil things, we are evil.

Balanced decisions are good decisions.

In order to be balanced the will should be equally affected by the emotions and intellect.

An **unbalanced decision** is either too emotional or too intellectual.

Many people make wrong decisions, because they allow either the emotions or intellect to override the other.

Through the *five senses* satan directs his attacks at our intellect, emotions and will.

This causes us to have sinful thoughts, feelings and make wrong decisions.

The decisions we make are effected by:

The images we see

The sounds we hear

The odors we smell

The things we taste

The feelings we feel

All incoming information comes in through these five senses.

It passes **through our sensory nerves** along **neural pathways** to a part of our mind called **perception**.

These sensory deposits into our mind can never be voluntarily discarded.

This incoming information passes **through our sub-conscious to our mind**.

Our mind is like a computer and all information pended into it is channeled to different compartments and stored in the memory.

What we observe depends upon the condition we are in.

The Three Dimensions of Man

If we are sober and sane the information received will be clear and balanced.

If not it will be blurred and inaccurate.

All information is processed through seven different compartments:

1. Perception
2. Reason
3. Imagination
4. Comparison (Within the Memory)
5. Emotions
6. Thought formulation
7. Will.

It then will effect and cause our behavior.

Understanding Perception

The light of God shines brightly within a Christian, within their perception.

MATTHEW 6:22

"The light of the body is the eye: if therefore thine eye be single, thy whole body shall be full of light."

Jesus teaches that if our eye (perception) is **"single"** our whole body will be full of light.

It is single and correctly discerns incoming information:

1. It **sees good** and accepts it
2. It **sees evil** and rejects it
3. It **sees self**, how it is affected by the information and deals with it

Understanding Reason

Deposits of information pass **through perception to our imagination.**

We may imagine things in two ways:

1. **In Faith** - imagining things to be positive and possible.
2. **In Uncertainty** - imagining things to be negative or impossible.

These imaginations then pass to our emotions and we experience positive or negative feelings and reactions to them.

Imaginations of Faith produce expectancies of success.

Imaginations of Uncertainty produce expectancies of fear.

These expectancies are then formulated into positive or negative thoughts.

The Three Dimensions of Man

Understanding Thoughts

Paul gives us an example of what Godly thoughts are made of:

PHILIPPIANS 4:8

"Finally, brethren, whatsoever things are true, whatsoever things are honest, whatsoever things are just, whatsoever things are pure, whatsoever things are lovely, whatsoever things are of good report; if there be any virtue, and if there be any praise, think on these things."

These Godly thoughts are:

1. *True*
2. *Honest*
3. *Just*
4. *Pure*
5. *Lovely*
6. *Good*
7. *Praise*
8. *Godly*

They reflect the thoughts of a Christian who has a sound mind.

2 Timothy 1:7

"For God hath not given us the spirit of fear; but of power, and of love, and of a **sound mind**."

Understanding the Memory

All thoughts are stored away in our memory.

All new information coming in to us is first channeled to the memory where it is compared with past information and experiences that have been stored away.

This is called the Law of Apperception where we remember the good and bad decisions of the past.

We learn by our mistakes and should try to only make good decisions.

Understanding the Will

The will is the part of the Soul where good or bad decisions are made.

Whatever we decide is demonstrated in either positive or negative behavior.

Spiritual people demonstrate positive behavior and produce the nine Fruits of the Spirit:

1. *Love*
2. *Joy*
3. *Peace*

The Three Dimensions of Man

4. *Patience*
5. *Gentleness*
6. *Goodness*
7. *Faith and faithfulness.*
8. *Humility*
9. *Self-control*

GALATIANS 5:22-23

"But the fruit of the Spirit is love, joy, peace, longsuffering, gentleness, goodness, faith, meekness, temperance."

Sinful and carnal people demonstrate negative behavior through the carnal works of the flesh:

1. Adultery
2. Sexual promiscuity
3. Impure thoughts and deeds
4. Perversion
5. Idol worship
6. Witchcraft - (Reading horoscopes, fortune telling, communicating with the dead, participating in magic and satanism)
7. Hatred
8. Sowing discord
9. Jealousy

10. Fits of rage
11. Selfishness
12. Self-gratification
13. Murder
14. Unrestrained living - out of control eating and living habits

GALATIANS 5:19-21

"Now the works of the flesh are manifest, which are these; Adultery, fornication, uncleanness, lasciviousness, Idolatry, witchcraft, hatred, variance, emulations, wrath, strife, seditions, heresies, envying, murders, drunkenness and reveling."

The behavior of a person reveals the thoughts and feelings inside of them.

LUKE 6:45

"A good man out of the good treasure of his heart bringeth forth that which is good; and an evil man out of the evil treasure of his heart bringeth forth that which is evil: for of the abundance of the heart his mouth speaketh."

The Three Dimensions of Man

God sees us the way we are inside our heart:

1 Samuel 16:7

"For man looketh on the outward appearance, but the LORD looketh on the heart."

With this in mind, David prayed this prayer to God:

Psalm 139:23-24

"Search me, O God, and know my heart: try me, and know my thoughts:

And see if there be any wicked way in me, and lead me in the way everlasting."

Understanding our Behavior

It is beneficial for us to carefully examine our own behavior.
It will reveal the contents of our Mind, Emotion and Will.

Do we make wise or foolish decisions?

Do we feel contaminated inside?

Do we feel fearful and insecure?

Do we act in haste?

Do we behave irresponsibly?

Do we feel ashamed?

Do we feel worthless?

Do we feel inferior?

Do we think we are a failure?

Are we hurting or grieving?

Are we lonely?

Are we depressed?

Do we feel deceived?

Do we feel loss?

Do we feel anger?

Do we hate?

Do we have a proud and boastful attitude?

How do we deal with these negative things in us?

- We need to deal with them immediately.
- We should not try to temporarily numb or forget them.
- Negative thoughts must be taken captive.
- Negative imaginations must be cast down.

2 Corinthians 10:5

"Casting down imaginations, and every high thing that exalteth itself against the knowledge of God, and bringing into captivity every thought to the obedience of Christ;"

Understanding the Renewal of the Soul

From birth satan attacks our mind, emotion and will.

His goal is to negatively effect and destroy us.

He can do this within a short period of time or over many years.

God however wants to restore and renew these broken parts of the Soul.

Psalm 23:3

"The lord is my Shepherd ... He restores my Soul."

Romans 12:2

"But be ye transformed by the renewing of your mind."

God wants us to have beautiful new thoughts.

God wants us to have wonderful new feelings.

God wants us to be able to make right and powerful decisions.

3. The Spirit.

This is the part that connects the Soul of man with the Spirit realm.

God's Breath created the spirit of man within his Body and Soul.

Genesis 2:7

"And the LORD God formed man of the dust of the ground, and breathed into his nostrils the breath of life; and man became a living soul."

God warned Adam and Eve that if they were disobedient to Him their spirit would die.

Genesis 2:17

"But of the tree of the knowledge of good and evil, thou shalt not eat of it: for in the day that thou eatest thereof thou shalt surely die."

We know that they partook of the fruit of the tree of the knowledge of good and evil and it brought about the death of their spirit.

Spiritual death has come upon all men.

1 Corinthians 15:21-22

"For since by man came death, by man came also the resurrection of the dead.

For as in Adam all die, even so in Christ shall all be made alive."

Ever since this tragic moment every man and woman needs a new spirit.

This miracle of life in Jesus Christ is the renewal of our Spirit.

God provides us with a new spirit.

Ezekiel 11:19

"I will put a new spirit within you; and I will take the stony heart out of their flesh, and will give them an heart of flesh:"

The truth is that only those who are born again of the Holy Spirit, receive a new spirit and become Children of God.

Job 33:4

"The spirit of God hath made me."

This creative work of the Holy Spirit is described in:

Zechariah 12:1

"The burden of the word of the LORD ... formeth the spirit of man within him."

1 Peter 1:23

"Being born again, not of corruptible seed, but of incorruptible, by the word of God."

2 Corinthians 3:6

"For the letter killeth, but the spirit giveth life."

The process

The work of the Holy Spirit is to create the spirit of man within him by the **"Word"** of God.

The process by which the Holy Spirit does this is called **"being born again"** or spiritual birth.

These are the four realities:

1. We are born again by the seed of the Word of God sown into our hearts.
2. The Holy Spirit quickens and makes the seed come alive within us.
3. Then the Word of God forms the three parts of the spirit of man within him.
4. Our new human spirit is born.

Spiritual birth is very similar to that of physical birth.

In physical birth, an **ovum** is fertilized by spermatozoa and becomes an **embryo.**

The embryo **divides into three**, forming the three parts of the human body.

Nine months later **a beautiful baby is born** into the world.

Similarly the seed of the **Word of God** is sown into the heart of a person.

The Word **(spiritual ovum)** is given life by the Holy Spirit and it becomes a **spiritual embryo.**

The Three Dimensions of Man

The spiritual embryo then becomes the **three parts of the human spirit.**

A new spiritual Baby is born into God's family and **its new name** is recorded in the Book of Life in Heaven.

The Word of God has three characteristics.

Each affects one of the three parts of the spirit of man:

The three characteristics are:

1. Light.

Ps 119:105
"Thy word is a lamp unto my feet, and a light unto my path."

In this part of the human spirit, spiritual illumination takes place.

Jesus who is the Light of the world enters our heart and lights up our life.

I John 1:4-9
"In him was life; and the life was the light of men.

And the light shineth in darkness; and the darkness comprehended it not.

That was the true Light, which lighteth every man."

As children of light we abide and walk in light;

1 John 2:10
"He that loveth his brother abideth in the light."

Ephesians 5:8
"But now are ye light in the Lord: walk as children of light:"

1 John 1:7
"But if we walk in the light, as he is in the light, we have fellowship one with another."

This light brings a threefold conviction within our Spirit:

- Conviction of sin (Things that are wrong and what we should not do)
- Conviction of righteousness (Things that are right and what we should do)
- Conviction of judgment (The judgment of the enemy satan)

John 16:8
"And when he is come, he will reprove the world of sin, and of righteousness, and of judgment:"

This light manifests God's glory within us:

2 Corinthians 4:6
"For God, who commanded the light to shine out of darkness, hath shined in our hearts, to give the light of the knowledge of the glory of God in the face of Jesus Christ."

2. Truth.

John 17:17
"Sanctify them through thy truth: thy word is truth."

This part of the new spirit of a Christian is created for Truth and here the Holy Spirit reveals truth.

John 16:13
"Howbeit when he, the Spirit of truth, is come, he will guide you into all truth: for he shall not speak of himself; but whatsoever he shall hear, that shall he speak: and he will shew you things to come."

It is in this area of the human spirit that we receive a special impartation of truth and revelation knowledge and therefore walk in truth:

3 John 3
"For I rejoiced greatly, when the brethren came and testified of the truth that is in thee, even as thou walkest in the truth."

3. Power.

Hebrews 1:3
"And upholding all things by the word of his power."

It is in and through this part of the human spirit that the Holy Spirit manifests God's power.

- We receive power to strengthen our will to make the right decisions.
- We receive supernatural power to do miracles, exploits and work for God.

A Christian's spirit experiences a very special connection, relationship and fellowship with the Holy Spirit.

A Radio can be described as a special receiver that can receive sound waves.

Similarly the spirit of a Christian has been created by the Holy Spirit to communicate with Him in the spiritual dimension and fellowship with Him.

We fellowship and have communion with the Holy Spirit through **our five spiritual senses**

A Christian can see, hear, taste, smell and feel spiritual things with spiritual senses:

Hebrews 5:14

"But strong meat belongeth to them that are of full age, even those who by reason of use have **their senses** exercised to discern both good and evil."

Spiritually mature Christians are those who effectively use their five spiritual senses which are:

The Three Dimensions of Man

1. Spiritual Sight.

1 Corinthians 2:9
"Eye hath not seen, nor ear heard, neither have entered into the heart of man, the things which God hath prepared for them that love him."

2. Spiritual hearing.

Revelation 2:7
"He that hath an ear, let him hear what the Spirit saith."

3. Spiritual Taste.

Psalm 34:8
"O taste and see that the LORD is good:"

Romans 6:4-5
Those who have tasted of the heavenly gift, and were made partakers of the Holy Ghost, and have tasted the good word of God, and the powers of the world to come.

4. Spiritual Smell.

2 Corinthians 2:14
"Maketh manifest the savor (smell) of his knowledge by us in every place."

5. Spiritual Feeling.

ACTS 17:27
"That they should seek the Lord, if haply they might feel after him."

Through our spiritual senses the Holy Spirit communicates with us and we experience six things:

1. We can hear Him

2. He communicates with us

3. He leads and commands us

4. We obey Him

5. We walk after the things of the Holy Spirit

6. We walk in the Spirit

ROMANS 8:14
"For as many as are led by the Spirit of God, they are the sons of God."

GALATIANS 5:16
"This I say then, Walk in the Spirit, and ye shall not fulfill the lust of the flesh."

Every day we enjoy Fellowship with the Holy Spirit:

2 CORINTHIANS 13:14
"The communion of the Holy Ghost be with you all."

The Three Dimensions of Man

We enjoy comfort from the Holy Spirit:

John 14:16-17

"And I will pray the Father, and he shall give you another Comforter, that he may abide with you forever: Even the Spirit of truth;"

The Holy Spirit abides with us, teaches us and anoints us:

1 John 2:27

"But the anointing which ye have received of him abideth in you, and ye need not that any man teach you: but as the same anointing teacheth you of all things, and is truth, and is no lie, and even as it hath taught you, ye shall abide in him."

The Holy Spirit perfects our Body, Soul and Spirit to do God's work on earth:

1 Thessalonians 5:23

"And the very God of peace sanctify you wholly; and I pray God your whole spirit and soul and body be preserved blameless unto the coming of our Lord Jesus Christ."

CHAPTER 24

Last Things

The study of last things is known as Eschatology.

Man has an insatiable curiosity about the future.

This teaching will help us understand what the future holds.

All of us face the future and the inevitable experience of death.

The fact of death

HEBREWS 9:27

"And as it is appointed unto men once to die, but after this the judgment:"

Death is certain and Solomon reflects on the physical body of man that will be buried and experience decomposition.

ECCLESIASTES 3:18-20

"For that which befalleth the sons of men befalleth beasts; as the one dieth, so dieth the other; yea, they have all one breath; All go unto one place; all are of the dust, and all turn to dust again."

There are three aspects of death that we need to consider:

1. Death is inevitable.

All men will die and from the moment of birth every person experiences the systematic and constant decay of the body.

- Our body ages
- Our teeth decay
- Our hair changes color and eventually baldness sets in
- Our skin ages and wrinkles
- Body organs malfunction
- Finally the whole body collapses and dies

Last Things

2 Corinthians 5:1-4
"For we know that if our earthly house of this tabernacle were dissolved, we have a building of God, For in this we groan, earnestly desiring to be clothed upon with our house which is from heaven: For we that are in this tabernacle do groan, being burdened:"

2. The uncertainty of when we will die.

We do not know when we will die but death is an appointment that all will keep.

Hebrews 9:27
"And as it is appointed unto men once to die, but after this the judgment:"

Each person faces the reality of passing through the door of death alone.

We pass through it naked and leave all our possessions and loved ones behind.

On the other side of the door of death is eternity.

For many people eternity is uncertain and frightening.

3. Death is necessary.

It is a necessary law of nature that everyone must experience.

In death three things happen to man:

1. The Body of man returns to dust

2. The Soul of man appears before God in Judgment

3. The Spirit of man returns to God

ECCLESIASTES 12:7

"And the spirit shall return unto God who gave it."

The righteous and the wicked are separated after death.

They go to different places.

Jesus told this true story about a rich man and a beggar who died.

After death they found themselves in two different places.

LUKE 16:19-26

"There was a certain rich man, which was clothed in purple and fine linen, and fared sumptuously every day: And there was a certain beggar named Lazarus, which was laid at his gate, full of sores,

And it came to pass, that the beggar died, and was carried by the angels into Abraham's bosom: the rich man also died, and was buried: And in hell he lift up his eyes, being in torments,

And he cried and said, Father Abraham have mercy on me, for I am tormented in this flame.

But Abraham said, Son, remember that thou in thy lifetime receivedst thy good things, and likewise Lazarus evil things: but now he is comforted, and thou art tormented.

And beside all this, between us and you there is a great gulf fixed: so that they which would pass from hence to you cannot:"

The destiny of a Christian after death

Here is an example of the death of a Stephen who was a Christian:

Acts 7:59-60

"And they stoned Stephen, calling upon God, and saying, Lord Jesus, receive my spirit.

And he kneeled down, and cried with a loud voice;

Lord lay not this sin to their charge. And when he had said this, he fell asleep."

Paul assures us that at death Christians immediately go to be with the Lord.

2 Corinthians 5:8

"We are confident, I say, and willing rather to be absent from the body, and to be present with the Lord."

When the spirit of a Christian leaves their body at death, their Soul is ushered into the Presence of God.

Death is a blessed experience for Christians.

PHILIPPIANS 1:21

"For to me to live is Christ, and to die is gain."

Christians are given a wonderful promise about the resurrection of their body.

1 CORINTHIANS 15:51-52

"Behold, I shew you a mystery; we shall all be changed, at the last trump: for the trumpet shall sound, and the dead shall be raised incorruptible, and we shall be changed.

Christians are promised victory over death, immortality and incorruption:

1 CORINTHIANS 15:53-54

"For this corruptible must put on incorruption, and this mortal must put on immortality.

So when this corruptible shall have put on incorruption, and this mortal shall have put on immortality, then shall be brought to pass the saying that is written, Death is swallowed up in victory."

Martha referred to this resurrection when she spoke to Jesus about Lazarus her brother.

John 11:24

"Martha saith unto him, I know that he shall rise again in the resurrection at the last day."

Jesus is the key to a Christian's victorious Resurrection.

John 11:25

"Jesus said unto her, I am the resurrection, and the life: he that believeth in me, though he were dead, yet shall he live:"

When we are resurrected, every part of our decomposed body will be reassembled and glorified in a heavenly body.

2 Corinthians 5:1

"For we know that if our earthly house of this tabernacle were dissolved, we have a building of God, an house not made with hands, eternal in the heavens."

Philippians 3:21

"Who shall change our vile body, that it may be fashioned like unto his glorious body."

24 Doctrines of the Bible

Jesus appeared to the Disciples in His glorified Body. His intangible body was able to pass though closed doors as if invisible, yet it could be touched and eat food.

Luke 24:36-43

"And as they thus spake, Jesus himself stood in the midst of them, and saith unto them, Peace be unto you.

Behold my hands and my feet, that it is I myself: handle me, and see; for a spirit hath not flesh and bones, as ye see me have. And they gave him a piece of a broiled fish, and of an honeycomb.

And he took it, and did eat before them."

How wonderful it is for Christians to face the future with this hope, security and no fear of death.

1 Corinthians 15:55-57

"O death, where is thy sting? O grave, where is thy victory?

But thanks be to God, which giveth us the victory through our Lord Jesus Christ."

At death Christians:

- Leave their Earthly Body and it is buried.
- Occupy their Heavenly Body in the glorious presence of Almighty God.
- Take up residence in a Mansion that Jesus has prepared for them:

John 14:1-3

"Let not your heart be troubled: ye believe in God, believe also in me.

In my Father's house are many mansions: if it were not so, I would have told you. I go to prepare a place for you. And if I go and prepare a place for you, I will come again, and receive you unto myself; that where I am, there ye may be also."

There are two kinds of resurrections:

1. Christians experience the resurrection unto life.
2. Non-Christians experience the resurrection unto condemnation.

John 5:28-29

"Marvel not at this: for the hour is coming, in the which all that are in the graves shall hear his voice,

And shall come forth; they that have done good, unto the resurrection of life; and they that have done evil, unto the resurrection of damnation."

The best resurrection is the one experienced by Christians.

Hebrew 11:35

"That they might obtain a better resurrection:"

The time of the resurrections:

Paul reveals that the future resurrection of the Saints will take place at the sounding of the last trumpet when Jesus Christ returns for them.

It will precede the **"catching away"** of the Saints at Christ's coming.

1 Corinthians 15:52

"In a moment, in the twinkling of an eye, at the last trump: for the trumpet shall sound, and the dead shall be raised incorruptible, and we shall be changed."

John reveals that the resurrection of all Non-Christians will take place at the White Throne Judgment.

Revelation 20:11-12

"And I saw a great white throne, and him that sat on it, from whose face the earth and the heaven fled away; and there was found no place for them.

And I saw the dead, small and great, stand before God; and the books were opened:"

Last Things

The Return of our Lord Jesus Christ

Jesus said five things about His Coming:

1. He promised that He would return again.

JOHN 14:3
"And if I go and prepare a place for you, I will come again, and receive you unto myself; that where I am, there ye may be also."

2. He said His coming would be quick and unexpected.

MATTHEW 24:27
"For as the lightning cometh out of the east, and shineth even unto the west; so shall also the coming of the Son of man be."

3. He said that not all people will be caught up with Him when He comes.

MATTHEW 24:39-42
"So shall also the coming of the Son of man be.

Then shall two be in the field; the one shall be taken, and the other left.

Watch therefore: for ye know not what hour your Lord doth come."

4. He warned that only those ready for His coming would become His Bride and enter His marriage feast.

Matthew 25:10-13
"The bridegroom came; and they that were ready went in with him to the marriage: and the door was shut. Afterward came also the other virgins, saying, Lord, Lord, open to us.

But he answered and said, Verily I say unto you, I know you not.

Watch therefore, for ye know neither the day nor the hour wherein the Son of man cometh."

5. Jesus gives nine signs in **Matthew 24** that would indicate that His coming is near.

1. Wars

2. Famines

3. Viruses and diseases

4. Earthquakes

5. Persecution of Christians

6. False Prophets

7. Sin abounding everywhere

8. All the world hearing the Gospel

9. The rise of the Anti-Christ

Last Things

The two Men clothed in white also promised that Jesus would return.

Acts 1:10

"Behold, two men stood by them in white apparel;

Which also said; Ye men of Galilee, why stand ye gazing up into heaven?

This same Jesus, which is taken up from you into heaven, shall so come in like manner as ye have seen him go into heaven."

Paul describes this future event.

1 Thessalonians 4:16-17

"For the Lord himself shall descend from heaven with a shout, with the voice of the archangel, and with the trump of God: and the dead in Christ shall rise first:

Then we which are alive and remain shall be caught up together with them in the clouds, to meet the Lord in the air: and so shall we ever be with the Lord."

2 Thessalonians 1:7

"And to you who are troubled rest with us, when the Lord Jesus shall be revealed from heaven with his mighty angels,"

1 Corinthians 15:51-52

"Behold, I shew you a mystery; We shall not all sleep, but we shall all be changed,

In a moment, in the twinkling of an eye, at the last trump: for the trumpet shall sound, and the dead shall be raised incorruptible."

Paul warns that before Jesus comes, three things will happen:

1. The Church will experience a spiritual falling away.
2. The Antichrist will be revealed.
3. The Last Trumpet will sound.

2 Thessalonians 2:3

"Let no man deceive you by any means: for that day shall not come, except there come a falling away first, and that man of sin be revealed, the son of perdition;"

1 Corinthians 15:52

"In a moment, in the twinkling of an eye, at the last trump: for the trumpet shall sound, and the dead shall be raised incorruptible, and we shall be changed."

The Church is the Bride of Christ and will be prepared and adorned for His coming.

Last Things

Revelation 21:2

"Coming down from God out of heaven, prepared as a bride adorned for her husband."

Paul describes the wonderful relationship between Jesus Christ and the Church.

Ephesians 5:25-27

"Even as Christ also loved the church, and gave himself for it;

That he might present it to himself a glorious church."

John describes this glorious future event.

Revelations 19:7-9

"Let us be glad and rejoice, and give honour to him: for the marriage of the Lamb is come, and his wife hath made herself ready.

And to her was granted that she should be arrayed in fine linen, clean and white: for the fine linen is the righteousness of saints.

And he saith unto me, Write, Blessed are they which are called unto the marriage supper of the Lamb."

The Return or Coming of Jesus Christ has two parts:

1. The catching away "Rapture" of the Saints in the middle of the tribulation.
2. The triumphant return of Christ and the saints to the earth for His Millennial Reign, at the end of the tribulation.

The rapture is described as a mysterious catching up into heaven.

It will take place

- at the sounding of the **last trump.**

1 Corinthians 15:51

"Behold, I shew you a **mystery**; We shall not all sleep, but we shall all be changed. In a moment, in the twinkling of an eye, **at the last trump**: for the trumpet shall sound, and the dead shall be raised incorruptible, and we shall be changed."

This mystery is the rapture.

There are seven trumpets that are sounded by the Angel of the Lord during the time of the seven year tribulation.

The Saints have to wait until the sounding of the seventh and **last trumpet** for the mysterious rapture to take place.

Revelation 10:7

"But in the days of the voice of the **seventh angel,** when he shall begin to sound, the **mystery of God should be finished**, as he hath declared to his servants the prophets."

However the rapture will take place before the horrific events of the second half, called the hour of temptation.

Revelation 3:10-11

"Because thou hast kept the word of my patience, I also will keep thee from the hour of temptation, which shall come upon all the world, to try them that dwell upon the earth. Behold, I come quickly: hold that fast which thou hast, that no man take thy crown."

Christians will escape the horrific second half of the tribulation.

Luke 21:36

"Watch ye therefore, and pray always, that ye may be accounted worthy to escape all these things that shall come to pass, and to stand before the Son of man."

John describes the magnificent descent of Jesus Christ and His Bride, coming down from Heaven back to the Earth. This is at the end of the tribulation.

REVELATION 19:11-16

"And I saw heaven opened, and behold a white horse; and he that sat upon him was called Faithful and True, and in righteousness he doth judge and make war.

His eyes were as a flame of fire, and on his head were many crowns; and he had a name written, that no man knew, but he himself.

And he was clothed with a vesture dipped in blood: and his name is called The Word of God.

And the armies which were in heaven followed him upon white horses, clothed in fine linen, white and clean.

And out of his mouth goeth a sharp sword.

And he hath on his vesture and on his thigh a name written, KING OF KINGS, AND LORD OF LORDS."

Zechariah describes this coming of Jesus Christ.

ZECHARIAH 14:3-4

"Then shall the LORD go forth, and fight against those nations, as when he fought in the day of battle.

And his feet shall stand in that day upon the Mount of Olives, which is before Jerusalem on the east, and the Mount of Olives shall cleave in the midst thereof toward the east and toward the west."

He describes the reaction of the Jews when they see and recognize Jesus as their Messiah.

Zechariah 12:10

"And they shall look upon me whom they have pierced, and they shall mourn for him, as one mourneth for his only son."

The Second Coming of Jesus Christ has four purposes:

1. He will come to save the Jews.
2. He will overthrow and punish satan, the anti-christ and the false-prophet.
3. He will Judge the Nations.
4. He will establish His magnificent Millennial Kingdom on earth.

John gives a special promise to those who are faithful martyrs during the tribulation

They will be reign with Christ during the Millennium.

Revelation 20:4

"And I saw thrones, and they sat upon them, and judgment was given unto them: and I saw the souls of them that were beheaded for the witness of Jesus, and for the word of God, and which had not worshipped the beast, neither his image, neither had received his mark upon their foreheads, or in their hands; and they lived and reigned with Christ a thousand years."

At the end of the Millennial Reign of Christ the White Throne Judgment will take place.

Revelation 20:11-15

"And I saw a great white throne, and him that sat on it, from whose face the earth and the heaven fled away; and there was found no place for them.

And I saw the dead, small and great, stand before God; and the books were opened: and another book was opened, which is the book of life: and the dead were judged out of those things which were written in the books, according to their works.

And the sea gave up the dead which were in it; and death and hell delivered up the dead which were in them: and they were judged every man according to their works.

And death and hell were cast into the lake of fire. This is the second death.

And whosoever was not found written in the book of life was cast into the lake of fire."

There are three aspects to consider about this Judgment:

1. God is the Judge.

Hebrews 12:22-23
"But ye are come ... to God the Judge of all."

2. There are four principles of Judgment:

    1. It will be according to Truth

    2. The Works of men will be judged

    3. It will be Impartial

    4. It will be according to the Light people received

Romans 2:2

"But we are sure that the judgment of God is according to truth against them which commit such things."

Romans 2:6

"Who will render to every man according to his deeds:"

ROMANS 2:11

"For there is no respect of persons with God."

ROMANS 1:20

"For the invisible things of him from the creation of the world are clearly seen, being understood by the things that are made, even his eternal power and Godhead; so that they are without excuse:"

ROMANS 2:12

"For as many as have sinned without law shall also perish without law: and as many as have sinned in the law shall be judged by the law;"

3. There are three Judgments.

  1. The Judgment Seat of Christ where the Saints are judged

  2. The Great White Throne Judgment where humanity is judged

  3. The Judgment of the Fallen Angels

Christians will be judged and rewarded at the Judgment Seat of Christ and not be judged with the sinners of the world.

2 CORINTHIANS 5:10
"For we must all appear before the judgment seat of Christ; that every one may receive the

things done in his body, according to that he hath done, whether it be good or bad."

1 Corinthians 11:32
But when we are judged, we are chastened of the Lord, that we should not be condemned with the world."

Fallen angels are preserved for their own judgment.

2 Peter 2:4

"For if God spared not the angels that sinned, but cast them down to hell, and delivered them into chains of darkness, to be reserved unto judgment;"

Finally:

Let us be thankful to God for revealing many of the details of the events and things that await us.

- This enables us to be prepared for what lies ahead
- It causes us to be excited as we wait for the Glory we will soon experience.

Other books published by Ken Wooldridge

The Apocalypse then Glory (written as a novel)

When reading this book, you will have deeper insight into:

- The unfolding drama of the 7 year Tribulation.
- Powerful players and their roles in this end time drama.
- Dangers many will face.
- How you can ensure your salvation and escape.
- Amazing glories that await every true Christian in Heaven.
- Life in the Millennial New Jerusalem and New World.

Understanding the End Times

By reading this book, the following questions will be answered:

- What major world events are about to happen?
- What is the true world timeline? An amazing new discovery
- How will our lives be affected?
- How can we prepare ourselves?
- How can we ensure our salvation and escape?

Last Things

Living in difficult times

Ken Wooldridge was born in Botswana and raised in Africa

He has been living in Tennessee for over twenty years

He has learned the benefits of foraging wild edible and medicinal plants

This book provides information about:

- Emergency preparations
- Foraging wild edible foods
- Food recipes
- Making household products
- Making Personal Care products
- Herbal remedies

It is a must have book for survival in difficult times

These books with a spiritual accent will help you and those you love

Available on Amazon.com and other retailers.

www.ingramcontent.com/pod-product-compliance
Lightning Source LLC
Chambersburg PA
CBHW071308150426
43191CB00007B/540